WITHDRAWAL

A BIBLIOGRAPHY OF
LATIN AMERICAN BIBLIOGRAPHIES:

Social Sciences & Humanities

Volume I

Daniel Raposo Cordeiro

Editor

Solena V. Bryant; Haydée N. Piedracueva;
and Barbara Hadely Stein

Associate Editors

(Supplementing the original works
by Arthur E. Gropp)

The Scarecrow Press, Inc.
Metuchen, N.J. & London
1979

Library of Congress Cataloging in Publication Data

Cordeiro, Daniel Raposo.
  A bibliography of Latin American bibliographies--
social sciences and humanities.

  1. Bibliography--Bibliography--Latin America.
2. Latin America--Bibliography. I. Gropp, Arthur Eric,
1902-   II. Title.
Z1601.A2G67 1968   suppl. 2   [F1408]   016.01698
ISBN 0-8108-1170-7 (v. 1)   78-11935

TO
ARTHUR ERIC GROPP
AND ALL BIBLIOGRAPHERS

PREFACE

When Arthur E. Gropp revealed to the Committee on Bibliography of the Seminar on the Acquisition of Latin American
Library Materials (SALALM) that he would no longer engage
himself in the preparation of supplements to his bibliographies
of Latin American bibliographies, published by Scarecrow Press
in 1968 and 1976, plans were set in motion by the Committee to
insure supplementation. The Subcommittee on Reporting Bibliographic Activities, which had had as its charge an annual working paper listing bibliographies newly published and/or in progress, was subsequently re-named the Subcommittee on the
Bibliography of Latin American Bibliographies.

This first of periodic efforts to supplement Gropp is
a cumulation of the working papers for the years 1969 through
1974, prepared by Herman H. Cline, Daniel Raposo Cordeiro,
Gayle Hudgens Watson and Haydée N. Piedracueva, with ad-
ditional citations gathered from approximately 250 periodicals.
Imprint dates are, for the most part, from 1969 to 1974 for
monographs and from 1966 to 1974 for periodical articles.
Since complete runs of some of the periodicals were not located, we decided to postpone listing herein those which were
perused until further attempts have been made at complete
coverage.

With few exceptions, Gropp's format was followed,
i.e., subject arrangement with subheadings for political en-
tities when warranted by the number of citations. Our de-
sire to be as comprehensive as possible led us to forego
personal perusal of all the monographs cited. The National
Union Catalog (NUC) and the Ohio College Library Center
(OCLC) proved useful in the verification of those citations
which were initially gathered from book dealers' lists, publishers' catalogs, etc.

We wish to thank all of the above-mentioned compilers
of working papers for having provided us with the basis for

this offering. Additionally, we wish to thank the library administrations of Syracuse University, Columbia University, Queens College and Princeton University for the encouragement and support they gave the compilers of this bibliography, and we wish to thank the many persons who gave us valuable assistance through their contributions, especially Mayellen Bresie, Juan R. Freudenthal, Jane Garner, Glenn F. Read, Jr., David S. Zubatsky, Kenneth E. Ingram, Alma Jordan, Nelly Dodero Kopper, and Luis Alberto Musso Ambrosi. To the late good and dedicated Marjorie LeDoux we offer a prayer of thanks. Lastly, on behalf of all Latin Americanists, we thank all of the bibliographers whose works are represented herein.

Daniel Raposo Cordeiro
Chairman, SALALM Committee
on Bibliography and Bibliographer
for Latin America, Spain and
Portugal at Syracuse University
Libraries

September, 1978
New Bedford, Massachusetts

CONTENTS

THE BIBLIOGRAPHY

GENERAL WORKS

GENERAL

1 "America en la bibliografía española (reseñas informativas)." Historiografía y bibliografía americanistas, 14 (1969), 162-300.

2 American Universities Field Staff. A select bibliography: Asia, Africa, Eastern Europe, Latin America. Cumulative supplement, 1961-1971. New York, 1973. 357 p.

3 _____ . _____ . Supplement 1969. New York, 1970. 97 p.

4 _____ . _____ . Supplement 1971. New York, 1972. 89 p.

5 Anaya-Las Americas. Bibliographical index for Spanish and Spanish American studies in the United States. New York, 1974. viii, 589 p.

6 Benito, Miguel. "América latina en la bibliografía danesa, 1969-1971...." Ibero-Americana, 2:2 (1972), 26-38.

7 _____ . "América latina en la bibliografía sueca, 1970-1971 ... (con añadiduras para 1959-1969 ...)." Ibero-Americana, 2:1 (1972), 28-62.

8 _____ . "Amérique [sic] latina en las bibliografías finlandesa [sic] y noruega [sic] 1969-1971...." Ibero-Americana, 3:1 (1973), 25-37.

9 _____ . Latinamerika i svensk bibliografi. America Latina en la bibliografía sueca, 1959-1969. Stockholm: Kungliga Biblioteket & Latinamerika-institutet, 1971. xv, 134 p.

1

10   Blakemore, Harold. "Recent British books on Latin
     America." British book news; a guide to new books,
     (Dec., 1971), 939-944.

11   CBA; anuario. Montevideo.

12   Centro Regional para el Fomento del Libro en América
     Latina. Boletín bibliográfico. Año I, Núm. 1- ,
     Julio 1974- . Bogotá, 1974- .

13   Dequenne, Jean. Amérique latine; essai de bibliographie
     des ouvrages belges publiés sur l'Amérique latine,
     1875-1962. Bruxelles: Commission Belge de Bibli-
     ographie, 1965. 295 p. (Bibliographie Belgica, 88).

14   Dorn, Georgette M. Latin America, Spain and Portugal;
     an annotated bibliography of paperbacks. Washington:
     Library of Congress, 1971. 180 p. (Hispanic Founda-
     tion bibliographical series, 13).

15   Farrell, Robert V. and John F. Hohenstein. Latin
     America, books for high schools; an annotated bibli-
     ography. Edited by Karna S. Wilgus. New York;
     Center for Inter-American Relations, 1969. 28 p.

16   Grases, Pedro. Más incunables venezolanas. Caracas:
     Cromotip, 1960. 30 p.

17   Hasler, Juan A. "Bibliographía americanísta brevis."
     Universidad de Antioquia, 180 (ene./mar., 1971), 3-
     32; 181 (abr./jun., 1971), 33-64.

18   Institute of Jamaica, Kingston. Library. Bibliography
     of the West Indies (excluding Jamaica), by Frank
     Cundall. New York: Johnson Reprint, 1971. 179 p.
     Reprint of the 1909 ed.

19   Jamieson, Alfred. A selective annotated guide to ma-
     terials on Latin America suitable for use at the sec-
     ondary level. Albany: The University of the State of
     New York, Center for International Programs and
     Comparative Studies, 1971. 57 p.

20   Kobe, Japan. University. Institute of Economy and
     Administration. Catálogo de libros sobre Latino-
     américa; sección de lenguas extrangeras. Shozo Raten
     Amerika Shiryo Mokuroku-ocbun-hen. Kobe: Instituto
     de Economía y Administración, 1970. 192 p.

21 Latin America: a guide to periodical literature. New
York: Center for Inter-American Relations, 197?.

22 Latin America; an annotated list of materials for children selected by a committee of librarians, teachers
and Latin American specialists in cooperation with the
Center for Inter-American Relations. New York: Information Center on Children's Cultures, 1969. iv,
96 p.

23 Latinamerika-institutet i Stockholm. Handledning vid
samhällsvetenskaplig och historisk forskning rörande
Latinamerika. Utg. för Nordiska samarbetskommitén
för Latinamerika forskning (NOSALF). Stockholm,
1973. 32 p.

24 León Pinelo, Antonio Rodríguez de. Epítome de la
biblioteca oriental y occidental, náutica y geográfica.
Madrid: Gráf. Yagües, 1973-1974. 3 v. Facsimile
of the 1737-1738 ed.

25 Levy, Jurt L. Book list on Latin America for Canadians.
Liste de livres sur l'Amérique latine à l'intention des
canadiens. Ottawa: Canadian Commission for UNES-
CO, 1969. 51 p.

26 Libros en venta en Hispanoamérica y España..., preparado bajo la dirección de Mary C. Turner. Suplemento 1967-1968. Buenos Aires: Bowker Editores
Argentina, 1969. 565 p.

27 _____. Suplemento 1969-1970. Buenos Aires: Bowker
Editores Argentina, 1972. 524 p.

28 _____. Suplemento 1971. Buenos Aires: Bowker
Editores Argentina, 1972. 269 p.

29 Libros en venta en Hispanoamérica y España. 2d ed.
New York: Bowker, 1974. 2 v.

30 Lohmann, Jens. Litteratur om Latinamerika. Annoteret
bibliografi. Kobenhavn: Mellemfolkelig Samvirke,
Eksp: DBK, 1973. 155 p. (Mellemfolkeligt samvirke. Ms bibliografier, 7)

31 London. Commonwealth Institute. The Commonwealth in
the Caribbean; an annotated list. London: National
Book League, 1969. 16 p.

32 London. University. Institute of Latin American
Studies. <u>Latin American studies in the universities of</u>
<u>the United Kingdom; staff research in progress or</u>
<u>recently completed in the humanities and the social</u>
<u>sciences.</u> London. Annual.

33 McGill University, Montreal. French Canada Studies
Programme. Bibliothèque. <u>La Canada français et</u>
<u>l'Amérique latine; bibliographie.</u> Compiled by Pierre
Jetté and Jean Pierre Jolin. Montreal: Bibliothèque,
Centre d'Etudes Canadiennes Françaises, Université
McGill, 1969. i, 13 ℓ.

34 Millares Carlo, Agustín. <u>Prontuario de bibliografía</u>
<u>general.</u> Caracas: Universidad Católica Andrés
Bello, Instituto de Investigaciones Históricas, 1973.
144 p.

35 North American Congress on Latin America. <u>NACLA's</u>
<u>bibliography on Latin America.</u> New York, 1973.
48p.

36 "Publications commissioned by the Joint Committees or
deriving from fellowships and grants." In: Foreign
Area Fellowship Program. <u>Joint Committee on Latin</u>
<u>American Studies and Joint Committee on the Foreign</u>
<u>Area Fellowship Program; report on activities, 1959-</u>
<u>70.</u> New York, 1971. pp. 42-81.

37 Steele, Colin. <u>English interpreters of the Iberian New</u>
<u>World from Purchas to Stevens: a bibliographical</u>
<u>study, 1603-1726.</u> Oxford: Dolphin Book Co., 1974?
204 p. Appendix: "A bibliography of English translations of Spanish and Portuguese books on the Iberian
New World, 1603-1726."

38 Texas. University at Austin. Latin American Curriculum Project. <u>Teaching about Latin America in secon-</u>
<u>dary school; an annotated guide to instructional re-</u>
<u>sources.</u> Clark Gill and William Conroy, co-directors.
Austin, 1967. 71 p.

39 Thompson, Lawrence Sidney. <u>The new Sabin; books de-</u>
<u>scribed by Joseph Sabin and his successors, now de-</u>
<u>scribed again on the basis of examination of originals,</u>
<u>and fully indexed by title, subject, joint authors, and</u>
<u>institutions and agencies.</u> Troy, N.Y.: Whitston Pub.
Co., 1974- .

40   U. S. Department of the Army. Latin America and the
     Caribbean: analytical survey of literature. Washing-
     ton: U. S. Government Printing Office, 1969.   vii,
     319 p.

41   U. S. Foreign Service Institute. Center for Area and
     Country Studies. A selected functional and country
     bibliography for the Latin American area. Washing-
     ton: Dept. of State, 1969.   38 ℓ.

42   Wilgus, Karna S.   Latin America books; an annotated
     bibliography for high schools and colleges.   New York:
     Center for Inter-American Relations, 1974.   80 p.

ARGENTINA

43   Matijevic, Nicolás and Olga Hecimovia de Matijevic.
     Bibliografía patagónica y de las tierras australes.
     Bahía Blanca; Universidad Nacional del Sur, Centro
     de Documentación Patagónica, 1973- .

44   Villascuerna, Inés.   Bibliografía para el estudio histórico
     de la marginalidad en el Noroeste de Argentina.
     Buenos Aires: Instituto Torcuato Di Tella, Centro de
     Investigaciones Sociales, 1970.   88 p.   (Documento
     de trabajo, 71).

BELIZE

45   Minkel, Clarence W. and Ralph H. Alderman.   A bib-
     liography of British Honduras, 1900-1970.   East Lans-
     ing: Latin American Studies Center, Michigan State
     University, 1970.   vii, 93 p.   (Research report, 7)

BERMUDA

46   Bermuda Library, Hamilton, Bermuda Islands.   Bermu-
     diana; bibliography.   Hamilton, 1971.   26 p.

BOLIVIA

47   Exposición bibliográfica: el libro Alemán contemporáneo
     y literatura en Alemán sobre Bolivia.   La Paz:

Universitaria, 1973.   39 p.   "Auspiciado por la Universidad Boliviana Mayor de San Andrés, Embajada de la República Alemana, Los Amigos del Libro."

BRAZIL

48   Almeida, Horácio de.   Contribuição para uma bibliografia paraibana.   Rio de Janeiro: Apex Gráfica e Editora, 1972.   195 p.

48a   Araújo, Zilda Galhardo de.   Guia de bibliografia especializada.   Rio de Janeiro: Associação Brasileira de Bibliotecarios, 1969.   xvi, 207 p.

49   Barreto, Abeillard.   Bibliografia sul-riograndense.   Rio de Janeiro: Conselho Federal de Cultura, 1973-   .

50   Bibliografia brasileira de livros infantis.   no. 1 -   . 1967-   .   Rio de Janeiro: Sindicato Nacional dos Editores de Livros.

51   Boletim internacional de bibliografia luso-brasileira. v. 1:1 (1960)-14:4 (1973).   Lisboa: Fundação Calouste Gulbenkian.

52   Brazil.   Congresso.   Câmara de Deputados.   Brasília. Brasília: Centro de Documentação e Informação, 1972.   1078 p.   (Bibliografias, 3).

53   Casa de las Américas.   Biblioteca José Antonio Echeverría.   Bibliografía sobre el Brasil.   La Habana, 1972.   91 ℓ.

54   Costa e Silva, Genny de and Maria do Carmo Rodrigues. Bibliografia sôbre Goiana: aspectos históricos e geográficos.   Recife: Commissão Organizadora e Executiva das Comemorações do IV Centenário do Provoamento de Goiana, 1972.   421 p.

55   Domínguez, Camilo A.   Amazonia colombiana; bibliografía general preliminar.   Bogotá: Universidad Nacional de Colombia, Centro de Investigaciones para el Desarrollo, 1973.   94 p.

56   Franzbach, Martin.   "Brasiliana."   Jahrbuch für Geschichte von Staat, Wirthschaft und Gesellschaft Lateina-

7 GENERAL WORKS

merikas, 7 (1970), 146-200. Includes a list of German language works published in the period 1504-1800.

57 Knopp, Anthony. Brazil books; a guide to contemporary works. New York: Center for Inter-American Relations, 1970. 20 p.

58 Livros novos. Current books. Neuerscheinungen. São Paulo: Atlantis Livros, 1972- . monthly.

59 Moraes, Rubens Borba de. Bibliografia brasileira do período colonial; catálogo comentado das obras dos autores nascidos no Brasil e publicadas antes de 1808. São Paulo: Instituto de Estudos Brasileiros, 1969. xxii, 437 p.

60 Musso Ambrosi, Luis Alberto. Bibliografía uruguaya sobre Brasil. 2. ed. aumentada. Montevideo: Instituto de Cultura Uruguayo-Brasileño, 1973. 166 p. (Publicaciones, 20).

61 Paraná, Brazil (State). Universidade Federal. Instituto de Letras e Artes. Catálogo coletivo de literatura, história e geografia do Paraná. Curitiba, 1972. 327 p.

62 Rio de Janeiro. Biblioteca Nacional. Amazonia brasileira; catálogo da exposição organizada pela seção de exposições e inaugurada em 2 de dezembro de 1969. Rio de Janeiro, 1969. 91 p.

63 _____. O livro raro em seus diversos aspectos; exposição comemorativa do Ano Internacional do Livro. Catálogo organizado pela Bibliotecária Iracema Celeste Rodrigues Monteiro. Rio de Janeiro, 1972. 58 p.

64 _____. Nordeste brasileiro; catálogo da exposição organizada pela Seção de Exposições e inaugurada em 24 de novembro de 1970. Rio de Janeiro, 1970. 86 p.

65 Rio de Janeiro. Instituto Brasileiro de Bibliografia e Documentação. Amazônia; bibliografia. Rio de Janeiro, 1963-72. 2 v.

66 Schulten, Cornelis Maria. Bibliografie van Nederlandse publikaties over Brazilië, 1945-1965. s.l., Ambassade van Brazilië, 1965. 28 p.

GENERAL WORKS   8

67 Sodré, Nelson Werneck. O que se deve ler para con-
    hecer o Brasil. 4. ed. Rio de Janeiro: Editora
    Civilização Brasileira, 1973. 406 p. (Retratos do
    Brasil, 54).

68 União Cultural Brasil-Estados Unidos. Biblioteca
    "Thomas Jefferson." List of books published in
    English on Brazil. São Paulo, n.d. 8 ℓ.

69 Villas-Bôas, Pedro. Notas de bibliografia sul-rio-
    grandense: autores. Proto Alegre: A Nação, 1974.
    615 p.

70 _____. Roteiro do regionalismo; bibliografia. Porto
    Alegre, 1969. 1 v. unpaged.

CENTRAL AMERICA

71 Heredia Correa, Roberto. "Bibliografía del IPGH
    sobre América Central." Estudios sociales centro-
    americanos, 6 (sept./dic., 1973), 155-163.

CHILE

72 Feliú Cruz, Guillermo. Historia de las fuentes de la
    bibliografía Chilena; ensayo crítico. Introducción a
    la edición facsímilar de la Estadística bibliográfica
    de la literatura Chilena de Ramón Briseño, 1812-1876.
    Santiago de Chile, 1966-69. 4 v. "Obra realizada
    por la Biblioteca Nacional bajo los auspicios de la
    Comisión Nacional de Conmemoración del Centenario
    de la Muerte de Andrés Bello."

COLOMBIA

73 Bryant, Solena V. Colombia: a select bibliography,
    1960-1970. New York: Colombia Information Ser-
    vice, 1972. 86 ℓ.

74 Domínguez, Camila A. Amazonia colombiana; biblio-
    grafía general preliminar. Bogotá: Universidad
    Nacional de Colombia, Centro de Investigaciones para
    el Desarrollo, 1973. 94 p.

75 Watson, Gayle Hudgens. Colombia, Ecuador, and Ven-
    zuela: an annotated guide to reference materials in
    the humanities and social sciences. Metuchen, N. J. :
    Scarecrow Press, 1971. 279 p.

CUBA

76 Alisse, Elena L. "Cuban books." The Booklist, 70:1
    (Mar. 1, 1974), 719-721.

77 Duncan, Roland E. "Cuba: selected paperback library."
    Hispania, 56:1 (March, 1973), 165-167.

78 "Libros sobre Cuba publicados en el extranjero." Re-
    vista de la Biblioteca Nacional José Martí, 3a. época,
    10:1 (ene. /abr. , 1968), 135-144.

79 Valdés, Nelson P. "Inventario bibliográfico sobre
    Cuba." Aportes, 11 (ene. , 1969), 66-75.

DOMINICAN REPUBLIC

80 Librería Hispaniola. Libros dominicanos. Santo Do-
    mingo: Julio D. Postigo, Editores, 1971. 91 p.

ECUADOR

81 Bromley, R. J. Bibliografía del Ecuador: ciencias
    sociales, económicas y geográficas. Talence, France:
    Centre d'Etudes de Géographie Tropicale, 1970. 61 p.
    (Travaux et documents de géographie tropicales, 2).

82 _____ . _____ . Quito: Junta Nacional de Planifi-
    cación y Coordinación, 1970? 61, 2 p.

EL SALVADOR

82a Sevillano Colom, Francisco. Lista de materiales micro-
    filmados [Misión de la UNESCO en El Salvador]. San
    Salvador, 1958. 44 ℓ .

GUYANA

83   Cummings, Leslie P. Bibliography, section 2 [of a bibliography on the Guianas being prepared. George-town, Guyana? 1968?] 45 p.

HAITI

83a Debien, Gabriel. "Antillas de lengua francesa (1969-1970)." Historiografía y bibliografía americanistas, 15:2 (jul. , 1971), 283-291.

84   Gagner, Lorraine and Kenneth Cook. Haiti: a selected and partially annotated bibliography. New York: United Nations, Institute for Training and Research, 1972. ii, 5 p.

HONDURAS

85   Finney, Kenneth V. "Valiosa y muy rara bibliografía hondureña." Anales del Archivo Nacional, 10 (may. , 1971), 52-57.

86   Martinson, Tom L. An introductory bibliography on Honduras. Monticello, Ill.: Council of Planning Librarians, 1972. 17 p. (Exchange bibliography, 326).

JAMAICA

87   Institute of Jamaica, Kingston. Library. Bibliographia jamaicensis; a list of Jamaica books & pamphlets, magazine articles, newspapers, & maps, most of which are in the Library of the Institute of Jamaica, by Frank Cundall. New York: B. Jranklin, 1971. 83 p. Reprint of 1902 ed.

MARTINIQUE

88   Jardel, Jean Pierre; Maurice Nicolas and Claude Relou-zat. Bibliographie de la Martinique. Fort-de-France: Centre d'Etudes Régionales Antilles. Guyane, 1969- . (Les Cahiers du CERAG, 3).

MEXICO

89   Civeira Taboada, Miguel.   La Ciudad de México en 500
      libros.   México: Departamento del Distrito Federal,
      Secretaría de Obras y Servicios, 1973.   142 p.
      (Colección popular Ciudad de México, 6).

90   Colin, Mario.   Bibliografía general del Estado de Méx-
      ico.   Mexico: [Editorial Jus, 1963-1964].   3 v.
      (Biblioteca enciclopédica del Estado de México, 1-3).

91   Homenaje a Benito Juárez.   Testimonios bibliográficos
      sobre México, 1548-1872.   Roma: Instituto ítalo-
      latino americano, 1972.   69 p.

92   Mexican National Tourist Council, New York.   Library.
      Bibliography of reference materials published in the
      U.S. on Mexico.   New York, 1970.   34 ℓ.

93   Puttick and Simpson, auctioneers, London.   Bibliotheca
      Mejicana; a catalogue of an extraordinary collection
      of books & manuscripts, almost wholly relating to
      the history and literature of North and South America,
      particularly Mexico.   To be sold by auction....   New
      York: AMS, 1973.   312 p.   Reprint of 1869 ed.

PARAGUAY

94   Moscov, Stephen C.   Paraguay: an annotated bibliog-
      raphy.   Buffalo: Council on International Studies,
      State University of New York at Buffalo, 1972.
      104 ℓ.   (Special studies, 10).

PERU

95   Casa de las Américas.   Biblioteca José Antonio Eche-
      verría.   Bibliografía del Perú.   La Habana, 1971.
      111 ℓ.

96   Martínez, Gustavo Miguel.   Bibliografías regionales
      peruanas.   Lima: Universidad Nacional Mayor de
      San Marcos, Instituto Raúl Porrás Barrenechea,
      Escuela de Altos Estudios y de Investigaciones Peru-
      anistas, 1973-   .

97 Moreyra Paz Soldán, Carlos. Bibliografía regional
    peruana; colección particular. Lima: Librería
    Internacional del Perú, 1967. 518 p.

98 Rubluo Islas, Luis. "Sumaria bibliográfica mexicana
    sobre la cultura del Perú." In: Congreso Interna-
    cional de Historia de América, 5th, Lima, 1971.
    Quinto Congreso Internacional de Historia de Amér-
    ica, Lima, 31 de Julio-6 de Agosto de 1971. Lima:
    Comisión Nacional del Sesquicentenario de la Inde-
    pendencia del Perú, 1972. v. 3, pp. 341-349.

PUERTO RICO

99 Bravo, Enrique R. Bibliografía puertorriqueña selecta
    y anotada. An annotated, selected Puerto Rican bib-
    liography. New York: The Urban Center, Columbia
    University, 1972. iii, 115 p., ii, 114 p.

100 Hill, Marnesba D. Bibliography of Puerto Rican his-
    tory and literature. New York: Herbert H. Leh-
    man College Library, 1972. 31 ℓ.

101 Ledesma, Moises. Bibliografía cultural de Puerto
    Rico (anotada). New York: Plus Ultra Educational
    Publishers, 1970. 103 p.

102 New York (State). State Education Department. Books
    and materials in English on Puerto Rico and the
    Puerto Ricans. Albany, 1972.

103 Pedreira, Antonio Salvador. Bibliografía puertorri-
    queña (1493-1930). Foreword to the new ed. by
    Francesco Cordasco. New York: B. Franklin Re-
    prints, 1974. xxxii, 707 p. (Burt Franklin bib-
    liography & reference series, 496). Reprint of
    1932 ed.

104 Puerto Rican Research and Resources Center. The
    Puerto Ricans: an annotated bibliography, edited
    by Paquita Vivó. New York: Bowker, 1973. xv,
    299 p.

105/6 The Puerto Ricans: migration and general bibliography.
    New York: Arno Press, 1975. 55 p.

SURINAM

107 Ensberg, Louise. Boeken over Suriname; bibliografie
     van boeken bestaande uit of bevattende een beschrijv-
     ing van Suriname als geheel. n.p., 1969. 40 ℓ.

108 Instituut voor Taal- Land- en Volkenkunde. Bibliotheek.
     Literatuur-overzicht van de Nederlandse Antillen
     vanaf de 17e eeuw tot 1970..., compiled by G. A.
     Nagelkerke. Leiden, 1973. 147 p.

109 _____. Literatuur-overzicht van Suriname tot 1940./
     Literature-survey of Surinam until 1940..., compiled
     by G. A. Nagelkerke. Leiden, 1972. 199 p.

110 _____. Literatuur-overzicht van Suriname, 1940
     tot 1970 / A bibliography of Surinam, 1940-1970...,
     compiled by G. A. Nagelkerke. Leiden, 1971.
     96 p.

111 Nederlandse Stichting voor Culturele Samenwerking met
     Suriname en de Nederlandse Antillen. Bibliografie
     van Suriname. [Redakteur: W. Gordijn]. Amsterdam,
     1972. 256 p.

URUGUAY

112 Alisky, Marvin. Bibliography on Uruguay. Montevideo:
     American International Association, 1969. 11 p.

VENEZUELA

113 Venezuela. Universidad Central. Consejo de Desar-
     rollo Científico y Humanístico. Bibliografía de
     humanidades y ciencias sociales del profesorado de
     la U.C.V., 1967-1970. Caracas, 1973 [i.e. 1974].
     101 p.

114 _____. Catálogo de la investigación universitaria
     [1960-1963]. Caracas, 1963 [i.e. 1964]. 181 p.

115 Venezuela. Universidad Central. Escuela de Biblio-
     teconomía y Archivos. Catálogo bibliográfico de la
     Facultad de Humanidades y Educación, 1948-1968.

Caracas, 1969.   498 p.   (Indice de publicaciones oficiales de la Universidad Central de Venezuela, 1).

116 _____. Exposición de obras conmemorativas del sesquicentenario de nuestra independencia.... Caracas: Facultad de Humanidades y Educación, 1961. 21 p.

117 _____. Muestra antológica del libro de Guyana. Caracas, 1964. 24 p.

AGRICULTURE

GENERAL

118 "Açúcar, transporte, estoque e armazenagem; bibliografia." Brasil açucareiro, 78:1 (jul., 1971), 98-99.

119 "Agronomia açucareira: bibliografia." Brasil açucareiro, 78:4 (out., 1971), 107-109.

120 Aliaga de Vizcarra, Irma. Bibliografía boliviana de pastos y forrajes. La Paz: Ministerio de Asuntos Campesinos, División de Investigaciones, 1971. 10 p.

121 Bibliografía agrícola latinoamericana. v. 1, no. 1- . 1966- . Turrialba, Costa Rica: Asociatión Interamericana de Bibliotecarios y Documentalistas Agrícolas.

122 Birou, Alain. Bibliografía reciente (1965-69) sobre problemas agrarios en América Latina. Madrid, IEPAL, 1970. 56 ℓ. (Cursos y documentos).

123 Cardozo González, Armando and G. Uribe. Bibliografía de materiales de enseñanza. Quito: Instituto Interamericano de Ciencias Agrícolas de la OEA, 1971. 13 p.

124 "Educación agrícola en América Latina; bibliografía de publicaciones preparadas por organizaciones internacionales." Boletín para Bibliotecas Agrícolas, 8:1 (1971), 32-54.

125 "Folclore da cana-de-açúcar no Brasil; bibliografia."
Brasil açucareiro, 78:2 (ago., 1971), 148-149.

126 Havana. Biblioteca Nacional José Martí. Departamento
Metódico. Bibliografía sobre: a) equipo y maqui-
naria agrícola y de construcción; b) organización y
planificación rural. La Habana, 1969. 115 p.
(Folletos de divulgación técnica y científica, 27).

127 Instituto Brasileiro do Café. "Bibliografia agrícola:
1950-1970; livros em português existentes na Biblioteca do IBC." Boletim de documentação, 1:4
(set., 1971), 17-26.

128 _____. Bibliografia sobre custos de produção de
produtos agrícolas. Rio de Janeiro: Instituto
Brasileiro do Café, 1971.

129 Instituto de Pesquisas e Experimentação Agropecuarias
do Nordeste. Biblioteca. Levantamento bibliográfico sôbre cana-de-açucar, por Lúcia Maria Coêlho
de Oliveira e Maria de Fátima Vieira Peixoto.
Recife, 1970. 37 ℓ.

130 Inter-American Center for Documentation and Agriculture Information. Reforma agraria y tenencia de la
tierra: catálogo colectivo. Turrialba, Costa Rica:
Centro Interamericano de Documentación e Información Agrícola, 1972. vi, 229 p. (Bibliografías, 7).

131 Mayrink, Paulo Tarcisio and Maria Dias Bicalho.
2,000 livros agrícolas em português. Viçosa,
Minas Gerais: Universidade Federal de Viçosa e
AIBDA, 1973. 232 p.

132 Morales, María Victoria. Bibliografía sobre caña de
azúcar. La Habana: Departamento de Publicaciones
de la Biblioteca Nacional José Martí, 1970. 62 ℓ.
(Folletos de divulgación técnica y científica, 31).

133 Peru. Centro Nacional de Capacitación e Investigación
para la Reforma Agraria. Centro de Documentación
del Sector Agrario. Boletín bibliográfico. v. 1,
no. 1, ene./jul., 1974. Lima.

134 Sable, Martin Howard. Latin American agriculture: a
bibliography. Milwaukee: University of Wisconsin,

Center for Latin American Studies, 1970. v, 72 p.
(Special study, 1).

135 Thomé, Joseph R. Bibliografía temática sobre aspectos
jurídico institucionales del proceso de reforma agraria en América Latina con énfasis en el proceso
chileno de 1965-1970. Versión preliminar. Santiago de Chile, 1972. iii, 24 ℓ.

136 Uribe Contreras, Maruja and Guillermo Isaza Vélez.
Bibliografía selectiva sobre reforma agraria en
América Latina. Bogotá: Biblioteca Rodrigo Peña,
1972. ix, 381 p. (Boletín bibliográfico, 5).

137 Viçosa, Brazil. Universidade Federal. Biblioteca
Central. Seção de Bibliografia e Documentação.
Bibliografia do café (1952-1972), levantamento bibliográfico do material existente sobre café no acervo
da Biblioteca.... Viçosa, 1973. vi, 124 p. (Série
bibliografias especializadas, 3).

BOLIVIA

138 Aliaga de Vizcarra, Irma. Bibliografía agrícola boliviana. Suplemento. La Paz: Ministerio de Agricultura, Biblioteca, 1969- .

139 Bibliografía agrícola boliviana. v. 1- . Cochabamba:
Editorial Universitaria, 1970- .

140 Cardozo González, Armando. Catálogo de la bibliografía agrícola de Bolivia, 1900-1963, de Arturo Costa
de la Torre. La Paz, 1970. 14 ℓ. (Sociedad de
Ingenieros Agrónomos de Bolivia. Boletín bibliográfico, 11). "Compiled from Costa de la Torre's
Catálogo de la bibliografía boliviana."

BRAZIL

141 Bibliografia brasileira de ciencias agrícolas. 1966/
68- . Rio de Janeiro, Instituto Brasileiro de Bibliografia e Documentação, 1969- .

142 Brazil. Superintendência do Desenvolvimento do Nordeste. Departamento de Agricultura. Catálogo das
publicações editadas pelo Departamento de Agricul-

tura e Abastecimento da SUDENE. Recife, 1972. 54 p.

143 Sociedad Nacional de Agricultura, Rio de Janeiro. Bibliografia agrícola do Brasil, 1968. Rio de Janeiro, 1969. 315 p.

CENTRAL AMERICA

144 Lombardo, Heraclio A. Research on agricultural development in Central America. New York: Agricultural Development Council, 1969. 71 p.

COLOMBIA

145 Instituto Colombiano Agropecuario. Boletín bibliográfico. Bogotá, 1974. (Boletín promocional, 7).

COSTA RICA

146 Huertas, Maritza. Bibliografías agrícolas de América Central: Costa Rica. Turrialba, Costa Rica: Instituto Interamericano de Ciencias Agrícolas, Centro Interamericano de Documentación e Información Agrícola, 1972. vii, 166 p. (Bibliografías, 8).

ECUADOR

147 Cordozo González, Armando; Galo Romero R. and Francisco Cevallos T. Bibliografía ecuatoriana de cereales. Quito: Instituto Interamericano de Ciencias Agrícolas de la OEA, Instituto Nacional de Investigaciones Agropecuarias y Comisión Nacional del Trigo, 1970. 18 p.

148 Oviedo, M. Bibliografía forestal ecuatoriana. Suplemento no. 1. Quito: Instituto Interamericano de Ciencias Agrícolas, OEA, 1971. 7 p.

JAMAICA

149 Steer, Edgar S. A select bibliography of reference material providing and introduction to the study of Jamaican agriculture. Hope, Jamaica: Agricultural

Planning Unit, Ministry of Agriculture and Fisheries, 1970. 40 p.

MEXICO

150 Martínez Ríos, Jorge. Tenencia de la tierra y desarrollo agrario en México; bibliografía selectiva y
comentada, 1522-1968. México: Institute de Investigaciones Sociales, 1970. ix, 305 p.

151 Velazquez Gallardo, Pablo and Raúl F. Zertuche Ríos.
Bibliografía agrícola nacional, 25 años de agricul-
tura mexicana, 1946-1970. México: Alvarez y
Alvarez, 1973. 2 v.

PANAMA

152 Herrera, C. D. de. Bibliografías agrícolas de América Central: Panamá. Turrialba, Costa Rica: Instituto Interamericano de Ciencias Agrícolas, Centro
Interamericano de Documentación e Información
Agrícola, 1972. 142 p. (Bibliografías, 9).

PERU

153 Lima. Centro Nacional de Capacitación e Investigación
para la Reforma Agraria. CENCIRA Boletín bibliográfico. no. 1- . 1971- . Lima.

URUGUAY

154 Bibliografía agrícola de Uruguay. 1962/63- . Montevideo: Ministerio de Ganadería y Agricultura, Biblioteca Central, 1970- .

VENEZUELA

155 Márquez M., Orfila, Luisa Bustillos García and Belkys
Gutiérrez. Fuentes de información agrícola venezolana. Maracay: Oficina de Comunicaciones Agrícolas y Fondo Nacional de Investigaciones Agropecuarias, 1972. 52 ℓ.

GENERAL

156   Alcina Franch, José. "La antropología americanista
      en España: 1950-1970. " Revista española de antro-
      pología americana, 7:1 (1972), 17-58.

157   Bartholomew, Doris. "Boletín informativo sobre idio-
      mas indígenas de Latinoamérica. " América Indí-
      gena, 29:2 (abr. , 1969), 515-528.

158   Boggs, Ralph Steele. Bibliography of Latin American
      folklore: tales, festivals, customs, arts, magic,
      music. Detroit: B. Ethridge-Books, 1971. x,
      109 p. Reprint of 1940 ed.

159   Buenos Aires. Museo Mitre. Catálogo razonado de la
      sección de lenguas americanas, por Bartolomé
      Mitre. Con una introducción de Luis María Torres.
      Buenos Aires: Imprenta de Coni hermanos, 1909-
      1910 [i. e. 11] 3 v.

160   Forbes, Jean; Juan J. Arias and Carmen Anzures.
      "Registro bibliográfico de estudios antropológicos
      sobre América Latina: índice analítico. " América
      indígena, ·28:1 (ene. , 1968), 139-154.

161   García Icazbalceta, Joaquín. Apuntes para un catálogo
      de escritores en lenguas indígenas de América.
      New York: B. Franklin, 1970. xiii, 157·p. (Burt
      Franklin bibliography and reference series, 335).
      Reprint of 1866 ed.

162   Hasler, Juan A. Bibliographia americanistica brevis.
      Medellín: Universidad de Antioquia, 1973. 170 p.

163   "Inventario de los estudios en ciencias sociales sobre
      América Latina: antropología. " Aportes. [Regular
      feature.]

164   Kemper, Robert V. "Bibliografía comentada sobre la
      antropología urbana en América Latina. " Boletín
      bibliográfico de antropología americana, 33/34 (1970/
      71), 85-140.

165 Ochoa S., Lorenzo. "Bibliografía antropológica de 'La palabra y el hombre.' " Boletín bibliográfico de antropología americana, 33/34 (1970/1971), 141-153.

166 "Registro bibliográfico de estudios antropológicos sobre América Latina." America indígena. [Regular feature.]

167 "Revista de libros y revistas." Boletín bibliográfico de antropología americana. [Regular feature.]

168 Rogers, Susan W. Black spiritualism in Latin America: a bibliography of sources available in the Pan American Society of New England Library. Boston: Pan American Society of New England and Simmons College, 1973. 9 p.

169 Villa Rojas, Alfonso. "Resúmenes de trabajos presentados en la 66a. reunión anual de la Asociación Americana de Antropología (nov. 30-dic. 3, 1967)." América indígena, 28:2 (abr., 1968), 485-525.

170 _____. "Resúmenes de trabajos presentados en la 69a. reunión anual de la Asociación Americana de Antropología; noviembre 19-22, 1970." América indígena, 31:1 (ene., 1971), 163-206.

ARGENTINA

171 Berberián, Eduardo E. "Bibliografía antropológica de la Provincia de Córdoba, R. A., años 1874 a 1969." Boletín de la Academia Nacional de Ciencias, 47: 2/4 (1970), 163-257.

172 Cooper, John Montgomery. Analytical and critical bibliography of the tribes of Tierra del Fuego and adjacent territory. Oosterhout, N.B., The Netherlands: Anthropological Publications, 1967. ix, 233 p. Reprint of the 1917 ed.

BRAZIL

173 Baldus, Herbert. Bibliografia crítica da etnologia brasileira. Nendeln, Liechtenstein: Kraus Reprints, 1968-1970. 2 v. (Volkerkundliche Abhandlungen. Bd. 3-4).

174 Hartmann, Thekla. Panorama das investigações antropológicas no Brasil. São Paulo: Universidade de São Paulo, Faculdade de Filosofia, Ciências e Letras, 1968. 29 p.

175 Nascimento, Braulio do. Bibliografia do folclore brasileiro. Com a colaboração de Cydnéa Bouyer. Rio de Janeiro: Biblioteca Nacional, 1971. 353 p. (Coleção Rodolfo Garcia. Série B: Catálogos e bibliografias).

176 Rio de Janeiro. Biblioteca Nacional. Catálogo da exposição Dia Internacional do Folclore e Mello Moraes Filho. Rio de Janeiro, 1969. 41 p.

177 Salles, Vicente. "Bibliografia crítica do folclore brasileiro: Capoeira." Revista brasileira de folclore, 8:23 (jan./abr., 1969), 79-103.

CENTRAL AMERICA

178 Bozzoli de Wille, María E. "Bibliografía antropológica de Costa Rica." Estudios sociales centroamericanos, 7 (ene./abr., 1974), 169-183.

179 McGlynn, Eileen A. Middle American anthropology: directory, bibliography, and guide to the UCLA Library collections. Los Angeles: Latin American Center and University Library, University of California, 1975. viii, 131 p. (UCLA Library. Guides. Series B, 1).

180 Warren, K. B. Mesoamerica community studies, 1930-1970: a bibliography. Princeton, N.J.: Princeton University Library, 1973. iv, 32 ℓ.

CHILE

181 Dannemann Rothstein, Manuel. Bibliografía del folklore chileno, 1952-1965. Austin: Center for Intercultural Studies in Folklore and Oral History, University of Texas, 1970. xvi, 60 p. (Latin American folklore series, 2).

182 Montané M., Julio C. Bibliografía selectiva de

antropología chilena. (4a parte): Indice de autores.
La Serena: Imprenta Diario "El Día," 1965. 97 p.

COLOMBIA

183   Bernal Villa, Segundo. Guía bibliográfica de Colombia
de interés para el antropólogo. Bogotá: Ediciones
Universidad de los Andes, 1969. 782 p.

DOMINICAN REPUBLIC

184   "Bibliografía (sobre antropología, arqueología y pre-
historia dominicanas)." Universo, Santo Domingo,
1 (jul./sept., 1971), 58-59.

MEXICO

185   Almstedt, Ruth. Bibliography of the Diegueño Indians.
Ramona, Calif.: Ballena Press, 1974. 52 p.

186   Hellmuth, Nicolas M. A bibliography of the 16th-20th
century Maya of the Southern lowlands: Chol, Chol
Lacandon, Yucatec Lacandon, Quejache, Itza and
Mopan, 1524-1969. Greeley: Museum of Anthropology, University of Northern Colorado, 1970.
xviii, 114 ℓ. (Occasional publication in anthropology. Archaeology series, 2).

187   _____. Preliminary bibliography of the Chol, La-
candon, Yucatec Lacandon, Chol, Itza, Mopan, and
Quejache of the Southern Maya lowlands, 1524-1969.
Providence, 1969. i, 110 ℓ.

188   _____. _____. Greeley, Colo.: Museum of
Anthropology, University of Northern Colorado, 1970.
xviii, 142 ℓ. (Katunob. Occasional publications in
Mesoamerican anthropology, 4).

189   Hillyer, Mildred. Bibliography of Spanish and South
Western Indian cultures: library books. Grants,
N.M.: Grants Municipal Schools, 1969. 24 ℓ.

190   Licea Ayala, Judith. "Una contribución a la bibliografía sobre cultura náhuatl; índice de los artículos

23 ANTHROPOLOGY

sobre esta disciplina publicados en los 'Anales del
Museo Nacional' y en los 'Anales del Instituto de
Antropología e Historia'." Boletín del Instituto de
Investigaciones Bibliográficas, 1:1 (ene./jun., 1969),
151-173.

191 Marino Flores, Anselmo. "Bibliografía de antropología del Estado de Guerrero (México)." Boletín bibliográfico de antropología americana, 32 (1969),
139-169.

192 Navarette, Carlos. "Fuentes para la historia cultural
de los Zoques." Anales de antropología, 7 (abr./
jun., 1970), 207-246.

193 Robe, Stanley Linn. Index of Mexican folktales, including narrative texts from Mexico, Central America,
and the Hispanic United States. Berkeley: University of California Press, 1973. xxiii, 276 p.
(Folklore studies, 26).

PARAGUAY

194 Mareski, Sofía and Oscar Humberto Ferraro. Bibliografía sobre datos y estudios etnográficos y antropológicos del Paraguay. Asunción: Centro Paraguayo de Documentación Social, 1972. 143 p.
(Documentos y estudios bibliográficos, 2).

PERU

195 Aguirre Beltrán, Gonzalo; Hernán Castillo Ardiles and
Jorge Miranda Pelayo. "Bibliografía antropológica
en lengua castellana de la costa y de la sierra del
Perú durante los últimos veinticinco años." América indígena, 28:1 (ene., 1968), 155-263.

196 García Blasquez, Raúl and César Ramón Córdova.
"Bibliografía de los estudios y publicaciones del
Instituto Indigenista Peruano (1961-1969)." Amér-
ica indígena, 30:3 (jul., 1970), 761-827.

197 Summer Institute of Linguistics. Bibliografía del Instituto Lingüístico de Verano en el Perú, junio 1946-
junio 1971. Recopilación por Mary Ruth Wise S.

Sumarios por Paul Powlison F. Lima: Instituto
Lingüístico de Verano, 1971. 124 p.

VENEZUELA

198   Cardozo, Lubio. Bibliografía de la literatura indígena
      venezolana. Mérida: Universidad de los Andes,
      Centro de Investigaciones Literarias, 1970. 122 p.

199   "Publicaciones antropológicas sobre Venezuela desde
      1967 hasta el presente." Boletín bibliográfico de
      antropología americana, 31 (1968), 53-56.

WEST INDIES

200   Clermont, Norman. Bibliographie annotée de l'anthro-
      pologie physique des Antilles. Montreal: Centre de
      Recherches Caraíbes, 1972 [i.e. 1973]. 51 p.

ARCHITECTURE

201   Gutiérrez Z. , Ramón. Notas para una bibliografía his-
      panoamericana de arquitectura, 1526-1875. Resis-
      tencia, Argentina: Departamento de Historia de la
      Arquitectura, 1973? xc, 420 p.

ART

202   Almanzar, Alcedo. Latin American numismatic bibliog-
      raphy (including the Caribbean). San Antonio, Texas:
      Almanzar's Coins of the World, 1972. 42 p.

203   Chacón Torres, Mario. Arte virreinal en Potosí:
      fuentes para su historia. Sevilla: Escuela de Es-
      tudios Hispanoamericanos, 1973. 329 p. (Publica-
      ciones, 213).

204   Chevrette, Valerie. Annotated bibliography of the pre-
      columbian art and archaeology of the West Indies.
      New York: Library, Museum of Primitive Art, 1971.
      18 p. (Primitive art bibliographies, 9).

205 Heller, Joyce de. Bibliografía de orfebrería prehis-
     pánica de Colombia. Bibliography of pre-Hispanic
     goldwork of Colombia. Bogotá: Tall, Gráf. Banco
     de la República, 1971. 126 p. (Museo del Oro.
     Estudios, 1:1).

206 Kendall, Aubyn. The art of pre-Columbian Mexico: an
     annotated bibliography of works in English. Austin:
     Institute of Latin American Studies, University of
     Texas, 1973. x, 115 p. (Guides and bibliographies
     series, 5).

207 Mattos, Maria Virgínia Bastos de. Semana de arte
     moderna: 50 anos; bibliografia. São Paulo: Uni-
     versidade de São Paulo, Depto. Biblioteconomia e
     Documentação, Hemeroteca, 1972- .

208 Rio de Janeiro. Biblioteca Nacional. A moderna gra-
     vura brasileira; catálogo da exposição. Organizado
     por Eunice de Manso Cabral. Rio de Janeiro, 1974.
     20 p.

     BIBLIOGRAPHY OF BIBLIOGRAPHIES

209 Becerra, Bertha and Ana Rosa Núñez. "Lista selectiva
     de bibliografías en revistas cubanas." In: Seminar
     on the Acquisition of Latin American Library Mater-
     ials, 15th, Toronto, 1970. Final report and working
     papers. Washington: O. A. S., 1971. v. 2, pp.
     191-207.

210 Cardozo González, Armando. Bibliografía de bibliogra-
     fías agrícolas bolivianas. La Paz: Empresa Edi-
     tora Universo, 1969. 8 p.

211. _____. _____. 2 ed. Bogotá, 1974. 18 p.

212 Centro Latinoamericano de Pesquisas em Ciências So-
     ciais. "Bibliografías especializadas." América
     latina, 13:4 (oct. /dez., 1970), 93-96.

213 Cline, Herman H. and Daniel Raposo Cordeiro. "A
     report of bibliographic activities, 1969." In: Semi-
     nar on the Acquisition of Latin American Library
     Materials, 14th, San Juan, Puerto Rico, 1969.

Final report and working papers. Washington:
O. A. S. , 1970. v. 1, pp. 261-278.

214 Cordeiro, Daniel Raposo. "A report on bibliographic
activities, 1970." In: Seminar on the Acquisition
of Latin American Library Materials, 15th, Toronto,
1970. Final report and working papers. Washington: O. A. S. , 1971. v. 2, pp. 3-39.

215 Culebra de Soberanes, Cecilia. "Bibliografías sobre
América Latina: ciencias sociales." Foro internacional, 46 (oct. /dic. , 1971), 229-269.

216 Dardón Córdova, Gonzalo. La bibliografía en Guatemala; su desarrollo durante los siglos XIX y XX.
Guatemala: Facultad de Humanidades, Universidad
de San Carlos de Guatemala, 1969. ii, 118 ℓ.
"Bibliografía de bibliografías guatemaltecas": ℓ.
57-118.

217 Duke University. Library. Bibliography of recent bibliographies published in Latin America and elsewhere
on subjects of interest to Latin America. Compiled
by Jesús Leyte-Vidal and Celia Leyte-Vidal. Dur-
ham, N.C. , 1971. 9 ℓ.

218 Estación Experimental Agropecuaria Pergamino. Bibliografía de bibliografías argentinas en ciencias
agrícolas y naturales. Pergamino, 1969. 56 p.
(Serie bibliográfica, tomo 53, apéndice).

219 Geoghegan, Abel Rodolfo. Bibliografía de bibliografías
argentinas, 1807-1970. Buenos Aires: Casa Pardo,
1970. 164 p.

220 Havana. Biblioteca Nacional José Martí. Departa-
mento de Hemeroteca e Información de Humanidades.
Bibliografía de bibliografías cubanas (1859-1972).
Compilación, prólogo y notas por Tomás Fernández
Robaina. La Habana, 1973 [i.e. 1974]. 340 p.

221 Jaquith, James R. "Bibliography of anthropological
bibliographies of the Americas." América indígena,
30:2 (abr. , 1970), 419-469.

222 Jones, Cecil Knight. A bibliography of Latin American
bibliographies. 2nd. ed. rev. and enl. New York:
Greenwood Press, 1969. 307 p.

223 Lovera de Sola, R. J. "Contribución a la bibliografía de bibliografías venezolanas. " Boletín histórico, Caracas, 10:33 (sept. , 1973), 513-522.

224 Matas, Anguita, Blanca. "Bibliografía de bibliografías chilenas, 1963-1971. " In: Seminar on the Acquisition of Latin American Library Materials, 16th, Puebla, Mexico, 1971. Final report and working papers. Washington: O. A. S. , 1973. v. 2, pp. 313-324.

225 Pinto, Aloísio de Arruda and Maria das Graças Moreira Ferreira. Bibliografia de bibliografias agrícolas do Brasil. Viçosa, Brasil: Universidade Federal de Viçosa, Biblioteca Central, Seção de Bibliografia e Documentação, 1974. 86 p. (Série bibliografias especializadas, 6).

226 Siles Guevara, Juan. Bibliografía de bibliografías bolivianas. La Paz: Ministerio de Cultura, Información y Turismo, Impr. del Estado, 1969. 38 p. (Cuadernos de bibliografía, 1).

227 _____. _____. 2a. ed. La Paz, 1970. Separata de Estudios andinos, 1:1 (1970), 149-170.

228 Watson, Gayle Hudgens. "A report on bibliographic activities, 1971. " In: Seminar on the Acquisition of Latin American Library Materials, 16th, Puebla, Mexico, 1971. Final report and working papers. Washington: O. A. S. , 1973. v. 1, pp. 309-354.

BIBLIOGRAPHY--NATIONAL

ARGENTINA

229 Bibliografía argentina universitaria. no. 1- . ago. 1970- . La Plata, Argentina: Universidad Nacional de La Plata, Biblioteca.

230 Buenos Aires. Universidad. Instituto Bibliotecológico. Catálogo colectivo universitario del libro argentino (CUCLA), Letras A-B; material correspondiente a los ingresos en las bibliotecas universitarias en 1973. Buenos Aires, 1975. 100 p.

231 Exposición del libro argentino. Dirección General de
     Relaciones Culturales del Ministerio de Relaciones
     Exteriores y Culto, Fondo Nacional de las Artes,
     Cámara Argentina del Libro, Cámara Argentina de
     Editores de Libros. Buenos Aires: Edición del
     Fondo Nacional de las Artes, 196?. 115 p.

BOLIVIA

232 Catálogo del libro potosino. Potosí: Universidad
     Boliviana Mayor "Tomás Frías," 1973. 42 p.

233 Costa de la Torre, Arturo. Catálogo de la bibliogra-
     fía boliviana: libros y folletos, 1900-1963. La
     Paz: Editorial Universidad Mayor de San Andrés,
     1969-1973. 2 v.

BRAZIL

234 Bibliografia brasileira mensal. nov., 1967-dez., 1972.
     Rio de Janeiro: Instituto Nacional do Livro. Super-
     seded by Boletim bibliográfico de la Biblioteca Na-
     cional, as of v. 18, No. 1 (1973).

235 Brodbeck, Sully. Problemática da bibliografía sul-rio-
     grandense. Pôrto Alegre: Departamento de Educa-
     ção e Cultura, 1968. 9 ℓ.

236 Resenha bibliográfica. Rio de Janeiro: Sindicato Na-
     cional dos Editores de Livros, 1968-1972. 47 nos.

237 Resumo bibliográfico. Rio de Janeiro: Sindicato Na-
     cional dos Editores de Livros, 1973- . Supersedes
     Resenha bibliográfica.

238 Rio de Janeiro. Biblioteca Nacional. Exposição do
     livro brasileiro contemporâneo. Lisboa, 1957.
     245 p.

239 Rio de Janeiro. Instituto Nacional do Livro. Exposi-
     ção do livro brasileiro contemporâneo.... Col-
     chester, Essex: University of Essex, 1969. ix,
     217 p.

240 _____. I exposição da imprensa universitária, São

Paulo, 17 a 25 de junho, 1972; catálogo.   Brasília,
1972. 202 p.

241 Sindicato Nacional dos Editores de Livros.   Edições
     brasileiras: Frankfurt Book Fair.   Rio de Janeiro,
     1970. 101 p.

242 U. S. Library of Congress.   Library of Congress acces-
     sions list: Brazil. v. 1, no. 1- . Jan. 1975- .
     Rio de Janeiro.

CHILE

243 "Bibliografía chilena; selección de los libros y folletos
     ingresados a la Biblioteca Nacional (Sección Chilena)
     por concepto de la ley de depósito legal. "· Mapocho·
     [Regular feature.]

COSTA RICA

244 Dobles Segreda, Luis.   Indice bibliográfico de Costa
     Rica· San José, C. R. :   Impr. Lehmann, Associa-
     ción Costarricense de Bibliotecarios, 1927-1968.
     11· v. in 10.

CUBA

245 Bibliografía cubana· 1959/62- . La Habana: Con-
     sejo Nacional de Cultura·

246 Revolutionary Cuba; a bibliographical guide, 1966-1968.
     Coral Gables, Fla. :   University of Miami Press,
     1967-1970. 3 v.

EL SALVADOR

247 El Salvador. Biblioteca Nacional· Boletín bibliográ-
     fico; lista de obras incorporadas y materias.   San
     Salvador, 1968- .

GUATEMALA

248 Reyes Monroy, José Luis.   Bibliografía de la imprenta

en Guatemala (Adiciones de 1769 a 1900). Guatemala: Editorial "José de Pineda Ibarra," Ministerio de Educación, 1969. 143 p.

HAITI

249 Bissainthe, Max. Dictionnaire de bibliographie haitienne: premier supplément. Metuchen, N. J. : Scarecrow Press, 1973. 277 p.

HONDURAS

250 García, Miguel Angel. Anuario bibliográfico hondureño, 1961-1971. Tegucigalpa: Banco Central de Honduras, 1973. 512 p.

251 _____. Bibliografía hondureña. Tegucigalpa: Banco Central de Honduras, 1971-1972. 2 v.

MEXICO

252 Andrade, Vicente de Paula. Ensayo bibliográfico mexicano del siglo xvii. 2. ed. Mexico: J. Medina, 1971. vii, 803 p.

253 Bonner, A. R. "Mexican pamphlets in the Bodleian Library." Bodleian Library record, 8:4 (Apr., 1970), 205-213.

254 Cavazos Garza, Israel. "Algunos impresos jaliscienses del siglo XIX existente en el Archivo General del Estado de Nuevo León." Boletín del Instituto de Investigaciones Bibliográficas, 4 (jul./dic., 1970), 73-83.

PANAMA

255 Susto Lara, Juan Antonio. Panorama de la bibliografía en Panamá (1619-1967). Panamá: Editorial Universitaria, 1971. xix, 102 p.

PARAGUAY

256 Fernández-Caballero, Carlos Francisco Solano. Aran-
     dukâ ha kuatiañeé paraguai rembiapocué. The Para-
     guayan bibliography; a retrospective and enumerative
     bibliography of printed works of Paraguayan authors.
     Asunción/Washington: Paraguay Arandú, 1970. iii,
     143 p.

PUERTO RICO

257 "Bibliografía puertorriqueña, 1966." Revista del In-
     stituto de Cultura Puertorriqueña, 34 (ene./mar.,
     1967), 56-62.

URUGUAY

258 Montevideo. Biblioteca del Poder Legislativo. Sección
     Bibliografía Uruguaya. Bibliografía uruguaya, años
     1962 a 1968 inclusive. Montevideo, 1971. 2 v.

VENEZUELA

259 Bibliografía venezolana. año 1- . ene./mar. 1970- .
     Caracas: Centro Bibliográfico Venezolano.

260 Venezuela. Universidad Central. Biblioteca. Libros
     de Venezuela. Caracas, 1970. xxxvi, 107 p.

261 Venezuela. Universidad Central. Escuela de Bibliote-
     conomía y Archivos. Catálogo de la exposición de
     libros venezolanos y venezolanistas de los anos 1957-
     1959.... Caracas: Facultad de Humanidades y Edu-
     cación, 1959. 36 ℓ.

262 _____. Catálogo de la exposición "Publicaciones y
     hojas sueltas venezolanas desde 1800 a 1900." Cara-
     cas: Facultad de Humanidades y Educacion, 1960.
     15 p.

263 Villasana, Angel Raúl. Ensayo de un repertorio biblio-
     gráfico venezolano, años 1808-1950. Caracas:
     Banco Central de Venezuela, 1969- . (Colección
     Cuatricentenario de Caracas, 8).

BIOGRAPHY (COLLECTIVE)

COLLECTIVE

264   Behar, Eli.   Vultos do Brasil: dicionário biobibliográfico brasileiro·   São Paulo: Livraria Exposição
do Livro, 1967.   222 p.

265   Bittencourt, Adalzira.   Diccionario bio-bibliográfico de
mulheres ilustres, notáveis e intelectuais do· Brasil.
Rio de Janeiro: Pongetti, 1969-   .

266   Freitas, Edna Gondim de.   "Repertórios biográficos
brasileiros; bibliografia cronológica e índice onomás-
tico, geográfico e temático."   ·Revista do livro,
39:12 (1969), 127-166.

267   Hill, Marnesba D. and Harold B. Schleifer.   Puerto
Rican authors: a biobibliographic handbook.   Metuchen: Scarecrow Press, 1974.   277 p.

268   Iguíniz, Juan Bautista.   Bibliografía biográfica mexi-
cana·   México: Universidad Nacional, Instituto de
Investigaciones Históricas, 1969.   431 p.   (Serie
bibliográfica, 5).

269   Millares Carlo, Agustín.   "I: Notas para una bibliografía de obras generales sobre anónimos y seu-
dónimos de Latinoamerica·   II: Datos para una bibliografía de repertorios biográficos latino-ameri-
canos."   Boletín de la Biblioteca General de la Universidad del Zulia, 11/12:19/20 (jul. 1971/jun.
1972), 121-161.

270   Morales Padrón, Francisco.   "Guía de americanistas
españoles."   Historiografía y bibliografía americanistas, 15:2 (jul., 1971), 247-279.

271   _____·   Guía de americanistas españoles.   Sevilla:
Escuela de Estudios Hispanoamericanos, 1971.   33 p.

272   Oss, Adriaan van.   Latinoamericanistas en Europa; un
registro de datos biobibliográficos sobre 443 espe-
cialistas activos en los estudios latinoamericanos en
Europa, resultados de una encuesta realizada en el
otoño de 1973.   Amsterdam: Centro de Estudios y
Documentación Latinoamericanos, 1974.   84 p.

33 BIOGRAPHY (Collective)

273 Pittsburgh. University. Center for Latin American
Studies. Faculty publications on Latin America.
Pittsburgh, 1973. 16 p.

274 U.S. Library of Congress. Hispanic Foundation.
National directory of Latin Americanists; biographies
of 2,695 specialists in the social sciences & humanities. 2d ed. Washington, 1971. 684 p. (Hispanic
Foundation bibliographic series, 12).

BIOGRAPHY (INDIVIDUAL)

AGUIRRE, MANUEL

275 Rey Fajardo, José del. "Apuntes para una bibliografía
de Manuel Aguirre, S. J." SIC; revista venezolana
de orientación, 32:314 (abr., 1969), 157-158.

ALENCAR, JOSE MARTINIANO DE

276 "Correspondência passiva do Senador José Martiniano de
Alencar." Anais da Biblioteca Nacional, Rio de
Janeiro, 86 (1966), 1-468.

AMORIM, ENRIQUE

277 Rodríguez Urruty, Hugo. La bibliografía de Enrique
Amorim, poeta. Montevideo: Aries, 1970. 5 p.

ANAYA MONROY, FERNANDO

278 Castillo Farreras, José. "Fernando Anaya Monroy,
1910-1970." Boletín bibliográfico de anthropología
americana, 33/34 (1970/71), 315-331.

ANDRADE, MARIO DE

279 Lopez, Telê Porto A. "Cronologia geral da obra de
Mário de Andrade publicada em volume." Revista
do· Instituto de Estudos Brasileiros, 7 (1969), 139-
172.

280   Rio de Janeiro.   Biblioteca Nacional.   Exposiçao Mário
       de Andrade.   Rio de Janeiro, 1970.   73 p.

ARCHILA, RICARDO

281   Freites de Acosta, Alecia.   Ricardo Archila.   Caracas:
       Escuela de Biblioteconomía y Archivos, Universidad
       Central de Venezuela, 1968.   51 p.   (Serie biblio-
       gráfica, 7).

ARGUEDAS, JOSE MARIA

282   Rowe, William.   "Bibliografía de José María Arguedas."
       Revista peruana de cultura, Lima, 13/14 (1970),
       179-197.

ARMAS CHITTY, JOSE ANTONIO DE

283   Lemmo B., Angelina.   J. A. de Armas Chitty.   Cara-
       cas: Facultad de Humanidades y Educación, Escuela
       de Biblioteconomía y Archivos, Universidad Central
       de Venezuela, 1969.   102 p.   (Serie bibliográfica,
       10).

ARRAIZ, ANTONIO

284   Caracas.   Universidad Católica Andrés Bello.   Semi-
       nario de Literatura Venezolana.   Contribución a la
       bibliografía de Antonio Arráiz, 1903-1963.   Caracas:
       Gobernación del Distrito Federal, 1969.   199 p.
       (Colección· Bibliografías, 3).

ARRIETA, RAFAEL ALBERTO

285   Becco, Horacio Jorge·   "Bibliografía de Don Rafael
       Alberto Arrieta (1889-1968)."   Boletín de la Aca-
       demia Argentina de Letras, 33:127/128 (ene./jun.,
       1968), 15-21.

286   López, Susana Beatriz.   Contribución a la bibliografía
       de Rafael Alberto Arrieta.   Buenos Aires: Fondo
       Nacional de las Artes, 1969.   102 p.   (Bibliografía

argentina de artes y letras. Compilación especial,
37).

ARZE, JOSE ANTONIO

287   Arze, José Roberto. Ensayo de una bibliografía del
      Dr. José Antonio Arze. Cochabamba, Bolivia: Edi-
      torial Universitaria, 1968. 81 p.

ASTURIAS, MIGUEL ANGEL

288   Andrea, Pedro Frank de. "Miguel Angel Asturias:
      anticipio bibliográfico." Revista iberoamericana,
      35:67 (ene./abr.; 1969), 133-267.

289   Dumas, Jean-Louis. "Asturias en Francia." Revista
      iberoamericana, 35:67 (ene./abr., 1969), 117-
      125.

AVILA MARTEL, ALAMIRO

290   "Bibliografía de Don Alamiro de Avila Martel." Bole-
      tín de la Academia Chilena de la Historia, 38:85
      (1971), 86-93.

AYALA, FRANCISCO

291   Amoros, Andres. Bibliografía de Francisco Ayala.
      Syracuse, N. Y.: Centro de Estudios Hispánicos,
      Syracuse University, 1973. 93 p. (Bibliotheca
      hispana novíssima, 4).

AYESTARAN, LAURO

292   "Bibliografía de Lauro Ayestarán." Revista Histórica
      (Montevideo), 39 (1968), 525-589.

BAEZ-CAMARGO, GONZALO

293   Gringoire, Pedro. Semblanza biobibliográfica de Gon-
      zalo Báez-Camargo: sus sesenta años de escritor,
      1913-1973. México: B. Costa Amic, 1974. 63 p.

BALDUS, HERBERT

294 Comas, Juan. "Herbert Baldus (1899-1970)." Boletín bibliográfico de antropología americana, 35:1 (1972), 97-109.

BANCHS, ENRIQUE

295 Becco, Horacio Jorge. "Bibliografía de Don Enrique Banchs (1888-1968)." Boletín de la Academia Argentina de Letras, 33:127/128 (ene./jun., 1968), 27-29.

BANDELIER, ADOLPHE FRANCIS ALPHONSE

296 Binz, Ruth Irma. "Adolphe Francis Alphonse Bandelier." Boletín bibliográfico de antropología americana, 35:1 (1972), 111-132.

BARAJAS Y MORENO, PEDRO

297 Montejano y Aguiñaga, Rafael. "Biobibliografía del Ilmo. Sr. Dr. D. Pedro Barajas, primer obispo de San Luis Potosí." Boletín del Instituto de Investigaciones Bibliográficas (México), 4 (jul./dic., 1970), 289-297.

BARRERA, ISAAC J.

298 Larrea, Carlos Manuel. "Isaac J. Barrera." Revista de historia de América, 71 (ene./jun., 1971), 153-156.

BARRETO DE MENEZES, TOBIAS

299 Menezes, José F. Bibliografia sobre Tobias Barreto de Menezes. Tobias Barreto, Brasil, 1973. 20 p.

BARRIGA, ISIDRO

300 Márquez Tapia, Ricardo. "Bibliografía del General

Isidro Barriga. " Boletín de la Academia Nacional de Historia (Quito), 53:115 (ene./jun., 1970), 77-86.

BARROS, LEANDRO GOMES DE

301   Batista, Sebastiâo Nunes. Bibliografia prévia de Leandro Gomes de Barros. Rio de Janeiro: Biblioteca Nacional, 1971. 95 p. (Coleçâo Rodolfo Garcia. Serie B: Catálogos e bibliografias).

BECERRA SCHMIDT, GUSTAVO

302   "Catálogo cronológico clasificado de las obras del compositor Gustavo Becerra Schmidt." Revista musical chilena, 26:119/120 (jul./dic., 1972), 82-91.

BELAUNDE, VICTOR ANDRES

303   Pacheco Vélez, César. "Necrología: Victor Andrés Belaúnde (1883-1966)." Revista histórica (Lima), 29 (1966), 436-449.

BELGRANO, MANUEL

304   Argentina. Archivo General. Exposición en homenaje a Manuel Belgrano; catálogo. Buenos Aires, 1970. 97 p.

305   Furlong Cardiff, Guillermo. "Manuel Belgrano: ensayo bibliográfico." Investigaciones y ensayos, 9 (1970), 33-162.

BELLO, ANDRES

306   "[Bibliografía sobre Don Andrés Bello]" Boletín de la Biblioteca General de la Universidad del Zulia, 13/14:21/22 (jul. 1972/jun. 1973). Entire issue.

307   Millares Carlo, Agustín. "Don Andrés Bello; ensayo bibliográfico. Adiciones y correcciones." Boletín de la Biblioteca General de la Universidad del Zulia, 9/10:15/16 (jul. 1969/jul. 1970), 239-277.

308 _____. "Don Andrés Bello (1781-1865). Ensayo
     bibliográfico." Revista de historia de América,
     67/68 (ene./dic., 1969), 211-331.

BERNAL Y GARCIA PIMENTAL, IGNACIO

309 "Curriculum vitae del doctor Ignacio Bernal y García
     Pimentel." Memoria de El Colegio de México, 7:3
     (1972), 109-123.

BIOY CASARES, ADOLFO

310 Borello, Rodolfo A. "Bibliografía sobre Adolfo Bioy
     Casares (Algunas nuevas fichas)." Revista ibero-
     americana, 41:91 (abr./jun., 1975), 367-368.

311 Puig Zaldívar, Raquel. "Bibliografía de y sobre Adol-
     fo Bioy Casares." Revista iberoamericana, 40:86
     (ene./mar., 1974), 173-178.

BLANCO, EDUARDO

312 Caracas. Universidad Católica Andrés Bello. Escuela
     de Letras. Centro de Investigaciones Literarias.
     Contribución a la bibliografía de Eduardo Blanco,
     1838-1912. Caracas: Gobernación del Distrito
     Federal, 1971. 82 p. (Colección Bibliografías, 9).

BOLIVAR, SIMON

313 "Dos listas de libros existentes en la Casa Natal del
     Libertador." Revista de la Sociedad Bolivariana de
     Venezuela, 29:98/99 (19 de abr./24 de jul. 1969),
     82-99.

BONIFAZ NUÑO, RUBEN

314 "Curriculum vitae del doctor Rubén Bonifaz Nuño."
     Memoria de El Colegio de México, 7:3 (1972), 143-
     146.

BORGES, JORGE LUIS

315   Becco, Horacio Jorge. Jorge Luis Borges: bibliogra-
      fía total, 1923-1973. Buenos Aires: Casa Pardo,
      1973. 244 p.

316   Fiore, Robert L. "Toward a bibliography of Jorge
      Luis Borges (1923-1969)." Books abroad, 45 (Sum-
      mer 1971), 446-466.

317   _____. "Toward a bibliography on Jorge Luis
      Borges (1923-1969)." In: Dunham, Lowell and
      Ivar Ivask. The cardinal points of Borges. Nor-
      man: University of Oklahoma Press, 1971. pp.
      83-105.

318   Foster, David William. A bibliography of the works
      of Jorge Luis Borges. Tempe, Arizona: Center
      for Latin American Studies, Arizona State Univer-
      sity, 1971. 39 ℓ. (Special study, 6).

319   "Jorge Luis Borges in 'Books abroad' (1936-1971)."
      In: Dunham, Lowell and Ivar Ivask. The cardinal
      points of Borges. Norman: University of Oklahoma
      Press, 1971. pp. 111-112.

320   "Jorge Luis Borges in 'Books abroad' (1936-1970)."
      Books abroad, 45 (Summer, 1971), 469-470.

321   Lyon, Thomas E. "Jorge Luis Borges: selected bib-
      liography of first editions and English translations."
      In: Dunham, Lowell and Ivar Ivask. The cardinal
      points of Borges. Norman: University of Oklahoma
      Press, 1971. pp. 107-109.

322   _____. "Jorge Luis Borges: selected bibliography
      of first editions and English translations." Books
      abroad, 45 (Summer, 1971), 467-469.

BORHEGHYI, STEPHAN F. DE

323   Navarrete, Carlos. "Stephan F. de Borheghyi (1921-
      1969)." Estudios de Cultura Maya, 8 (1970), 427-
      435.

BRICENO PEROZO, MARIO

324   Ramírez Báez, Carmen Celeste.   Mario Briceño Perozo.   Caracas: Escuela de Biblioteconomía y Archivos, Facultad de Humanidades y Educación, Universidad Central de Venezuela, 1970.   232 p.   (Serie
bibliográfica, 12).

BROCA, JOSE BRITO

325   Brito Broca, 1903-1961.   Pequena biobibliografia comemorativa do décimo aniversário da morte do escritor.   Homenagem da Livraria S. José.   Rio de
Janeiro, 1971.   15 p.

BUSTAMANTE, CARLOS MARIA

326   O'Gorman, Edmundo.   Guía bibliográfica de Carlos
María de Bustamante.   México: UNAM, Centro de
Estudios de Historia de México, 1967.   227 p.

CALOGERAS, JOAO PANDIA

327   Matos, Odilon Nogueira de.   "Vultos de historiografia
brasileira: Pandia Calogeras, 1870-1934."   Revista
de história (São Paulo), 44:90 (abr. / jun., 1972),
531-534.

CÂMARA, HELDER

328   Leonard, Patrick J.   "Bibliography of Helder Câmara."
Latin American Research Review, 10:2 (Summer,
1975), 147-166.

CAPDEVILA, ARTURO

329   Becco, Horacio Jorge.   "Bibliografía de Arturo Capdevila (1889-1967)."   Boletín de la Academia Nacional de la Historia, Buenos Aires, 42 (1969), 335-
339.

330   _____.   "Bibliografía de Don Arturo Capdevila

(1889-1967)." Boletín de la Academia Argentina de Letras, 32:125/126 (jul./dic., 1967), 329-338.

CARDENAS H., MARTIN

331 Cardozo, Armando. Bibliografía del Dr. Martín Cárdenas H. La Paz: Sociedad de Ingenieros Agrónomos de Bolivia, 1970. 14 p. (Boletín bibliográfico, 12).

CARDONA, MIGUEL

332 "Contribución a la bibliografía de Miguel Cardona." In: Cardona, Miguel. Temas de folklore venezolano. Caracas: Ediciones del Ministerio de Educación, Dirección de Cultura y Bellas Artes, Departamento de Publicaciones, 1964. pp. xxv-xxxv.

CARPENTIER, ALEJO

333 Foster, David W. "A bibliography of the fiction of Carpentier, Cabrera Infante, and Lezama Lima: works and criticism," Abraxas, 1:3 (Spring, 1971), 305-310.

334 Havana. Biblioteca Nacional "José Martí." Alejo Carpentier: 45 años de trabajo intelectual. La Habana, 1966. 39 p.

CARRERA ANDRADE, JORGE

335 Harth, Dorothy E. Jorge Carrera Andrade: a bibliography, 1922-1970. Syracuse, N.Y.: Centro de Estudios Hispánicos, Syracuse University, s.d. (Bibliotheca hispana novíssima, 2).

CARRILLO FLORES, ANTONIO

336 "Curriculum vitae del doctor Antonio Carrillo Flores." Memoria de El Colegio de México, 7:3 (1972), 169-173.

CASAL, JULIAN DEL

337 Figueroa Amaral, Esperanza. "Bibliografía cronológica de la obra de Julián del Casal." Revista iberoamericana, 35:68 (may./ag., 1969), 387-399.

338 Geada de Prulletti, Rita. "Bibliografía de y sobre Julián del Casal (1863-1893)." Revista iberoamericana, 33:63 (ene./jun., 1967), 133-139.

CASCUDO, LUIS DA CAMARA

339 Lima Filho, Diógenes da Cunha. Bibliografia de Luís de Câmara Cascudo. Natal: Imp. Universitária, 1965. 14 p.

340 Mamede, Zila. Luís da Câmara Cascudo: 50 anos de vida intelectual, 1918-1968; bibliografia anotada. Natal, Brazil: Fundaçao José Augusto, 1970. 2 v. in 3.

CASO, ALFONSO

341 Bernal, Ignacio. "Alfonso Caso, 1896-1970." Boletín bibliográfico de antropología americana, 33/34 (1970/71), 301-314.

CASTILLO, MADRE DE

342 "Ficha biográfica y bibliográfica de la Madre de Castillo." Boletín de la Academia Colombiana, 22:91 (feb./mar., 1972), 5-7.

CASTRO, FIDEL

343 Bonachea, Rolando P. "A briefly annotated bibliography of Fidel Castro's works, 1959-1970." Cuban studies newsletter/Boletín de estudios sobre Cuba, 3:2 (Jun., 1973), 1-69.

344 _____ and Nelson P. Valdés. "The making of a revolutionary: a Fidel Castro bibliography (1947-

1958.." Latin American research review, 5:2 (Summer, 1970), 83-88.

345 _____ and _____. "Una bibliografía de Fidel Castro (1948-1958)." Aportes, 18 (oct., 1970), 120-130.

346 Valdés, Nelson P. and Rolando E. Bonachea. "Documento: una bibliografía de Fidel Castro (1948-1958)." Aportes, 18 (oct., 1970), 120-130.

CASTRO ALVES, ANTÔNIO DE

347 Castro Alves (1847-1871). Pequena bio-bibliografia comemorativa do centenário da morte do poeta. Homenagem da Livraria S. José. Rio de Janeiro, 1971. 19 p.

CECUNA, VICENTE

348 "Obras del doctor Vicente Cecuna en la Biblioteca de la Academia Nacional de la Historia." Boletín de la Academia Nacional de la Historia, Caracas, 53:212 (oct./dic., 1970), 644-649.

CHAVEZ, EZEQUIEL A.

349 Cameron, Alberto Perry. "Vida y obras de Ezequiel A. Chávez." Boletín bibliográfico de la Secretaría de Hacienda y Crédito Público, Mexico, 15:426 (1969), 11-13; 15:427 (1969), 10-11; 15:428 (1969), 15-16; 15:429 (1969), 12, 14-15.

CHAVEZ OROZCO, LUIS

350 Sierra, Carlos J. Bibliohemerografía de Luis Chávez Orozco. México: Secretaría de Hacienda y Crédito Público, 1966.

CLAVIJERO, FRANCISCO JAVIER

351 Pasquel, Leonardo. Bibliografía de Clavijero. México: Editorial Citlaltépetl, 1971. 157 p.

CLINE, HOWARD FRANCIS

352   Ross, Stanley Robert.   "Howard Francis Cline (1915-
      1971)."   Revista de historia de América, 73/74
      (ene./dic., 1972), 203-215.

COELHO NETTO, HENRIQUE

353   Coelho Netto, Paulo and Neuza do Nascimento Kuhn.
      Bibliografia de Coehlo Netto.   Brasília: Instituto
      Nacional do Livro 1972. 326 p. (Coleção Docu-
      mentos, 4).

COMAS CAMPS, JUAN

354   "Juan Comas Camps."   Boletín bibliográfico de antro-
      pología americana, 33/34 (1970/71), 225-247. A
      continuation of the bibliography which appeared in
      the BBAA, vol. 5 (1941).

COMTE, AUGUSTE

355   Rio de Janeiro. Biblioteca Nacional.   Comemoração do
      I centenario da morte de Auguste Comte.   Exposição
      realizada na ..., de 5 a 28 de setembro. Rio de
      Janeiro, 1957.

CORTAZAR, JULIO

356   Paley de Francescato, Martha.   "Bibliografía de y
      sobre Julio Cortázar."   Revista iberoamericana,
      39:84/85 (jul./dic., 1973), 698-726.

CORTES, HERNAN

357   Valle, Rafael Heliodoro.   Bibliografía de Hernán Cortés.
      New York: Burt Franklin, 1970. viii, 269 p. Re-
      print of the 1953 ed.

COSTA PEREIRA FURTADO DE MENDONCA, HIPOLITO
   JOSE DA

358   Rio de Janeiro. Biblioteca Nacional. Hipólito José da

45   BIOGRAPHY (Individual)

Costa e a imprensa no Brasil: catálogo da exposição. Rio de Janeiro, 1974. 41 p.

CREMA, EDOARDO

359 Venezuela. Universidad Central. Facultad de Humanidades y Educación. Catálogo bibliográfico de las
obras publicades por el profesor Edoardo Crema.
Caracas, 1962. 14 p.

CUENCA, AGUSTIN F.

360 Kuehne, Alyce G. de. "Hemerografía de Agustín F.
Cuenca." Boletín de la Biblioteca Nacional, Mexico,
17:3/4 (1966), 53-72.

CUMBERLAND, CHARLES CURTIS

361 "Charles Curtis Cumberland (1914-1970)." Hispanic
American historical review, 53:2 (May, 1973), 299-
301.

CUNHA, EUCLIDES DA

362 Reis, Irene Monteiro. Bibliografia de Euclides da Cunha. Rio de Janeiro: Instituto Nacional do Livro,
1971. xxv, 417 p. (Coleção Documentos, 2).

DARIO, RUBEN

363 Del Greco, Arnold Armand. Repertorio bibliográfico
del mundo de Rubén Darío. New York: Las Américas, 1969. 666 p.

364 Havana. Biblioteca Nacional "José Martí." Centro de
Información Humanística. Bibliografía Rubén Darío,
en homenaje al centenario de su nacimiento. La
Habana, 1967. vii, 11 p.

365 Hebblethwaite, Frank P. "Una bibliografía de Rubén
Darío (1945-1966)." Inter-American review of bibliography, 17:2 (Apr./Jun., 1967), 202-221.

366 Panama (City) Universidad.   Biblioteca.   Bibliografía
de y sobre Rubén Darío,   Panamá, 1967.   25 ℓ.

367 Woodbridge, Hensley Charles.   Rubén Darío, a selective classified and annotated bibliography.   Metuchen,
N. J. : Scarecrow Press, 1975.   xix, 231 p.

DAVALOS HURTADO, EUSEBIO

368 Gurría Lacroix, Jorge.   "Eusebio Dávalos Hurtado,
1909-1968. " América indígena, 28:2 (abr. , 1968),
563-566.

369 Marino Flores, Anselmo.   "Eusebio Davalos Hurtado,
1909-1968. " Boletín bibliográfico de antropología
americana, 31 (1968), 59-66.

DELGADO OCANDO, JOSE MANUEL

370 Quintana, Ignacio.   "José Manuel Delgado Ocando, bibliografía; consideraciones sobre su filosofía, " Boletín de la Biblioteca General de la Universidad del
Zulia, 9/10:15/16 (jul. 1969/jul. 1970), 9-19.

DENEVI, MARCO

371 Yates, Donald A.   "Para una bibliografía de Marco
Denevi. " Revista iberoamericana, 33:63 (ene. / jun. ,
1967), 141-146.

DIAS, ANTÔNIO CONÇALVES

372 Bibliografía gonçalvina, centenario de Antônio Gonçalves
Dias, 1864-1964.   São Luis, Brasil: Departamento
de Cultura do Estado, 1964.   45 p.

373 "Correspondência passiva de Antônio Gonçalves Dias. "
Anais da Biblioteca Nacional, Rio de Janeiro, 91
(1971), 3-356.

DIAZ DIAZ, OSWALDO

374 Lee López, Alberto.   "Oswaldo Díaz Díaz: nota bio-

bibliográfica." Boletín de historia y antigüedades,
55 (1968), 5-19.

DIAZ RODRIGUEZ, MANUEL

375 Caracas. Universidad Católica Andrés Bello. Seminario de Literatura Venezolana. Contribución a la
bibliografía de Manuel Díaz Rodríguez, 1871-1927.
Caracas: Gobernación del Distrito Federal, 1970?
156 p. (Colección Bibliografías, 2).

DIAZ SANCHEZ, RAMON

376 Caracas. Universidad Católica Andrés Bello. Seminario de Literatura Venezolana. Contribución a la
bibliografía de Ramón Díaz Sánchez, 1903-1968.
Caracas: Gobernación del Distrito Federal, 1970.
249 p. (Colección Bibliografías, 5).

DIEGO, ELISEO

377 García-Carranza, Araceli. Bibliografía de Eliseo
Diego. La Habana: Biblioteca Nacional José Martí,
1970. 24 p.

DURAND, LUIS

378 Escudero, Alfonso M. "Fuentes consultables sobre
Luis Durand." Revista iberoamericana, 32:61 (ene./
jun., 1966), 131-138.

ECHEVERRIA, ESTEBAN

378a Kisnerman, Natalio. Contribución a la bibliografía
sobre Estéban Echeverría (1805-1970). Buenos
Aires: Universidad de Buenos Aires, Instituto de
Literatura Argentina Ricardo Rojas, 1971. 123 p.
(Guías bibliográficas, 9).

EYZAGUIRRE GUTIERREZ, JAIME

379 Pereira Salas, Eugenio. "Jaime Eyzaguirre Gutiérrez

(1908-1968). " Revista de historia de América, 67/
68 (ene./dic., 1969), 346-347.

FALABELLA CORREA, ROBERTO

380 Merino, Luis. "Catálogo de la obra musical de Roberto Falabella." Revista musical chilena, 27:121/122
(ene./jun., 1973), 100-112.

FELICIANO MENDOZA, ESTER

381 Alamo de Torres, Daisy. Bibliografía de Ester Feliciano Mendoza. San Juan: Sociedad de Bibliotecarios
de Puerto Rico, 1971. 33 p. (Cuadernos bibliotecológicos, 5).

FERNANDEZ DE MIRANDA, MARIA TERESA

382 Romero Castillo, Moisés. "María Teresa Fernández
de Miranda." Boletín bibliográfico de antropología
americana, 31 (1968), 137-138.

FIGUEIREDO, FIDELINO DE

383 Paula, Eurípedes Simões de. "Fidelino de Figueiredo
de a renovação dos estudos históricos em Portugal
e no Brasil." Revista de história (São Paulo), 34:
70 (abr./jun., 1967), 321-330.

FIGUERES, JOSE

384 Kantor, Harry. Bibliography of José Figueres.
Tempe: Arizona State University; Center for Latin
American Studies, 1972. 50 p.

FLASCHE, HANS

385 Studia Iberica. Festschrift für Hans Flasche. Hrg.
von Karl Hermann Körner und Klaus Ruhl. Bern,
München: Francke, 1973. Includes a bibliography
of the works of Flasche--pp. 705-709.

FRANCO, AFONSO ARINOS DE MELO

386   Guaraná, Hélio. "Bibliografia de/sobre Afonso Arinos."
      Revista do livro, 11:33 (1968), 143-155.

FRIAS, HERIBERTO

387   Brown, James W. "Bibliografía de Heriberto Frías."
      Boletín bibliográfico de la Secretaría de Hacienda y
      Crédito Público, México, 17:463 (1971), 26-32.

388   _____. _____. Boletín del Instituto de Investi-
      gaciones Bibliográficas (México), 2:1 (ene./jun.,
      1970), 137-152.

FUENTE, JULIO DE LA

389   Aguirre Beltrán, Gonzalo. "Julio de la Fuente, 1905-
      1970." América indígena, 30:3 (jul., 1970), 844-
      850.

FUENTE, RAMON DE LA

390   "Curriculum vitae del doctor Ramón de la Fuente."
      Memoria de El Colegio de México, 7:3 (1972), 195-
      199.

FUENTES, CARLOS

391   "Curriculum vitae del Señor Carlos Fuentes." Memoria
      de El Colegio de México, 7:3 (1972), 215-221.

392   Reeve, Richard M. "An annotated bibliography on Car-
      los Fuentes, 1949-69." Hispania (Am. Assoc. of
      Teachers of Spanish & Portuguese), 53 (Oct., 1970),
      597-652.

FUENZALIDA VILLEGAS, HUMBERTO

393   Flores Silva, Eusebio. "El profesor Humberto Fuenza-
      lida." Revista chilena de historia y geografía, 134
      (1966), 96-115.

GALLEGOS, ROMULO

394   Caracas.   Universidad Católica Andrés Bello.   Seminario de Literatura Venezolana.   Contribución a la
bibliografía de Rómulo Gallegos, 1884-1969.   [Bajo
la dirección de Efraín Subero].   Caracas: Gobernación del Distrito Federal, 1969.   405 p.   (Colección
bibliografías, 1).

395   Shaw, Donald L.   "Rómulo Gallegos: suplemento a una
bibliografía."   Revista iberoamericana, 37:75 (abr. /
jun., 1971), 447-457.   [Supplements the above].

GAOS, JOSE

396   Bibliografía de José Gaos (1900-1969)."   Bibliografía
filosófica mexicana, 2:2 (1969), [49]-94.

GARCIA CRUZ, MIGUEL

397   Ramos V., Roberto.   "Bio-bibliografía del Ingeniero
Miguel García Cruz."   Boletín bibliográfico de la
Secretaría de Hacienda y Crédito Público, Mexico,
18:470 (1972), 24-32.

GARCIA MARQUEZ, GABRIEL

398   Mendoza, Roseanne B. de.   "Bibliografía de y sobre
Gabriel García Márquez."   Revista iberoamericana,
41:90 (ene. /mar., 1975), 107-143.

GARCIA ROBLES, ALFONSO

399   "Curriculum vitae del Licenciado Alfonso García Robles."
Memoria de El Colegio de México, 7:3 (1972), 249-
253.

GARIBAY KINTANA, ANGEL MARIA

400   León-Portilla, Miguel.   "Angel María Garibay K.,
1892-1967."   América indígena, 28:1 (ene., 1968),
265-271.

401 _____. "Bibliographie du docteur Garibay." Journal de la Societé des Americanistes, 56:1 (1967), 255-259.

GARVEY, MARCUS

402 Institute of Jamaica, Kingston. West India Reference Library. Marcus Mosiah Garvey, 1887-1940; a reading list of printed material in the West India Reference Library. Compiled by Audrey Leigh. Kingston, 1973. 13 p.

GIMENEZ FERNANDEZ, MANUEL

403 Malagón Barceló, Javier. "In memoriam: Manuel Giménez Fernández." The Americas, 26:1 (Jan., 1969), 77-86.

404 Pérez de Tudela, Juan. "Don Manuel Giménez Fernández." Revista de Indias, 28:113/114 (1968), 533-540.

GODOI, JUAN SILVANO

405 California. University, Riverside. Latin American Studies Program. Research guide to the Godoi-Díaz Pérez Collection in the Library of the University of California, Riverside, by Pastora Montoro de López-Román, et al. Riverside, 1973. 60 p. (Research guide series, 1).

GOMEZ PEREZ, JOSE

406 Vaz Araujo, Lino. "José Gómez Pérez: ensayo de una biobibliografía." Boletín de la Biblioteca General de la Universidad del Zulia, 10/11:17/18 (ag., 1970/jun., 1971), 11-37.

GOMEZ RESTREPO, ANTONIO

407 Ortega Torres, José J. "Bibliografía de don Antonio Gómez Restrepo." In: Cuervo, Rufino José.

Epistolario de Rufino José Cuervo y Miguel Antonio Caro con Antonio Gómez Restrepo. Bogotá: Instituto Caro y Cuervo, 1973. pp. 1v-cxx.

GONZALEZ, MANUEL PEDRO

408 Roggiano, Alfredo A. "Manuel Pedro González (1893-1974)." Revista iberoamericana, 40:89 (oct./dic., 1974), 689-692.

GONZALEZ MARTINEZ, ENRIQUE

409 Sierra, Carlos J. "La obra de Enrique González Martínez." Boletín bibliográfico de la Secretaría de Hacienda y Crédito Público, Mexico, 17:460 (1971), 17-27.

GRIECO, AGRIPPINO

410 Rio de Janeiro. Instituto Nacional do Livro. Bibliografia e crítica de Agrippino Grieco; coletânea org. em comemoração do octogésimo aniversário do nascimento do escritor.... Rio de Janeiro, 1968. 401 p.

GUEVARA, ERNESTO

411 Scauzillo, Robert J. "Ernesto Che Guevara: a research bibliography." Latin American research review, 5:2 (Summer, 1970), 53-82.

GUILLEN, JORGE

412 "A Jorge Guillén bibliography." Books abroad, 42:1 (Winter, 1968), 58-59.

413 "Jorge Guillén in 'Books abroad' (1929-68)." Books abroad, 42:1 (Winter, 1968), 60.

GUIMARAENS, AFONSO HENRIQUES DE

414 Rio de Janeiro. Biblioteca Nacional. Alphonsus de

Guimaraens; catálogo da exposição comemorativa do
centenário do nascimento, 1870-1970.   Rio de Janeiro, 1970.   37 p.

GURVITCH, GEORGES

415   "Georges Gurvitch."   América latina, 9:1 (jan./mar.,
1966), 133-137.

GUSINDE, MARTIN

416   Binz, Ruth Irma.   "P. Martin Gusinde."   Boletín bibliográfico de antropología americana, 35:1 (1972),
133-157.

HEINE, HEINRICH

417   Owen, Claude R.   Heine im spanischen Sprachgebiet;
eine kritische Bibliographie.   Münster/Westfalen:
Ashendorff, 1968.   xlviii, 336 p.   (Spanische For-
schungen der Görresgesellschaft.   2. Reihe, Bd.
12).

HERAS, CARLOS

418   Caillet-Bois, Ricardo R.   "Carlos Heras; bibliografía
de obras."   Boletín del Instituto de Historia Argentina "Doctor Emilio Ravignani," 2a série, 14/15
(1967), 384-387.

419   Timpanaro, Horacio Enrique.   "Contribución a la bibliografía de Carlos Heras."   Trabajos y comunicaciones (Facultad de Humanidades y Educación, Departamento de Historia, Universidad Nacional de la
Plata), 17 (1967), 205-232.

HEREDIA, JOSE MARIA

420   Havana.   Biblioteca Nacional "José Martí."   Bibliografía sobre José María Heredia, compilado por Tomas
F. Robaina.   La Habana, 1970.   111 p.

HERNANDEZ, JOSE

421   Barbato, Martha J. "José Hernández y Martín Fierro; nuevo aporte a su bibliografía." Logos; revista de la Facultad de Filosofía y Letras, Universidad de Buenos Aires, 7:12 (1972), 259-318.

422   Sara, Walter. "José Hernández: cien años de bibliografía: periódicos y revistas." Revista iberoamericana, 38:81 (oct./dic., 1972), 681-774.

423   Texas. University at Austin. Library. Catalogue of Martín Fierro materials in the University of Texas Library. Edited and introduced by Nettie Lee Benson. Susan Klipfel, cataloguer. Adán Benavides, Jr., compiler of articles and reviews. Austin: Institute of Latin American Studies, University of Texas, 1972. xi, 135 p. (Guides and bibliographies series, 6).

HERRERA, ANTONIO DE

424   Bejarano Díaz, Horacio. "Los cronistas de Indias. Antonio de Herrera y Antonio de Solís." Boletín de la Academia Colombiana, 24:105 (1975), 455-466.

HERRERA, LUIS ALBERTO DE

425   Montevideo. Biblioteca Nacional. Luis Alberto de Herrera; centenario de su nacimiento, 1873-1973: exposición bibliográfica. Montevideo, 1973. 49 p.

HERRERA CARRILLO, PABLO

426   Mendirichaga y Cueva, Tomás. "Pablo Herrera Carrillo. Notas bio-bibliográficas." Abside; revista de cultura mejicana, 30:1 (ene./mar., 1966), 98-104.

HOLMBERG, ALLAN RICHARD

427   Vázquez, Mario C. "Allan Richard Holmberg, 1909-1966." América indígena, 27:1 (ene., 1967), 131-134.

HOUSSAY, BERNARDO A.

428 Becco, Horacio Jorge. "Bibliografía del Doctor Bernardo A. Houssay." Boletín de la Academia Argentina de Letras, 36:141/142 (jul./dic., 1971), 273-275.

HUIDOBRO, VICENTE

429 Hey, Nicholas. "Bibliografía de y sobre Vicente Huidobro." Revista iberoamericana, 41:91 (abr./jun., 1975) 293-353.

IGUIÑIZ, JUAN B.

430 Dávila Garibi, J. Ignacio. "Juan B. Iguíñiz." Et Caetera, 22 (1971), 3-11.

431 Perales de Mercado, Alicia. "Don Juan B. Iguíñiz, El Maestro." Boletín del Instituto de Investigaciones Bibliográficas (México), 4 (jul./dic., 1970), 39-43.

432 Rublúo, Luis. "Bibliografía de un bibliógrafo (la del Dr. Juan B. Iguíñiz)." Boletín del Instituto de Investigaciones Bibliográficas (México), 4 (jul./dic., 1970), 55-71.

433 Villaseñor y Villaseñor, Ramiro. "Bibliografía de Juan B. Iguíñiz." Et Caetera, 22 (1971), 23-35.

INGENIEROS, JOSE

434 Roig, Arturo Andrés. "Contribución para una bibliografía de José Ingenieros." Inter-American review of bibliography, 23:2 (Apr./Jun., 1973), 141-163.

ISAACS, JORGE

435 McGrady, Donald. Bibliografía sobre Jorge Isaacs. Bogotá: Instituto Caro y Cuervo, 1971. 75 p. (Publicaciones. Serie bibliográfica, 8).

JIMENEZ, JUAN RAMON

436   Campoamor González, Antonio.   "Bibliografía funda-
mental de Juan Ramón Jiménez."   La Torre, 16:62
(oct./dic., 1968), 1·77-231; 17:6·3 (ene./mar., 1969),
177-213; 17:64 (abr./jun., 1969), 113-145; 17:65
(jul./sept., 1969), 145-179; 17:66 (oct./dic., 1969),
131-168.

JIMENEZ RUEDA, JULIO

437   Vázquez, Edward A.   "Julio Jiménez Rueda y sus
obras dramáticas."   Boletín bibliográfico de la
Secretaría de Hacienda y Crédito Público, Mexico, 19:483 (1973), 15-19; 19:486 (1973), 25-
27.

JOBOATÃO, ANTÔNIO DE SANTA MARIA, BROTHER

438   Wílleke, Venâncio.   "Frei Antônio de Santa Maria
Joboatão, OFM."   Revista de história (São Paulo),
46:93 (jan./mar., 1973), 47-67.

JUAREZ, BENITO

439   Avilés, René.   Bibliografía de Benito Juárez.   México:
Sociedad Mexicana de Geografía y Estadística, ·1972.
345 p.

KONETZKE, RICHARD

440   Herterich, Günter and Günter Kahle.   "Bibliographie
der Werke von Richard Konetzke."   Jahrbuch fur
Geschichte von Staat, Wirtschaft und Gesellschaft
Lateinamericas, 4 (1967), xxvii-xxxi.

LAVAL, RAMON A.

441   Feliú Cruz, Guillermo.   Ramón A. Laval (1862-1929).
La bibliografía de bibliografías chilenas.   Santiago de Chile: Bibliógrafos Chilenos, 1969.
46 p.

LAVIN A. , CARLOS

442 Dannemann R. , Manuel. "Bibliografía folklórica y
     etnográfica de Carlos Lavín A." Revista musical
     chilena, 21:99 (ene. /mar. , 1967), 85-88.

LAZO BAEZA, OLEGARIO

443 Escudero, Alfonso M. "Bio-bibliografía de Olegario
     Lazo Baeza (1878-1964). " Revista iberoamericana,
     32:61 (ene. /jun. , 1966), 121-130.

LECUNA, VICENTE

444 "Obras del doctor Vicente Lecuna en la Biblioteca de
     la Academia Nacional de la Historia. " Boletín de la
     Academia de la Historia, Caracas, 53:212 (oct. /dic. ,
     1970), 644-649.

LEJANZA INCHAURRAGA, FIDEL DE

445 Tormo, Leandro. "El P. Fidel de Lejanza Inchaurraga. "
     Revista de Indias, 31:125/126 (jul. /dic. , 1971), 379-
     386.

LEON ECHAIZ, RENE

446 "Bibliografía de René León Echaíz." Revista chilena
     de historia y geografía, 142 (1974), 199-204.

LEON -PORTILLA, MIGUEL

447 "Curriculum vitae del Doctor Miguel León-Portilla. "
     Memoria de El Colegio Nacional, México, 7:2 (1971),
     129-144.

LEON Y GAMA, ANTONIO

448 Moreno, Roberto. "Ensayo biobibliográfico de Antonio
     de León y Gama. " Boletín del Instituto de Investi-
     gaciones Bibliográficas (México), 2:1 (ene. /jun. ,
     1970), 43-135.

LEONI, GIULIO DAVIDE

449   Bibliografia das obras publicadas pelo Exmo. Prof.
Dr. Giulio Davide Leoni; homenagem de ex-alunas
para celebrar o XXX aniversário do mestre como
lente nas escolas superiores brasileiras, 1940-1969.
São Paulo: Impresso nas Escolas Profissionais
Salesianas, 1970. 46 p.

LETELIER MADARIAGA, VALENTIN

450   Schlinger, Peter J.   "El desarrollo intelectual y la
influencia de Valentín Letelier: un estudio bibliográfico." Revista chilena de historia y geografía
136 (1968), 250-284.

LEVILLIER, ROBERT

451   Caillet-Bois, Ricardo R.   "Robert Levillier (1886-1969)."
Revista de historia de América, 71 (ene./jun., 1971),
156-160.

452   Ezquerra, Ramón.   "Bibliografía de don Roberto Levillier." Revista de Indias, 31:125/126 (jul./dic.,
1971), 396-402.

LINS, ALVARO

453   Fonseca, Edson Nery.   "Alvaro Lins: bibliografia com
notas remissivas." Revista do Livro, 13:43, 4.
trimestre (1970), 128-137.

LISBOA, ANTÔNIO FRANCISCO

454   Hogan, James E.   "Antônio Francisco Lisboa, 'O Aleija-
dinho': an annotated bibliography." Latin American
research review, 9:2 (Summer, 1974), 83-94.

LORENZANA, FRANCISCO ANTONIO

455   Malagón Barceló, Javier.   "Los escritos del Cardenal
Lorenzana." Boletín del Instituto de Investigaciones

Bibliográficas (México), 4 (jul. /dic. , 1970), 223-
[263].

LOZANO, PEDRO

456 Fúrlong Cardiff, Guillermo.   Pedro Lozano, S. J. , y
     sus "Observaciones a Vargas," 1750.   Buenos Aires:
     Librería del Plata, 1959.   176 p.   (Escritores
     coloniales rioplatenses, 9).

LUCENA, HENRIQUE BEREIRA DE LUCENA, BARAO DE

457 Pernambuco, Brazil (State) Arquivo Público.   Arquivo
     do barão de Lucena: catálogo.   Recife, Secretaria
     do Interior e Justiça, 1956.   xv, 285 p.

LUGONES, LEOPOLDO

458 Lermon, Miguel.   Contribución a la bibliografía de
     Leopoldo Lugones....   Buenos Aires: Ediciones
     Maru, 1969.   255 p.

MACHADO DE ASSIS, JOAQUIM MARIA

459 Rio de Janeiro.   Biblioteca Nacional.   Exposição comem-
     orativa do sexagésimo aniversário de falecimento do
     Joaquim Maria Machado de Assis.   Rio de Janeiro,
     1968.   39 p.

MALDONADO KOERDELL, MANUEL

460 Heredia Correa, Roberto.   "Manuel Maldonado Koerdell
     (1908-1972)."   Revista de historia de América, 73/
     74 (ene. /dic. , 1972), 215-218.

MARASSO, ARTURO

461 Becco, Horacio Jorge.   "Bibliografía de Don Arturo
     Marasso (1890-1970)."   Boletín de la Academia
     Argentina de Letras, 35:135/136 (ene. /jun. , 1970),
     15-22.

MARMOL, JOSE

462   Giannangeli, Liliana.   Contribución a la bibliografía de
      José Mármol.   La Plata: Universidad Nacional de
      La Plata, Facultad de Humanidades y Ciencias de
      la Educación, 1972.   ii, 254 p.   (Textos, documen-
      tos y bibliografía, 5).

MARTENS, CONRAD

463   James, David.   "Conrad Martens en Sudamérica."
      Traducción y prólogo por Eugenio Pereira Salas.
      Boletín de la Academia Chilena de la Historia,
      38:85 (1971), 169-199.   Includes: "Catálogo gen-
      eral de los dibujos y acuarelas originales ejecu-
      tades por Conrad Martens en Sudamérica."--
      pp. 191-199.

MARTI, JOSE

464   Quintana, Jorge.   Cronolía [i.e. cronología] biobib-
      liográfica de José Martí.   Caracas, 1964.
      262 p.

MARTINEZ DURAN, CARLOS

465   Dardón Córdova, Gonzalo.   Cincuenta años de la produc-
      ción literaria del doctor Carlos Martínez Durán
      (1923-1973); bibliografía descriptiva compilada por
      ... con la colaboración de Ofelia Aguilar Pellecer en
      la sección de artículos publicados en El Imparcial,
      en los años comprendidos en 1963 a 1973.   Guate-
      mala, Facultad de Humanidades, Universidad de San
      Carlos de Guatemala, 1973.   ii, 21 ℓ.

MARTINEZ ESTRADA, EZEQUIEL

466   Adam, Carlos.   Bibliografía de Ezequiel Martínez
      Estrada.   Advertencia preliminar por Juan Carlos
      Ghiano.   La Plata: Universidad Nacional, Instituto
      de Letras, 1968.   247 p.   (Textos, documentos y
      bibliografías, 3).

61   BIOGRAPHY (Individual)

467   Echevarría, Israel. "Don Ezequiel Martínez Estrada
      en Cuba: contribución a su bibliografía." Revista
      de la Biblioteca Nacional José Martí, 3a ser.,
      10:2 (may./ago., 1968), 113-165.

MARTIUS, KARL FRIEDRICH PHILIPP VON

468   Rio de Janeiro. Biblioteca Nacional. Exposição co-
      memorativa do centenário de morte de Karl Fried-
      rich Philipp von Martius, 1868-1968. Rio de Janei-
      ro, 1968. 46 p.

MAZA CUADRA, FRANCISCO DE LA

469   Gorráez Arcaute, Luz. "Francisco de la Maza
      Cuadra, 1913-1972." Anales del Instituto de In-
      vestigaciones Estéticas, U.N.A.M., 11:41 (1972),
      141-175.

MEADE, JOAQUIN

470   Montejano y Aguiñaga, Rafael. "Joaquín Meade (1896-
      1971)." Revista de historia de América, 73/74
      (ene./dic., 1972), 219-227.

471   Rubio Mañé, J. Ignacio. "Nota necrológica: Joaquín
      Meade, 1896-1971." Boletín del Archivo General
      de la Nación, Mexico, 2d ser., 12:1/2 (1971),
      237-246.

MENDOZA, VICENTE T.

472   Moedano Navarro, Gabriel. "Bibliografía del professor
      Vicente T. Mendoza." In: 25 estudios de folk-
      lore. México: Universidad Nacional de México,
      Instituto de Investigaciones Estéticas, 1971.
      pp. 23-55.

MENENDEZ PIDAL, RAMON

473   Havana. Biblioteca Nacional "José Martí." Breve

bibliografía: Ramón Menéndez Pidal in memoriam, 1869-1968, compilado por Tomás F. Robaina. La Habana, 1970. 60 p.

MILLARES CARLO, AGUSTIN

474 Vaz Araujo, Lino. Agustín Millares Carlo (Testimonios para una bibliografía). Maracaibo, Venezuela: Universidad del Zulia, Dirección de Cultura, 1968. 229 p.

MITRE, BARTOLOME

475 Biblioteca Municipal Pública del Partido de General Pueyrredón. Bibliografía sobre Bartolomé Mitre. Mar del Plata, Argentina, 1971. 16 ℓ.

476 Fúrlong Cardiff, Guillermo. "Bartolomé Mitre: el hombre, el soldado, el historiador, el político." Investigaciones y ensayos, 11 (jul./dic., 1971), 325-522.

MITTELHOLZER, EDGAR AUSTIN

477 Guyana. Public Free Library. Edgar Austin Mittelholzer, 1909-1965. Georgetown, 1968. 23, 13 p.

MOLINARI, JOSE LUIS

478 Guérin, Miguel A. and Susana M. Ramírez. "Bibliografía del académico de número José Luis Molinari." Boletín de la Academia Nacional de la Historia (Buenos Aires), 44 (1971), 505-523.

MONTES DE OCA Y OBREGON, IGNACIO, ABP.

479 Montejano y Aguiñaga, Rafael. Bibliografía de Don Ignacio Montes do Oca. San Luis de Potosí, México: Academia de Historia Potosina, 1969. 51 p. (Biblioteca de historia potosina. Serie cuadernos, 3).

MORALES GALAVIS, ANTONIO

480 Elias Ortiz, Sergio. "Biblioteca del prócer doctor
Antonio Morales Galavís." Boletín cultural y
bibliográfico, 12:7 (1969), 10-16.

MOREIRA, JOÃO ROBERTO

481 "Professor João Roberto Moreira." América latina,
10:2 (abr. /jun., 1967), 139-142.

MORON, GUILLERMO

482 Academia Nacional de la Historia, Caracas. Guillermo
Morón. Caracas, 1974. 295 p. (Colección bibliográfica, 2).

MORTARA, GIORGIO

483 Paiva, Helena Gomes de and Hespéria Zuma de Rosso.
"Bibliografia das obras do Prof. Giorgio Mortara."
Revista brasileira de estatística, 30:120 (out. /dez.,
1969), 399-519.

MOSHINSKY, MARCOS

484 "Curriculum vitae del Doctor Marcos Moshinsky."
Memoria de El Colegio de México, 7:3 (1972), 271-
284.

MUELLE, JORGE C.

485 Ravines, Roger; Duccio Bonavia and Rosalía Avalos de
Matos. "Bio-bibliografía de Jorge C. Muelle."
Revista del Museo Nacional, Lima, 40 (1974), 459-
470.

NALE ROXLO, CONRADO

486 Becco, Horacio Jorge. "Bibliografía de Don Conrado
Nalé Roxlo (1898-1971)." Boletín de la Academia

Argentina de Letras, 36:141/142 (jul./dic., 1971), 263-267.

NARANJO, PLUTARCO

487 Bibliografía del Dr. Plutarco Naranjo (1942-1971). Quito, 1972? 26 ℓ.

NAVARRO TOMAS, TOMAS

488 Beardsley, Theodore S. Tomás Navarro Tomás: a tentative bibliography, 1908-1970. Syracuse, N. Y. : Centro de Estudios Hispánicos, Syracuse University, 1971. 12 p. (Cuadernos, 1).

NERUDA, PABLO

489 Chile. Congreso. Biblioteca. Pablo Neruda, Premio Nobel de literatura 1971; bibliografía selectiva .... Santiago de Chile, 1971. 49 ℓ.

490 Loyola, Hernán. Exposición bibliográfica de la obra de Pablo Neruda, Biblioteca Nacional, del 20 al 31 de agosto. Santiago de Chile: Nascimento, 1969. 69 p.

491 Morelli, Gabriele. "Bibliografía de Neruda en Italia." Revista iberoamericana, 39:82/83 (ene./jun., 1973), 369-371.

492 "Pablo Neruda in 'Books abroad' (1929-72)." Books abroad, 46 (Winter, 1972), 54-55.

493 Volek, Emil. "Pablo Neruda: bibliografía complementaria selectiva." Revista iberoamericana, 39:82/83 (ene./jun., 1973), 363-368.

NETO, SIMÕES LOPES

494 Dantes, Macedo. "Vida e obra de Simões Lopes Neto." Revista do Arquivo Municipal (São Paulo), 179 (out./ dez., 1969), 91-109.

NOGUERA, EDUARDO

495   "Eduardo Noguera. " Boletín bibliográfico de antropolo-
      gía americana, 33/34 (1970/1971), 249-257.

NORDENSKIÖLD, ERLAND

496   Kaudern, Walter Alexander and Stig Rydén.   "Erland
      Nordenskiöld, 11-VII-1877--5-VII-1932. " Archives
      ethnos, 1: Series C, 1 (May, 1948), 1-13.

NUÑEZ, ENRIQUE BERNARDO

497   Caracas. Universidad Católica Andrés Bello. Semin-
      ario de Literatura Venezolana. Contribución a la
      bibliografía de Enrique Bernardo Nuñez, 1895-1964.
      Caracas: Gobernación del Distrito Federal, 1970.
      205 p. (Colección Bibliografías, 6).

OBLIGADO, PEDRO MIGUEL

498   Becco, Horacio Jorge. "Bibliografía de Pedro Miguel
      Obligado (1890-1967)." Boletín de la Academia Ar-
      gentina de Letras, 32:123/124 (ene. /jun. , 1967),
      169-173.

OLIVEIRA LIMA, MANUEL DE

499   Macedo, Neusa Dias de. Bibliografia de Manoel de
      Oliveira Lima; com estudio biográfico e cronologia.
      Pref. de Edson Nery da Fonseca. Recife: Arquivo
      Público Estadual, 1968.   88 p.

OLIVER BELMAS, ANTONIO

500   Gutiérrez-Vega, Zenaida. "Antonio Oliver Belmás
      (1903-1968). " Abside, 38:4 (1974), 440-448.

ONETTI, JUAN CARLOS

501   Frankenthaler, Marilyn. "Complemento a la bibliografía

de y sobre Juan Carlos Onetti." Revista iberoamericana, 41:91 (abr. /jun. , 1975), 355-365.

502   Verani, Hugo J. "Contribución a la bibliografía de
Juan Carlos Onetti." Revista iberoamericana, 38:
80 (jul. /sept. , 1972), 523-548.

ONIS Y SANCHEZ , FEDERICO DE

503   Arrigoitia, Luis de. "Bibliografía de Federico de
Onis." La Torre, 16:59 (mar. , 1968), 229-262.

503a   Florit, Ricardo. "Federico de Onis: bibliografía."
Revista hispánica moderna, 34:1/2 (1968), 95-100.

ORE, LUIS JERONIMO DE

504   Heras, Julián. "Bio-bibliografía de Fray Luís Jeró-
nimo de Oré, O. F. M. (1554-1630)." Revista histórica, Lima, 29 (1966), 173-192.

ORIA, JOSE O.

505   Becco, Horacio Jorge. "Bibliografía de Don José O.
Oría (1892-1970)." Boletín de la Academia Argentina de Letras, 35:135/136 (ene. /jun. , 1970), 33-
37.

ORTIZ FERNANDEZ, FERNANDO

506   Havana. Biblioteca Nacional José Martí. Bio-bibliografía de don Fernando Ortíz. Compilado por Araceli García-Carranza. La Habana, 1970. 250 p.

507   Le Riverend, Julio. "Fernando Ortíz, 1881-1969."
América indígena, 29:3 (jul. , 1969), 892-898.

OTERO Y ARCE, MIGUEL

508   Alcocer Andalon, Alberto. "El Dr. Miguel Otero y
Arce: bibliografía." Archivos de historia potosina,
18 (dic. , 1973), 83-103.

OYARZUN, LUIS

509 Chile. Congreso. Biblioteca. Luis Oyarzún Peña
(1920-1972): [bibliografía]. Santiago de Chile,
1974. 11 ℓ. (Bibliografía, 56: Serie A: 1).

PAEZ, JOSE ANTONIO

510 "Contribución a la bibliografía del General José Antonio
Páez (1790-1873)." Boletín histórico, Caracas, 31
(ene., 1973), 101-179.

511 Lovera De-Sola, R. J. "El General Paéz y su tiempo:
bibliografía venezolana publicada con ocasión del
centenario de su muerte." Boletín histórico, Cará-
cas, 34 (ene., 1974), 157-172.

PARDO Y ALIAGA, FELIPE

512 Cachay Díaz, Roselena. "Felipe Pardo y Aliaga,
1806-1868: Biobibliografía." Boletín de la Biblioteca Nacional (Lima), 22/23:45/48 (1968), 3-27.

PARRA, TERESA DE LA

513 Caracas. Universidad Católica Andrés Bello. Escuela
de Letras. Centro de Investigaciones Literarias.
Contribución a la bibliografía de Teresa de la Parra,
1895-1936. Caracas: Gobernación del Distrito
Federal, 1970. 135 p. (Colección bibliografías, 7).

PAZ, OCTAVIO

514 "Octavio Paz in 'Books abroad' (1951-72)." Books
abroad, 46 (Autumn, 1972), 613-614.

515 Roggiano, Alfredo A. "Bibliografía de y sobre Octavio
Paz." Revista iberoamericana, 37:74 (ene./mar.,
1971), 269-297.

516 "Selected bibliography [of Octavio Paz]." Books abroad,
46 (Autumn, 1972), 611-613.

517   Valencia, Juan and Edward Coughlin. Bibliografía se-
      lecta y crítica de Octavio Paz. Cincinnati: Univer-
      sity of Cincinnati; México: Universidad Autónoma
      de San Luis Potosí, 1973. 87 p.

PAZ CASTILLO, FERNANDO

518   Calvo de Elcoro, Miren Zorkunde. Contribución a la
      bibliografía de Fernando Paz Castillo, 1893....
      Caracas: Gobernación del Distrito Federal, 1974.
      332 p. (Colección Bibliografías, 11).

PELLICER, CARLOS

519   Lara Barba, Othón. "Carlos Pellicer: testimonios
      (ensayo biblio-iconográfico ilustrado con textos). "
      Boletín del Instituto de Investigaciones Bibliográficas
      (México), 5 (ene. /jun. , 1971), 9-117.

PEREGRINO DA SILVA, MANUEL CICERO

520   Rio de Janeiro. Biblioteca Nacional. Manuel Cícero
      Peregrino da Silva, 1866-1966; exposição comemora-
      tiva do centenário de nascimento. Rio de Janeiro,
      1966. 22 p.

PEREYRA, CARLOS

521   Rublúo, Luis. "Carta historiográfica para Carlos
      Pereyra, 1871-1971. " Boletín bibliográfico de la
      Secretaría de Hacienda y Crédito Público, Mexico,
      18:468 (1971), 3-15.

PEREZ-BUSTAMANTE, CIRIACO

522   Seco Serrano, Carlos. "Don Ciriaco Pérez-Bustamente. "
      Revista de Indias, 29:115/118 (ene. /dic. , 1969),
      27-30.

PICON-SALAS, MARIANO

523   Grases, Pedro. "Contribución a la bibliografía de

Mariano Picón Salas. " Revista nacional de cultura, 27:167/169 (ene. /jun. , 1965), 112-117.

PILLADO, JOSE ANTONIO

524   Fariní, Juan Angel.   José Antonio Pillado.   Buenos Aires, 194?, 35 p.   (Bibliografía de los miembros de número de la Academia Nacional de la Historia, 10).

POCATERRA, JOSE RAFAEL

525   Caracas.   Universidad Católica Andrés Bello.   Seminario de Literatura Venezolana.   Contribución a la bibliografía de José Rafael Pocaterra, 1890-1955. Caracas: Gobernación del Distrito Federal, 1969. 96 p.   (Colección Bibliografías, 4).

PORTINARI, CANDIDO

526   "Portinari; bibliografia. "   Compilada pela Biblioteca da Faculdade de Arquitectura e Urbanismo, Universidade de São Paulo.   Revista de história, São Paulo, 44: 90 (abr. /jun. , 1972), 557-664.

PRATA, RANULFO

527   Carvalho-Neto, Paulo de.   "Un lugar para Ranulfo Prata (contribuição bibliográfica). "   Inter-American review of bibliography, 24:1 (Jan. /Mar. , 1974), 3-30.

PRIETO, GUILLERMO

528   McLean, Malcolm Dallas.   Bibliography on Guillermo Prieto, Mexican poet-statesman.   Fort Worth: Texas Christian University Press, 1968.   vii, 399 p. Sobretiro del Boletín bibliográfico de la Secretaría de Hacienda y Crédito Público, 366 (mayo de 1967).

PUCCIARELLI, EUGENIO

529   Ruiz de Galaretta, Juan.   "Bibliografía de Eugenio

Pucciarelli. " Boletín bibliográfico de la Biblioteca
Pública de La Plata, 20 (1969), 9-15.

PUTNAM, SAMUEL

530   Gardiner, Clinton Harvey.   Samuel Putnam, Latin
Americanist; a bibliography.   Carbondale: Southern
Illinois University, Libraries, 1970.   xvi, 48 p.
(Bibliographic contributions, 5).

QUIROGA, HORACIO

531   Rela, Walter.   Horacio Quiroga: repertorio bibliográfico anotado, 1897-1971.   Buenos Aires: Casa
Pardo, 1972.   145 p.

RAGUCCI, RODOLFO MARIA

532   Becco, Horacio Jorge.   "Bibliografía del Pbro.   Don
Rodolfo María Ragucci, S. D. B. (1887-1973). "
Boletín de la Academia Argentina de Letras, 38:
147/148 (ene. /jun. , 1973), 19-23.

RAMOS MEJIA, JOSE MARIA

533   Fariní, Juan Angel.   Doctor José María Ramos Mejía.
Buenos Aires, 194?.   32 p.   (Bibliografía de los
miembros de número de la Academia Nacional de
la Historia, 9).

RÊGO, JOSE LINS DO

534   Kelly, John R.   "An annotated bibliography of the early
writings of José Lins do Rêgo. "   Luso-Brazilian review, 9:1 (Summer, 1972), 72-85.

REICHENBERGER, ARNOLD G.

535   Geiver, Gail R. and José M. Regueiro.   "Publications
of Arnold G. Reichenberger. "   Hispanic review,
special issue, 41 (1973), 143-150.

RESTREPO POSADA, JOSE

536   León Helguera, J. "Apreciaciones breves sobre la
      obra y bibliografía del Monseñor José Restrepo
      Posada, 1924-1972." Boletín de historia y anti-
      güedades (Academia Colombiana de Historia), 61:703
      (ene./mar., 1974), 27-78.

REYLES, CARLOS

537   Montevideo. Biblioteca Nacional. Exposición Carlos
      Reyles; centenario de su nacimiento, 1868-1968.
      Montevideo, 1968. 35 p.

RIVERA, JOSE EUSTASIO

538   Lozano, Hernán. "La vorágine": ensayo bibliográfico.
      Bogotá: Instituto Caro y Cuervo, 1973. Unpaged.

RODRIGUES, JOSE CARLOS

539   "Correspondencia passiva de José Carlos Rodrigues."
      Anais da Biblioteca Nacional (Rio de Janeiro), 90
      (1970), 3-339.

RODRIGUEZ, CAYETANO JOSE

540   Fernández, Belisario. "Fray Cayetano José Rodríguez.
      Guía bio-bibliográfica (1761-1823)." Investigaciones
      y ensayos, Buenos Aires, 3 (jul./dic., 1967), 243-
      269.

RODRIGUEZ MOÑINO, ANTONIO

541   Quintana, José. "Antonio Rodríguez-Moñino: El Menén-
      dez Pelayo de la bibliografía española." Boletín de
      la Biblioteca General de la Universidad del Zulia,
      10/11:17/18 (ag. 1970/jun. 1971), 389-396.

RODRIGUEZ RIVERA, VIRGINIA

542   Moedano Navarro, Gabriel. "Biografía de la profesora

Virginia Rodríguez Rivera. " In: 25 estudios de folklore. México: Universidad Nacional de México, Instituto de Investigaciones Estéticas, 1971. pp. 57-72.

ROMO ARMERIA, JESUS

543 "Curriculum vitae del Doctor Jesús Romo Armería. " Memoria de El Colegio de México, 7:3 (1972), 303-318.

ROSENBLUETH, EMILIO

544 "Historial académico del Doctor Emilio Rosenblueth. " Memoria de El Colegio de México, 7:3 (1972), 329-340.

ROYS, RALPH LOVELAND

545 Thompson, J. Eric S. "Ralph Loveland Roys, 1879-1965. " Estudios de Cultura Maya, 6 (1967), 421-431.

RULFO, JUAN

546 Lioret, E. Kent. "Continuación de una bibliografía de y sobre Juan Rulfo. " Revista iberoamericana, 40: 89 (oct. /dic. , 1974), 693-705.

546a Ramírez, Arthur. "Hacia una bibliografía de y sobre Juan Rulfo. " Revista iberoamericana, 40:86 (ene. / mar. , 1974), 135-171.

RYDEN, STIG

547 Mörner, Magnus. "Necrología: Stig Ryden. " Revista de Indias, 26:103/104 (1966), 191-194.

SABATO, ERNESTO

548 Petersen, Fred. "Ernesto Sábato: una bibliografía. "

La Palabra y el hombre, 47 (jul./sept., 1968), 425-435.

SACO, JOSE ANTONIO

549   Codina Carreira, Pablo. "Ensayo para una biografía de José Antonio Saco: la realidad de su pensamiento." Revista de Indias, 27:107/108 (1967), 89-135.

SALAS, JULIO CESAR

550   "Bibliografía del Dr. Julio César Salas." Anuario del Instituto de Antropología e Historia, Universidad Central de Venezuela, 3 (1966), 459-470.

SALMERON, FERNANDO

551   "Curriculum vitae del Doctor Fernando Salmerón." Memoria de El Colegio de México, 7:3 (1972), 347-363.

SANCHEZ, FLORENCIO

552   Rela, Walter. Repertorio bibliográfico anotado sobre Florencio Sánchez, 1891-1971. Buenos Aires: Universidad de Buenos Aires, Facultad de Filosofía y Letras, Instituto de Literatura Argentina Ricardo Rojas, 1973- . (Guías bibliográficas, 2).

SANCHEZ-ALBORNOZ Y MENDUINA, CLAUDIO

553   Bibliografía de Claudio Sánchez-Albornoz; homenaje con ocasión de sus cuarenta años de docencia universitaria. Buenos Aires: Coni, 1957. 45 p.

SANTA MARIA DE ORO, JUSTO

554   González, Ruben C. "Bibliografía de Fray Justo de Santa María de Oro, O.P." Archivum; revista de la Junta de Historia Eclesiástica Argentina, 8 (1966), 51-72.

SANTIANA, ANTONIO

555 Comas, Juan. "Antonio Santiana, 1914-1966. " América indígena, 27:2 (abr. , 1967), 333-337.

SANZ, CARLOS

556 "Homenaje a don Carlos Sanz. " Revista de Indias, 27:109/110 (jul. /dic. , 1967), 493-505.

SARDUY, SEVERO

557 González Echevarría, Roberto. "Para una bibliografía de y sobre Severo Sarduy (1955-1971). " Revista iberoamericana, 38:79 (abr. /jun. , 1972), 333-343.

SCHELLENBERG, THEODORE R.

558 Ulibarri, George S. "Theodore R. Schellenberg (1903-1970). " Revista de historia de América, 69 (ene. / jun. , 1970), 133-137.

SCOBIE, JAMES

559 Wright, Antônio Fernanda Almeida. "A contribuição do Professor James Scobie para a historiografia argentina. " Revista de história, São Paulo, 33:68 (out. / dez. , 1966), 515-547.

SERIS, HOMERO

560 Beardsley, Theodore S. , Jr. "Publications of Homero Serís. " Hispanic Review, 37 (1969), 555-565.

SIERRA, JUSTO

561 Mantecón Navasal, José Ignacio; Irma Contreras García and Ignacio Osorio Romero. Bibliografía general de Don Justo Sierra. México: UNAM, Instituto de Investigaciones Bibliográficas, 1969. xiv, 273 p. (Publicaciones, 12).

SILVA CASTRO, RAUL

562 MacHale, Tomás P.   "Bibliografía de Raúl Silva Castro (1903-1970). " Inter-American review of bibliography, 22:1 (Jan. /Mar. , 1972), 30-44.

SMITH, ROBERT SYDNEY

563 Rubio Mañé, J. Ignacio. "Nota necrológica: Robert Sydney Smith, 1904-1969. " Boletín del Archivo General de la Nación, México, ser. 2, 10:3/4 (jul. / dic. , 1969), 601-608.

SOLIS FOLCH DE CARDONA, JOSE

564 Lyday, León F.   "El Virrey Solís en las letras colombianas (bibliografía). " Boletín cultural y bibliográfico, 12:3 (1969), 53-63.

SOUZA, THOMAZ MARCONDES DE

565 Silva, Nicolau Duarte. "Homenagem: Prof. Thomaz Marcondes de Souza. " Revista de história, São Paulo, 38:77 (jan. /mar. , 1969), 3-9.

SPELL, JEFFERSON REA

566 Spell, Lota M.   "Bibliografía de Jefferson Rea Spell. " Revista iberoamericana, 34:66 (jul. /dic. , 1968), 356-364.

SPINDEN, HERBERT JOSEPH

567 Ruz Lhuillier, Alberto. "Herbert Joseph Spinden (1879-1967). " Estudios de Cultura Maya, 8 (1970), 437-442.

SWADESH, MAURICIO

568 Rendón, Juan José.   "Mauricio Swadesh, 1909-1967. " América indígena, 27:4 (oct. , 1967), 735-746.

TASCON, JORGE H.

569 "Doctor Jorge H. Tascon.   Noticia bio-bibliográfica."
Boletín colombiano de historia y antigüedades, 55
(1968), 182-184.

TERMER, FRANZ

570 Ruz Lhuillier, Alberto.   "Franz Termer (1894-1968)."
Estudios de Cultura Maya, 7 (1968), 401-406.

TERERRA, GUILLERMO ALFREDO

571 Terrera, Guillermo Alfredo.   Curriculum vitae.   [2.
ed. ampliada].   Buenos Aires, 1973.   40 p.

TORO, FERMIN

572 Moron, Guillermo.   "El Archivo de Fermín Toro."
Revista nacional de cultura, 38:174/175 (1966),
49-57.

TORRE REVELLO, JOSE

573 Fúrlong Cardiff, Guillermo.   José Torre Revello, "a
self-made man"; su biografía y su biobibliografía.
Buenos Aires: Universidad del Salvador, Instituto
de Historia Argentina y Americana, 1968.   339 p.
(Colección Indices y bibliografías, 2).

TORRES RIOSECO, ARTURO

574 Roggiano, Alfredo A.   "Obras de Arturo Torres Rioseco."   Revista iberoamericana, 38:78 (ene./mar.,
1972), 28-29.

URBANEJA ACHELPOHL, LUIS MANUEL

575 Caracas.   Universidad Católica Andrés Bello.   Escuela
de Letras.   Centro de Investigaciones Literarias.
Contribución a la bibliografía de Luis Manuel

Urbaneja Achelpohl, 1873-1937.   Caracas: Governación del Distrito Federal, 1971. 115 p. (Colección bibliografías, 8).

USIGLI, RODOLFO

576 Scott, Wilder P. "Toward an Usigli bibliography (1931-1971)." Latin American theatre review, 6:1 (Fall, 1972), 53-63.

USLAR PIETRI, ARTURO

577 Caracas. Universidad Católica Andrés Bello. Escuela de Letras. Centro de Investigaciones Literarias. Contribución a la bibliografía de Arturo Uslar Pietri ... realizado por María Zoraída Lange de Cabrera ... et al. Caracas: Gobernación del Distrito Federal, 1973? 396 p. (Colección Bibliografías, 10).

578 García González, Dunia. "Contribución a la bibliografía del Doctor Arturo Uslar Pietri." Boletín de la Biblioteca General de la Universidad del Zulia, 10/11:17/18 (ag. 1970/jun. 1971), 287-317.

VALLE ARIZPE, ARTEMIO DE

579 Quintana, José Miguel. "Don Artemio de Valle Arizpe." Boletín bibliográfico de la Secretaría de Hacienda y Crédito Público, México, 17:455 (1971), 4-8.

VALLEJO, CESAR

580 González Poggi, Uruguay. Exposición: César Vallejo, 1892-1938. Montevideo: UNESCO, 1970. 23 p.

581 Roggiano, Alfredo. "Mínima guía bibliográfica [César Vallejo]." Revista iberoamericana, 36:71 (abr./jun., 1970), 353-358.

VEDIA Y MITRE, MARIANO

582 Fariní, Juan Angel. "Bibliografía de Mariano de

Vedia y Mitre." Boletín de la Academia Nacional de la Historia, Buenos Aires, 43 (1970), 423-447.

VEGA, CARLOS

583 Suarez Urtubey, Pola. "Contribución a la bibliografía de Carlos Vega." Revista musical chilena, 21:101 (jul./sept., 1967), 73-86.

VESPUCCI, AMERIGO

584 Fúrlong Cardiff, Guillermo. "Bibliografía [sobre Américo Vespucio]." Investigaciones y ensayos, 6/7 (ene./dic., 1969), 45-53.

VIANA, HELIO

585 Matos, Odilon Nogueira de. "Vultos da historiografia brasileira: Helio Viana (1908-1972)." Revista de história, São Paulo, 46:93 (jan./mar., 1973), 201-203.

VILLAVICENCIO, PABLO DE

586 Olea, Héctor R. Panfletografía de El Payo del Payo del Rosario (semblanza de Pablo Villavicencio). México, 1969. 97 p. (Testimonios de Atlacomulco, 37).

VILLEGAS BASAVILBASO, BENJAMIN

587 Caillet-Bois, Ricardo R. "Retrato del Dr. Benjamín Villegas Basavilbaso." Boletín del Instituto de Historia Argentina "Doctor Emilio Ravignani," 2a série, 11:18/19 (1969), 278-280.

WEITLANER, ROBERTO J.

588 Olivera de V., Mercedes. "La presencia y la ausencia del Maestro Weitlaner." Boletín bibliográfico de antropología americana, 31 (1968), 119-127.

589 "Roberto J. Weitlaner, 1883-1968." América indígena,
     28:4 (oct., 1968), 1156-1162.

COMMERCE AND TRADE

590 Argentina. Consejo Nacional de Desarrollo. Secre-
     taría. Celulosa y papel; bibliografía. Buenos
     Aires, 1968. 203 p.

591 Banco de México (Founded 1925). Biblioteca. Comer-
     cio exterior de México, 1943-1967. México, 1968.
     89 p. (Its Serie de bibliografías especiales, 8).

592 Banco Industrial del Perú. Biblioteca. Pequeña in-
     dustria y artesanía: bibliografía. Lima, 1972.
     vi, 59 p. (Its Serie bibliográfica, 1).

593 "Bibliografía sobre comercio exterior." Revista de
     política e administraçao fiscal, 2:2 (mar./abr.,
     1970), 195-204.

594 Buenos Aires. Bolsa de Comercio. Biblioteca.
     Sociedades anónimas; bibliografía. Buenos Aires,
     1966. 147 p.

595 Escuela de Administración de Negocios para Graduados,
     Lima. Biblioteca. Promoción y gestión de exporta-
     ciones; guía bibliográfica. Compilada por Biblioteca
     "Alan B. Coleman." Lima, 1972. xv, 191 p.

596 Latin American Center for Economic and Social Docu-
     mentation. Bibliografía sobre promoción de exporta-
     ciones. 1. ed. Santiago de Chile: Centro Latino-
     americano de Documentación Económica y Social,
     1973. x, 371 p.

597 Organization of American States. Bibliografía de
     comercio exterior. Bogotá, 1968. 73 ℓ.

DISSERTATIONS

598 Baa, Enid M. Doctoral dissertations and selected
     theses on Caribbean topics accapted [sic] by

universities of Canada, United States and Europe, from 1778-1968. St. Thomas, V.I.: Bureau of Public Libraries & Museums, 1969. iv, 91 p.

599 _____. Theses on Caribbean topics, 1778-1968. San Juan: Institute of Caribbean Studies, University of Puerto Rico Press, 1970. v, 146 p. (Caribbean bibliographic series, 1).

600 Bogotá. Universidad de los Andes. Comité de Investigaciones. Catálogo de tesis, 1960-1973. Bogotá, 1973. 55, 41 p.

601 Brown, Larry C. "Report on lists of doctoral dissertations and master's theses on Latin America." Latin American research review, 6:3 (Fall, 1971), 127-129.

602 Buenos Aires. Universidad. Facultad de Ciencias Económicas. Tesis doctorales aprobadas desde el lo. de enero hasta el 31 de diciembre de 1968; resúmenes. Buenos Aires, 1970. 47 p. (Serie de divulgación bibliográfica económica, 43).

603 Buenos Aires. Universidad. Instituto Bibliotecológico. Tesis presentadas a la Universidad de Buenos Aires, 1961-1962. Buenos Aires, 1965 [i.e. 1966]. ii, 61 ℓ.

604 _____. Tesis presentadas a la Universidad de Buenos Aires, 1963-1964. Buenos Aires, 1968. ii, 67 p.

605 _____. Tesis presentadas a la Universidad de Buenos Aires, 1965-1966. Buenos Aires: Universidad de Buenos Aires, 1970.

606 Bustelo, Blanca Margarita. Monografías y tesis universitarias sobre industrialización en el Uruguay, presentadas en la Facultad de Ciencias Económicas y de Administración, Universidad de la República, Montevideo, Uruguay, (1937-1972). Montevideo: Comcorde, Secretaría Técnica, 1973. 40 p.

607 Caldeira, Paulo da Terra and Sonia Maria Penido de Freitas. "Trabalho de conclusão de curso; bibliografia analítica dos trabalhos de conclusão de curso

dos alunos da Escola de Biblioteconomia da UFMG referente ao período de 1956 a 1972, arranjada por assunto." Revista da Escola de Biblioteconomia (Universidade Federal de Minas Gerais), 2:1 (mar., 1973), 86-138.

608 Cardozo González, Armando. Bibliografía de tesis de grado y postgrado de ingenieros agrónomos del Ecuador. Quito: Instituto Interamericano de Ciencias Agrícolas de la OEA y AIBDA, 1971. 60 p.

609 "Catalogue des theses et memoires sur l'Amérique Latine soutenus en France de 1970 à 1974." Cahiers des Ameriques Latines, Série sciences de l'homme, 9/10 (1974), 283-366.

610 Chaffee, Wilber A. and Honor M. Griffin. Dissertations on Latin America by U.S. historians, 1960-1970: a bibliography. Austin: Institute of Latin American Studies, University of Texas, 1973. xi, 62 p. (Guides and bibliographies series, 7).

611 Colombia. Universidad, Bogotá. Facultad de Derecho y Ciencias Políticas. Biblioteca. Tesis existentes en la Biblioteca ..., 1898-1968. Preparada por Lucía Belmonte Román. Bogotá, 1968. xiii, 200 p.

612 Costa Rica. Universidad. Biblioteca. Lista de tesis de grado de la Universidad de Costa Rica, 1967. San José, 1969. 72 p. (Serie bibliotecología, 24).

613 _____. Lista de tesis de grado de la Universidad de Costa Rica, 1969-1971. San Pedro de Montes de Oca: Universidad de Costa Rica, Depto. de Publicaciones, 1973. 203 p. (Serie bibliotecología, 28).

614 Dossick, Jesse J. Doctoral research on Puerto Rico and Puerto Ricans. New York: New York University, 1967. 34 p.

615 _____. "Doctoral research on the Caribbean and circum Caribbean accepted by American, British and Canadian universities, 1968-1970." Caribbean studies, 11:2 (Jul., 1971), 127-155.

616 Fernández-Torriente, Gastón. "Tesis de grado escritas en los Estados Unidos sobre Colombia." Boletín cultural y bibliográfico, 11:11 (1968), 76-82.

617   Garner, Jane; Don Gibbs and Mary Ellis Kahler.   "Pro-
      visional list of dissertations on Latin American
      topics, 1972."   Newsletter of the Latin American
      Studies Association, 5:3 (Sept., 1974), 47-105.

618   Gibbs, Don and Mary Ellis Kahler.   "Provisional list
      of dissertations on Latin American topics, 1973."
      LASA Newsletter, 6:2 (June, 1975), 13-77.

619   Glick, Thomas F.   "Lists of doctoral dissertations and
      master's theses on Latin America: addenda."
      Latin American research review, 7:2 (Summer,
      1972), 148.   Additions to Larry C. Brown's report
      which appeared in LARR,   6:3 (Fall, 1971), 127-129.

620   Griffin, Ernst C. and Clarence W. Minkel.   A bibliog-
      raphy of theses and dissertations on Latin America
      by U.S. geographers, 1960-1970.   Washington: U.S.
      National Section, Pan American Institute of Geog-
      raphy and History, 1970.   16 p.   (Special publica-
      tion, 2).

621   Hanson, Carl A.   "Dissertations on Luso-Brazilian
      topics: a bibliography of dissertations completed in
      the United States, Great Britain and Canada, 1892-
      1970:   Part I."   The Americas, 30:2 (Oct., 1973),
      251-267.

622   _____. "_____: Part II, with addendum."   The
      Americas, 30:3 (Jan., 1974) 373-403.

623   Hills, Theo L.   Caribbean topics: theses in Canadian
      university libraries.   Montreal: Centre for Develop-
      ing-Area Studies, McGill University, 1967.   11 ℓ.

624   _____. _____. 3d ed.   Montreal: Centre for
      Developing-Area Studies, McGill University, 1971?
      21 p.

625   _____. _____. 4th ed.   Montreal: McGill Uni-
      versity, Centre for Developing-Area Studies, 1973.
      v, 25 ℓ.

626   Hulet, Claude L.   "Dissertations in the Hispanic lan-
      guages and literatures."   Hispania.   [A regular
      feature.]

627 London. University. Institute of Latin American
Studies. Theses in Latin American studies at British universities in progress and completed. London.

628 Lozano Rivera, Uriel. Resúmenes de tesis presentadas
por los candidatos al título de licenciado en bibliotecología de 1960-1970. Medellín, Colombia: Universidad de Antioquia, 1972. xiii, 126 ℓ. (Escuela
Interamericana de Bibliotecología. Serie bibliografías, 19).

629 MacHale, Tomas P. Bibliografía de las memorias de
grado sobre la literatura chilena, 1918-1967. Santiago de Chile: Biblioteca Nacional, 1969. 39 p.

630 Mederos, Amelia. "Contribution to a bibliography of
published and unpublished theses written by Cubans
or on Cuba, located at Harvard University. Apended
is a list of theses submitted at the University of
Miami." In: Seminar on the Acquisition of Latin
American Library Materials, 15th, Toronto, 1970.
Final report and working papers. Washington:
O. A. S., 1971. v. 2, pp. 177-189.

631 Mendez Norma, Enrique. Resúmenes de tesis presentadas en el Departamento de Estudios Graduados de
la Facultad de Pedagogía. Río Piedras: Universidad de Puerto Rico, 1969- .

632 Meyer, Michael C. "Dissertations on Mexican history
since 1810 completed or in progress at universities
in the United States, Great Britain and France,
1967-1969." Conference on Latin American History,
Newsletter, n. s., 5:2 (Oct., 1969), 27-32.

633 Miranda P., Jorge. "Tesis doctorales en antropología
social y cultural." América indígena, 27:2 (April,
1967), 365-382.

634 Morales, Engracia Martínez de. Tesis y disertaciones
presentadas en El Colegio de México. México: El
Colegio de México, Biblioteca, Sección de Servicios
Públicos, 1975. 20 ℓ.

635 Paley, Nicholas M. Tesis profesionales de la Universidad Interamericana, 1942-1969. Saltillo, México:
Ediciones Universitarias, 1969. 51 p.

636 Panama. Universidad. Biblioteca. Bibliografía de
     los trabajos de graduación presentados en la Univer-
     sidad de Panamá, 1961-1970. Panamá, 1972.

637 Puerto Rico. University. College of Social Sciences.
     Compendios de las tesis de maestría presentadas
     ante la facultad del Departamento de Economía,
     1959-1969. Río Piedras, 1970. 151 p. (Mono-
     grafías de investigación, 1).

638 "Referencias bibliográficas de tesis." Revista de in-
     vestigación de la Universidad Nacional de San Agus-
     tín, Arequipa, Perú, 2:1 (1971), 175-201.

639 Romero Padilla, Emilio. Investigación bibliográfica de
     las tesis y seminarios de investigación de la Biblio-
     teca de la Facultad de Contaduría y Administración.
     México, 1973. [Thesis; UNAM].

640 "Tesis con contenido centroamericano de la Universidad
     de Florida." Estudios sociales centroamericanos,
     1:1 (ene./abr., 1972), 161-162.

641 "Tesis con contenido latinoamericano de la Universidad
     de Tulane." Estudios sociales centroamericanos, 1
     (ene./abr., 1972), 165-189.

642 "Tesis de grado publicadas en Estados Unidos sobre
     Colombia." Boletín cultural y bibliográfico, 9:8
     (1966), 1596-1606.

643 "Tesis doctorales relacionadas con América Latina,
     defendidas en Polonia." Estudios latinoamericanos
     (Polska Akademia Nauk, Instytut Historii/Academie
     de Ciencias de Polonia, Instituto de Historia), 2
     (1974), 311-317.

644 Texas. University at Austin. Institute of Latin Ameri-
     can Studies. Latin American research and publica-
     tions at The University of Texas at Austin, 1893-
     1969. Austin, 1971. viii, 187 p. (Guides and bib-
     liographies series, 3).

645 Torres, Leida I. La realidad de Puerto Rico; biblio-
     grafía de las tesis presentadas en la Universidad
     de Puerto Rico, recinto de Río Piedras. Río
     Piedras: Universidad de Puerto Rico, Escuela
     Graduada de Bibliotecología, 1973. xi, 101 p.

646   "Universidad de Costa Rica: lista de tesis de grado
      presentadas en la Facultad de Economía - años
      1960-1972." Estudios sociales centroamericanos,
      3 (sept./dic., 1972), 211-222.

647   "Universidad de San Carlos de Guatemala: lista de
      tesis de egresados de la Facultad de Ciencias Eco-
      nómicas desde el año de 1960." Estudios sociales
      centroamericanos, 4 (ene./abr., 1973), 229-253.

648   Xerox University Microfilms. Latin America: a cata-
      log of dissertations. Ann Arbor, 1974. 70 p.

649   Zubatsky, David S. Doctoral dissertations in history
      and the social sciences on Latin America and the
      Caribbean accepted by universities in the United
      Kingdom, 1920-1972. London: University of Lon-
      don, Institute of Latin American Studies, 1973.
      16 p.

650   _____. A list of Washington University theses and
      dissertations in the field of Ibero-American studies
      held by Olin Library. St. Louis: Washington Uni-
      versity, Library, 1970. i, 14 ℓ.

651   _____. "United States doctoral dissertations on Cu-
      ban studies." Cuban studies newsletter/Boletín de
      estudios sobre Cuba, 4:2 (Jun., 1974), 33-55.

                        ECONOMY

GENERAL

652   Anderson, Teresa J. "A description of sources for
      legal and social science research on Latin America:
      land tenure and agrarian reform." In: Seminar on
      the Acquisition of Latin American Library Materials,
      15th, Toronto, 1970. Final report and working pa-
      pers. Washington: O.A.S., 1971. v. 2, pp. 95-
      125.

653   Bibliografía de América Latina y el desarrollo. Ma-
      drid: Ciudad Universitaria, Centro de Información
      y Sociología de la OCSHA, n.d., 36, 29 p. (Bole-
      tín bibliográfico iberoamericano).

654 "Bibliografía inicial y básica conducente en último término a una teoría del derecho de la integración."
Revista de la Facultad de Derecho, Universidad Central, Caracas, 52 (ag., 1972), 47-50.

655 Bibliografía sobre colonización en América Latina.
Turrialba, Costa Rica: Instituto Interamericano de
Ciencias Agrícolas, 1972. 70 p. (Bibliografías, 10).

656 Centro de Estudios Monetarios Latinoamericanos. Bibliografía seleccionada sobre integración económica;
lista de libros, artículos y documentos incluídos en
una biblioteca básica reunida por el Centro de Estudios Monetarios Latinoamericanos y el Banco Interamericano de Desarrollo. México, 1968. 20 p.

657 Centro de Estudios para el Desarrollo e Integración de
América Latina. Desarrollo y revolución, Iglesia
y liberación (bibliografía). Complemento a la bibliografía. Bogotá, 1973. 2v. (Boletín bibliográfico, A-1, B-1).

658 Centro Interamericano de Promoción de Exportaciones.
Red interamericana de información comercial; guía
bibliográfica para el establecimiento de centros de
información comercial en función de las exportaciones. Bogotá, 1972? iv, 99 p.

659 Chile. Universidad, Santiago. Centro de Estudios
Socioeconómicos. Bibliografía para la investigación
sobre relaciones de dependencia en América Latina.
Santiago, 1969. 160 ℓ. (Its Archivo bibliográfico, 1).

660 Dokumentationsdienst Lateinamerika. Boletín de documentación latinoamericana. Hamburg: Dokumentations-Leitstelle am Institut für Iberoamerika-Kunde.

661 Escuela de Administración de Negocios para Graduados,
Lima. Biblioteca. Integración económica. Lima,
1970. viii, 175 p. (Serie bibliográfica, 6).

662 _____. _____ [trabajo de compilación, I. Olivera
R., L. Zapata]. Lima, 1973. viii, 130 p.

663 Estrada R., Gerardo. "Bibliografía sobre integración

económica de América Latina." Revista mexicana
de ciencia política, 16:60 (abr./jun., 1970), 265-
286.

664 Hernández de Caldas, Angela. Publicaciones periódicas
económicas latinoamericanas. Bogotá: Centro de
Información y Documentación Económica, 1971.
55 ℓ.

665 International Mining Congress, 6th, Madrid, 1970. La
minería hispánica e iberoamericana; contribución a
su investigación histórica; estudios, fuentes, bibliografía. León: Cátedra de San Isidoro, 1970. 7 v.

666 "Inventario de los estudios en ciencias sociales sobre
América Latina. Desarrollo económico." Aportes.
[Regular feature.]

667 McGreevey, William Paul. A bibliography of Latin
American economic history, 1760-1960. Berkeley:
Center for Latin American Studies, University of
California, 1968. iv, 60 p.

668 _____. "Recent research on the economic history
of Latin America." Latin American research review, 3:2 (Spring, 1968), 89-117.

669 Sautter, Hermann. Wirtschaft und Entwicklung Lateinamerikas. Ausgewahlte, neuere Literatur. Hamburg: (Institut für Iberoamerika-Kunde), 1967-1968.
3 v. (Reihe "Bibliographie und Dokumentation,"
Heft 11).

670 Simposio sobre historia económica en América Latina,
1st, Lima, 1970. La historia económica de América
Latina. (XXXIX Congreso Internacional de Americanistas, Lima, Peru, Agosto, 1970.) México: Secretaría de Educación Pública, 1972. 2 v. (Sep-
Setentas, 37, 47). V. 2: Desarrollo, perspectivas
y bibliografía.

671 Tambs, Lewis A. "Latin American geopolitics; a basic
bibliography." Revista geográfica, Rio de Janeiro,
73 (dez., 1970), 71-105.

672 United Nations. Centro Latinoamericano de Documentación Económica y Social. Bibliografía analítica de

la Comisión Especial de Coordinación Latinoamericana (CECLA); documentos básicos y resoluciones
hasta marzo de 1972. Santiago de Chile, 1972.
65 p. (Colección bibliografías).

673 United Nations. Economic Commission for Latin
America. Bibliografía analítica del Instituto Latino-
americano de Planificación Económica y Social
(ILPES). Santiago de Chile: Naciones Unidas,
CEPAL, CLADES, 1972. 24 p.

674   . Bibliografía de la CEPAL, 1948-1972. Por
Lilian Pessoa. Santiago de Chile: CEPAL, 1973.
xi, 165 p.

675   . Disposiciones, acuerdos y bibliografía sobre
unión aduanera. Santiago de Chile: Comisión Económica para la América Latina, 1972. 56 p.

676 Vivó, Paquita. Latin America: a selected list of
sources. Washington: Latin American Service,
1972? 61 p. "First published in 1971 under title:
Sources of current information on Latin America."

677   . Sources of current information on Latin
America. Washington: Squirrel Publications, 1971.
iii, 38 p.

678 Weaver, Jerry L. Latin American development; a selected bibliography (1950-1967). Santa Barbara,
Calif.: ABC-Clio, 1969. v, 87 p. (Bibliography
and reference series, 9).

ARGENTINA

679 Argentina. Congreso. Biblioteca. Cuenca del Plata.
Buenos Aires: Servicio de Referencia, Departamento de Bibliografía, 1973. 16 p. (Serie bibliográfica, 2).

680 Argentina. Consejo Federal de Inversiones. Bibliografía región de desarrollo Comahué; material bibliográfico existente en la Biblioteca a mayo de 1971.
Buenos Aires, 1971. 115 ℓ.

681   . Desarrollo económico y planificación en la

República Argentina: selección bibliográfica, 1930-
1972. Compilación y selección: Alfredo Estévez.
Buenos Aires, 1972. 394 p. (Serie técnica, 13).

682 _____. Material bibliográfico existente en la Biblioteca del ... sobre la región noroeste y las provincias que la integran: Catamarca, Jujuy, Salta,
Santiago del Estero y Tucumán. Buenos Aires,
1970.

683 _____. Los parques industriales en la República
Argentina, 1961-1971; selección bibliográfica.
Buenos Aires, 1971.

684 Argentina. Consejo Nacional de Desarrollo. Bibliografía preliminar sobre Cuenca del Plata. Buenos
Aires, 1969- .

685 Argentina. Consejo Nacional de Desarrollo. Biblioteca.
Bibliografía sobre sistema nacional de planeamiento
y acción para el desarrollo. Buenos Aires, 1969- .

686 _____. Boletín bibliográfico. Buenos Aires.

687 _____. Catálogo acumulativo de publicaciones,
1962-69. Buenos Aires, 1970. 75 p.

688 Halperin, Delia R. de and Alicia L. Boraso. Bibliografía preliminar sobre aprovechamiento e industrialización de las algas marinas bentónicas. Buenos
Aires: Instituto Nacional de Tecnología Industrial,
1971. 152 p. (Centro de Investigación de Biología
Marina. Contribución técnica, 8).

689 Luvecce Massera, Galo. Bibliografía sobre economía
de la Provincia de Córdoba (período, 1950-1972).
Córdoba: Universidad de Córdoba, Facultad de
Ciencias Económicas, 1972. 45 l.

690 United Nations. Development Programme. Oficina del
Representante Residente en Argentina. Estudios tec-
nicos sobre Argentina, 1956-1971, preparados por
organismos del sistema de las Naciones Unidas segun
indicativas del Gobierno de la República. Revisión
2. Buenos Aires, 1971. vi, 66 p.

BAHAMAS

691 Posnett, N. W. and P. M. Reilly. Bahamas. Surbiton, England: Foreign and Commonwealth Office, Land Resources Division, 1971. v, 74 p. (Land resources bibliography, 1).

BELIZE

692 Posnett, N. W. and P. M. Reilly. Belize (British Honduras). Surbiton: Foreign and Commonwealth Office, Overseas Development Administration, Land Resources Division, 1973. v, 92 p. (Land resources bibliography, 3).

BOLIVIA

693 Torrico Arze, Armando and Irma Aliaga de Vizcarra. Bibliografía boliviana de economía agrícola. La Paz: Sociedad de Ingenieros Agrícolas de Bolivia, 1967. 27 ℓ. (Boletín bibliográfico, 6).

BRAZIL

694 Banco da Amazonia. Departamento de Estudos Econômicos. Bibliografia BASA, 1943-1968. Belém: Divisão de Documentação e Divulgaçao, 1968. 14 ℓ. (Documento, 6).

695 Banco do Nordeste do Brasil, Fortaleza. Departamento de Estudos Econômicos do Nordeste. Sumários dos trabalhos publicados pelo BNB. Preparado por Juracy Portela Pimentel. 3a. ed. rev. e ampliada. Fortaleza, 1969. 88 p.

696 Bibliografia brasileria de transportes. 1969/1972- . Rio de Janeiro: Grupo de Estudos para Integração da Política de Transportes.

697 "Bibliografia de história econômica do Brasil." Anais de historia, Faculdade de Filosofia, Ciências e Letras de Assis, 2 (1970), 46-64.

698 Brandão, José Mussoline and Maria do Socorro Cabral.

Bibliografía selecionada de pesca.   Part 1:   libros.
Recife: SUDENE, 1970.   94 ℓ.

699   Brasil.   Grupo de Estudos para Integração da Política
de Transportes.   Centro de Documentação.   Catálogo
bibliográfico GEIPOT, Centro de Documentação.
Rio de Janeiro, 1973-   .

700   Brazil.   Superintendência do Desenvolvimento do Nordeste.   Departamento de Administração Geral.   Biblioteca.   Bibliografia sôbre SUDENE e o nordeste.
Recife, 1969.   385 p.

701   Brasil.   Superintendência do Desenvolvimento do Nordeste.   Setor de Informação Técnico-Científica.
Lista de revistas sôbre transporte e rodovias existentes nas bibliotecas das seguintes escolas superiores e instituções: 1.   Departamento de Estradas
de Rodagem do Estado de Pernambuco, Recife.
2.   Escola de Engenharia da Universidade Federal
de Pernambuco, Recife.   Recife, 1969.   17 ℓ.

702   Ferreira, Carmosina N.; Lieny do Amaral and Eliza-
beth Tolomei Moletta.   Bibliografia seletiva sobre
desenvolvimento econômico no Brasil.   Rio de
Janeiro: Instituto de Planejamento Econômico e
Social, Setor de Documentação, 1972.   96 p.
(Serie bibliográfica, 1).

703   Furtado, Dilma Ribeiro.   Indice de periódicos brasileiros de economia.   Colaboração de Lygia de
Lourdes Saide.   Introdução de Mário Ferreira da
Luz.   Rio de Janeiro: Biblioteca Nacional, 1968.
266 p.

704   Grupo de Estudos para Integração da Política de Transportes, Rio de Janeiro.   Catálogo bibliográfico.
v. 1-   .   no. 1-   .   1972-   .   Rio de Janeiro,
1973-   .

705   Moraes, Doralice Didier de.   Bibliografia sôbre cooperativismo.   Recife: Superintendência do Desenvolvimento do Nordeste, Divisão de Documentação,
1970.   104 p.   (Cooperativismo, 3).

706   Moreira, Eidorfe.   Roteiro bibliográfico de Marajó.
Belém, Brasil: Instituto do Desenvolvimento

Econômico e Social do Pará, 1969. 67 p. (Cadernos paraenses, 4).

707 Pernambuco, Brasil (State). Conselho de Desenvolvimento de Pernambuco. Pernambuco: uma bibliografia básica sôbre desenvolvimento. Recife, 1973. 63 ℓ.

708 Petróleo Brasileiro, S.A. Centro de Pesquisas e Desenvolvimento. Divisão de Documentação Técnica e Patentes. Catálogo coletivo de periódicos brasileiros (até junho de 1969). Direção: Delce Silva. Organização: Marlene Machado Laura Silva. Rio de Janeiro, 1970. viii, 50 p.

709 Petróleo Brasileiro, S.A. Divisão de Treinamento. Setor de Documentação. Coleção bibliográfica do Setor de Documentação da Divisão de Treinamento, 1968. Rio de Janeiro, 1968? 115 ℓ.

710 Rio de Janeiro. Biblioteca Nacional. Transportes no Brasil; exposição comemorativa da I Semana Nacional dos Transportes. Organizada pela Seção de Exposições da Biblioteca Nacional, em colaboração com o Serviço de Documentação do Ministério dos Transportes, e inaugurada em 25 de julho de 1969. Rio de Janeiro: Ministério dos Transportes, Serviço de Documentação, 1969. 48 p.

CARIBBEAN

711 Institute of Jamaica, Kingston. West Indian Reference Library. Caribbean economic integration: short reading list. Prepared by Rosalie Williams. Kingston: Institute of Jamaica, 1970. 5 p.

CENTRAL AMERICA

712 Arce Behrens, Fernando. "Integración centroamericana: selección bibliográfica." Foro internacional, 24 (abr./jun., 1966), 556-605.

713 González Dubon, Cristina Idalia. Bibliografía analítica sobre la integración económica centroamericana. Guatemala: Tipografía Nacional, 1970. 384 p.

CHILE

714   Instituto de Investigación de Recursos Naturales. Bib-
      liografía de recursos naturales (1966-1971). San-
      tiago de Chile, 1973. 266 p. (Publicaciones, 10).

715   Livingstone, Mario and Solange Phillips. Bibliografía
      sobre participación en la empresa industrial. San-
      tiago de Chile, Universidad Católica de Chile, Cen-
      tro de Estudios de Planificación Nacional, 1973.
      91 ℓ.

716   Moraga Neira, René and Paulina Sanhueza Vargas.
      Bibliografía económica de Chile; guía de publica-
      ciones periódicas, libros, folletos e informes
      técnicos publicados por instituciones chilenas de
      carácter económico entre los años 1960 y 1968.
      Santiago de Chile: Biblioteca, Banco Central de
      Chile, 1969. v, 196 p.

COLOMBIA

717   Bryant, Solena V. The Colombian economy: 1964-
      1971. New York: Colombia Information Service,
      1972. 59 ℓ.

718   Instituto Colombiano de Comercio Exterior. Centro de
      Documentación. Catálogo del Centro de Documenta-
      ción, INCOMEX: publicaciones registradas en el
      periódo 1 Agosto 1973-30 Abril 1974. Comp. de
      José Ignacio Bohórquez C. Bogotá, 1974. 415 ℓ.

719   Piedrahita P., Dora. Indice económico colombiano,
      1967-1970. Medellín: Universidad de Antioquia,
      1973. v, 132 ℓ.

720   Serna C., Himilce O. Indice económico colombiano
      1961-1966. Medellín: Escuela Interamericana de
      Bibliotecología, 1967. xviii, 381 ℓ.

721   Suaza Vargas, María Cristina. Indice económico
      colombiano, 1960-1966. Medellín: Editorial Uni-
      versidad de Antioquia, 1968. xi, 263 ℓ. (Publica-
      ciones de la Escuela Interamericana de Bibliotecolo-
      gía. Serie Bibliografías, 23). "Continuación del
      Indice económico colombiano, 1951-1960."

CUBA

722 Bertot, Eladio. Bibliografía sobre la economía y la sociedad de la colonia, con referencia a América y en especial a Cuba. La Habana: Biblioteca Nacional José Martí, 1969. 64 p.

723 Havana. Biblioteca Nacional José Martí. Departamento Metódico. Bibliografía de los recursos marinos y fluviátieles de Cuba. La Habana, 1968. 61 p. (Folletos de divulgación técnica y científica, 21).

724 _____. Bibliografía sobre café. La Habana, 1968. 66 p. (Folletos de divulgación técnica y científica, 23).

725 _____. Bibliografía sobre petróleo. La Habana, 1968. 104 p. (Folletos de divulgación técnica y científica, 22).

GUATEMALA

726 Banco de Guatemala. Departamento de Investigaciones Agropecuarias e Industriales. Indice de estudios técnicos del ..., 1963-1967. Guatemala, 1968.

GUYANA

727 Bank of Guyana. Research Department. Bibliography of documents relating to the economy of Guyana. Georgetown, 1968. 23 ℓ.

728 Guyana. National Library. Guyana and Caribbean integration: a bibliography. Georgetown, Guyana, 1973. vi, 26 p.

MEXICO

729 "Bibliografía sobre desarrollo regional." El Mercado de valores. [Regular feature.]

730 Hurtado Márquez, Eugenio. "Bibliografía sobre empleo." Revista mexicana del trabajo, 1 (ene./mar., 1972), 82-93.

731 Martínez Ríos, Jorge. Tenencia de la tierra y desarrollo agrario en México; bibliografía selectiva y
comentada, 1522-1968. México: Instituto de Investigaciones Sociales, 1970. ix, 305 p.

732 Reynolds, Clark Winton. A selective bibliography
of Mexican economic history; sources and
analysis. Stanford: Food Research Institute,
1969. 30 p.

PARAGUAY

733 Mareski, Sofía and Oscar Humberto Ferraro. Bibliografía sobre datos y estudios económicos en el
Paraguay. Asunción: Centro Paraguayo de Documentación Social, 1972. 82 ℓ. (Documentos y estudios bibliográficos, 1).

PERU

734 Peru. Oficina Regional de Desarrollo del Norte.
Centro de Documentación. Boletín bibliográfico.
Chiclayo, 1970- .

PUERTO RICO

735 Andic, Fuat M. and Suphan Andic. "An annotated bibliography of the economy of Puerto Rico, 1954-
1969." Handbook of Latin American studies, 31
(1969), 574-588.

736 _____ and _____. An annotated bibliography of
the economy of Puerto Rico, 1960-1969. Río Piedras: University of Puerto Rico, Department of
Economic Research, 1969. 23 ℓ.

VENEZUELA

737 Lollet C., Carlos Miguel. Repertorio de la bibliografía
venezolana económica y social. Prefacio de Pedro
Grases. Cuernavaca: Centro Intercultural de Documentación, 1968. 4-46 p. (CIDOC cuaderno, 12).

738   Maggiolo V., Lorenzo and Augusto Celis M.   Biblio-
       grafía sobre cooperativas.   Valencia, Venezuela:
       Universidad de Carabobo, Centro de Planficación y
       Desarrollo Económico, 1968.   65 p.

EDUCATION

GENERAL

739   Ajo González de Rapariegos, Cándido María.   Historia
       de las universidades hispanicas; origenes y desarrollo
       desde su aparación a nuestros dias.   Madrid: Imp.
       Lit. Ed. La Normal, 1957- .   V. 6: Manuscritos
       y fuentes inéditas.   V. 7: Mas fuentes y manuscri-
       tos.

740   Arnove, Roberto E.   "A survey of literature and re-
       search on Latin American universities."   Latin
       American research review, 3 (Fall, 1967), 45-63.

741   "Artículos en materia de educación superior, apare-
       cidos en publicaciones periódicas."   Universidades,
       13:51 (mar., 1973), 173-194.

742   Bibliografía: educación superior universitaria y no
       universitaria.   Santa Fé, Argentina: Universidad
       Nacional del Litoral, 1973.   151 p.

743   "Bibliografía selectiva sobre recreación y temas afines."
       Boletin del Instituto Interamericano del Niño, 43:169
       (jun., 1969), 267-288.

744   Boschi, Renato Raul.   Bibliografia internacional comen-
       tada sóbre imigração e retorno de pessoal qualifi-
       cado.   Rio de Janeiro: Instituto Brasileiro de Rela-
       ções Internacionais, 1971.   45 ℓ.   (Projeto Retorno.
       Documento, 1).

745   "Catálogo de libros sobre educación circulante."   Bole-
       tín bibliográfico, Biblioteca Pública de La Plata,
       20 (1969), 117-135.

746   Centro Interamericano de Investigación y Documentación
       sobre Formación Profesional.   Catálogo de manuales
       latinoamericanos sobre formación profesional.   Mon-
       tevideo: CINTERFOR, 1969.   89 p.

747 Centro Regional de la UNESCO en el Hemisferio Occidental. Centro de Documentación Pedagógica. Bibliografía anotada sobre medios audiovisuales en la educación. La Habana, 1968. 36 p.

748 La educación en América Latina. Madrid: Ciudad Universitaria, Centro de Información y Sociología de la OCSHA, n.d. (Boletín bibliográfico iberoamericano).

749 Gómez Figueroa, Carlos. "Análisis cuantitativo de la planeación educacional: revisión bibliográfica." Revista mexicana de sociología, 33 (ene./mar., 1971), 183-200.

750 Lisboa, Hadjine Guimaraes. "Bibliografia sobre educação permanente e lazer." Revista brasileira de estudos pedagógicos, 51:113 (ene./mar., 1969), 94-113.

751 Love, Joseph. "Sources for the Latin American student movement: Archives of the U.S. National Student Association." Journal of developing areas, 1 (1967), 215-226.

752 Mexico. Centro de Información Técnica y Documentación. Servicio Nacional ARMO. Indice de artículos sobre educación y adiestramiento. México.

753 Puerto Rico. University. Centro de Investigaciones Pedagógicas. Bibliografía anotada de preescolares. Preparada por Jennie Rivera Damiany et al. Río Piedras, 1971. 67 ℓ.

754 Resumenes analíticos de educación. Santiago de Chile: Centro de Investigación y Desarrollo de la Educación, 1972?- .

755 UNESCO. Oficina Regional de Educación para América Latina y el Caribe. Publicaciones periódicas de educación de América Latina y el Caribe; repertorio. Santiago de Chile, 1972. 103 p.

756 Universidad Nacional del Litoral. Servicios de Pedagogía Universitaria. Sección de Información y Documentación. Bibliografía analítica temática universitaria. Santa Fé, Argentina, 1974 [i.e. 1975]. 37 p. (Serie bibliográfica, 3).

ARGENTINA

757 Argentina. Centro Nacional de Documentación e Información Educativa. Referencias bibliográficas. Buenos Aires, 1972. 12 ℓ.

758 Bibliografía argentina: educación. v. 1- . La Plata: Instituto de Bibliografía.

BRAZIL

759 "Bibliografia sôbre reforma universitária no Brasil, 1966-1968." América Latina, 12:1 (jan./mar., 1969), 116-126.

760 "Bibliografia sôbre TV educativa." Revista brasileira de estudos pedagógicos, 52:116 (out./dez., 1969), 396-408.

761 Instituto Euvaldi Lodi. Pesquisa bibliográfica sobre integração universidade-indústria, jun. 1970/jul. 1972; segundo levantamento bibliográfico sobre integração universidade-indústria. Rio de Janeiro, 1972. 66 p.

762 McNeill, Malvina Rosat. Guidelines to problems of education in Brazil; a review and selected bibliography. New York: Teachers College, 1970. vi, 66 p.

CARIBBEAN

763 Shinebourne, John. A bibliography on technical education in the Caribbean. Georgetown, 1970. 34 p. (University of Guyana Library Series, 1).

CHILE

764 Maurin F., Carlos. Catastro bibliográfico sobre educación de adultos, Provincia de Santiago. Santiago de Chile: Ministerio de Educación, Centro de Perfeccionamiento, Experimentación e Investigaciones Pedagógicas, 1973. 56 p.

99 EDUCATION

765 Museo Pedagógico de Chile, Santiago de Chile. Bibliografía de artículos y documentos publicados en revistas chilenas de educación, 1825-1899. Santiago
de Chile: Dirección de Bibliotecas, Archivos y
Museos, 1970. 135 p.

766 Scherz García, Luis. Pensamiento e investigación
sobre la universidad; bibliografía. Santiago de
Chile: Corporación de Promoción Universitaria,
1974. 278 p.

COLOMBIA

767 Bogotá. Universidad Pedagógica Nacional. Departamento de Bibliotecología y Recursos Educativos.
Indice de documentos sobre educación. Bogotá,
1974. 167 p.

768 Montoya, Amanda and Juan María Hidalgo. Indice
colombiano de educación. Preparado por ... con
la colaboración de Ernestina Rojas de Correa.
Bogotá: Instituto Colombiano para el Fomento de
la Educación Superior, División de Documentación
y Fomento Bibliotecario, 1974- .

MEXICO

769 Ibarrola Nicolín, María de. La enseñanza media en
México, 1900-1968; guía bibliográfica. México:
Instituto de Investigaciones Sociales, Universidad
Nacional Autónoma de México, 1970. x, 266 p.

770 Ocampo V., Tarsicio. México: conflicto estudiantil,
1968; documentos y reacciones de prensa. Cuernavaca: Centro Intercultural de Documentación, 1969.
2 v. (CIDOC dossier, 23).

771 Rosa, Martín de la and Margarita González T. "Bibliografía comentada del movimiento estudiantil mexicano." Revista del Centro de Estudios Educativos,
1:2 (1971), 135-146.

PARAGUAY

772 Mareski, Sofía and Oscar Humberto Ferraro.

Bibliografía sobre datos y estudios de educación
paraguaya. Asunción: Centro Paraguayo de Documentación Social, 1972. 120 p. (Documentos y
estudios bibliográficos, 3).

PERU

773 Paulston, Rolland G. Educación y el cambio dirigido
de la comunidad; una bibliografía anotada con referencia especial al Perú. Cambridge, Mass.: Harvard University, Graduate School of Education, Center for Studies in Education and Development, 1969.
ii, 190 p. (Occasional papers in education and development, 3).

URUGUAY

774 "Bibliografía educacional del Uruguay." Perspectiva,
Montevideo (nov., 1973), 31-48.

FINANCE

775 Alegre, Lucy. Banco de desarrollo; bibliografía.
Lima: Asociación Latinoamericana de Instituciones
Financieras de Desarrollo, 1971. 101 p.

776 Argentina. Congreso. Biblioteca. Inversiones ex-
trangeras. Buenos Aires, 1973. 8 ℓ. (Serie
bibliográfica, 3).

777 Argentina. Consejo Nacional de Desarrollo. Biblioteca. Bibliografía sobre problemas actuales del
sistema monetario internacional. Buenos Aires,
1969. 36 ℓ.

778 Asociación Latinoamericana de Instituciones Financieras
de Desarrollo. Banca de desarrollo; bibliografía.
Lima, 1971. 101 p.

779 _____. Bibliografía preliminar sobre banca de
desarrollo. Lima, 1970. 74 p.

780 Banco de México (Founded 1925). Biblioteca. Bibliografía fiscal de México, 1940-1967. México, 1968.
56 p. (Serie de bibliografías especiales, 9).

101　　　　FINANCE

781　"Bibliografia: reforma bancaria." Boletim da Biblioteca da Cámara de Deputados, Brasília, 11:1 (jan./jun., 1972), 193-211.

782　"Bibliografia sôbre processo fiscal." Revista de política e administração fiscal, 2:3 (mai./jun., 1970), 209-220.

783　Hernández de Caldas, Angela. "Bibliografía sobre inversiones multinacionales." Revista de la Cámara de Comercio de Bogotá, 1:4 (sept., 1971), 57-64.

784　_____. "Bibliografía sobre temas monetarios en Colombia." Revista, Cámara de Comercio de Bogotá, 2:6 (mar., 1972), 145-167.

785　_____. Inversiones multinacionales: bibliografía. Bogotá: Cámara de Comercio de Bogotá, Centro de Información Económica, 1971. 13 p. (Bibliografía especializada, 1).

786　Maia, Adelaide Prestes and Alvaro Costa e Silva. "Livros selecionados: II, administração financeira." Revista de administração municipal, 16:96 (set./out., 1969), 626-632.

787　Puerto Rico. University. College of Social Sciences. Department of Economics. Bibliografía de hacienda pública. Bibliography of public finance. Preparada con la cooperación de Ana T. Dávila. Río Piedras, 1969. 110 ℓ.

788　Sierra, Carlos J. and Rogelio Martínez Vera. Bibliografía de la Hacienda Pública. México: Secretaría de Hacienda y Crédito Público, 1972-1974. 4 v.

789　Stanzick, Karl Heinz and María Teresa Medina. La inversión privada extranjera en América Latina; bibliografía selecta. Santiago de Chile: Instituto Latinoamericano de Investigaciones Sociales, 1971. 147 p.

GEOGRAPHY

790　Barbieri de Santamerina, Estela; Alicia T. García and Hilda M. Díaz. Nueva bibliografía geográfica de

Tucumán. Tucumán: Universidad Nacional de Tucumán, Departamento de Geografía, 1972. 182 p. (Serie monográfica, 20).

791 Brazil. Superintendência do Desenvolvimento da Amazônia. SUDAM bibliografia; bibliografia da Amazônia. v. 1, no. 1, jul./dez., 1970- . Belém.

792 Chile. Congreso. Biblioteca. Canal Beagle. Santiago de Chile, 1972. 45 ℓ. (Bibliografía selectiva, 43).

793 Denevan, William M. A bibliography of Latin American historical geography. Washington: U.S. National Section, Pan American Institute of Geography and History, 1971. iv, 32 p. (Special publication, 6).

794 Geografia da Amazônia; bibliografia, por Alda das Mercês Moreira da Cunha et al. Belém: Universidade Federal do Pará, Centro de Filosofia e Ciências Humanas, 1974. 85 ℓ.

795 Gunn, Drewey Wayne. Mexico in American and British letters: a bibliography of fiction and travel books, citing original editions. Metuchen, N.J.: Scarecrow Press, 1974. vii, 150 p.

796 Louisiana. State University and Agricultural and Mechanical College. Latin American Studies Institute. Some geographical aspects of Ecuador: an annotated critical bibliography of periodical and serial literature. Baton Rouge, n.d. 50 p. (Working papers, 2).

797 Meléndez Chaverri, Carlos and Manuel Argüello M. "Bibliografía de las principales obras geográficas de Costa Rica." Revista geográfica, Instituto Panamericano de Geografía e Historia, 69 (dic., 1968), 181-187.

798 Muñoz Reyes, Jorge. Bibliografía geográfica de Bolivia. La Paz: Academia Nacional de Ciencias de Bolivia, 1967. 170 p. (Publicación, 16).

799 Rey Balmaceda, Raúl Ceferino. Bibliografía geográfica referida a la República Argentina; primera contribución. Buenos Aires: GAEA, 1975. 648 p.

800 _____. "Contribución para una bibliografía de bibliografías geográficas sobre Argentina." Inter-American review of bibliography, 18:2 (Apr./Jun., 1968), 150-159.

801 Silva, Genny da Costa e and Maria do Carmo Rodrigues. Bibliografia sôbre Goiana; aspectos históricos e geográficos. Recife: Comissão Organizadora e Executiva das Comemorações do IV Centenário do Povoamento de Goiana, 1972. 421 p.

802 Wilgus, Alva Curtis. Latin America in the nineteenth century; a selected bibliography of books of travel and description published in English. Metuchen, N.J.: Scarecrow Press, 1973. x, 174 p.

HISTORY

GENERAL

803 Avila Martel, Alamiro de. "Presencia de Bolívar en Chile en 1819." Boletín de la Academia Chilena de la Historia, 38:85 (1971), 39-77. Includes: "Noticias en los periódicos chilenos, de 1812 a 1819, acerca de la revolución en Venezuela, Nueva Granada y Ecuador y de los hechos de Bolívar."-- pp. 61-77.

804 "Bibliografía de historia de América." Revista de historia de América. [A regular feature, edited by Roberto Heredia Correa.]

805 "Bibliographia de historia Societatis Iesu: Amérique." Archivum historicum Societatis Iesu. [Regular feature.]

806 Bromley, Rosemary. "Parish registers as a source in Latin American demographic and historical research." Bulletin of the Society for Latin American Studies, Portsmouth, England, 19 (Jan., 1974), 14-21.

807 Butler, Ruth (Lapham). Guide to the Hispanic American historical review, 1918-1945. New York: Kraus Reprint Co., 1970. xviii, 251 p. Reprint of 1950 ed.

808   Coker, William S. "Research possibilities and re-
       sources for a study of Spanish Mississippi." Jour-
       nal of Mississippi history, 34:2 (May, 1972), 117-
       128.

809   _____ and Jack D. L. Holmes. "Sources for the
       history of the Spanish borderlands." In: Dibble,
       Ernest F. and Earle W. Newton. Spain and her
       rivals on the Gulf Coast. Pensacola, Fla.: His-
       torical Pensacola Preservation Board, 1971.
       pp. 129-141.

810   Committee on Latin America. Latin American history
       with politics: a serials list, edited on behalf of the
       Committee by C. J. Koster, with a preface by
       R. A. Humphreys and a note on periodical indexes
       by A. J. Walford. Farnborough: Hants, Gregg,
       1973. 165 p. (Latin American Serials, 2).

811   Denevan, William M. A bibliography of Latin American
       historical geography. [Washington]: Pan American
       Institute of Geography and History, U.S. National
       Section, 1971. iv, 32 p. (Special publication, 6).

812   Díaz-Trechuelo Spínola, María Lourdes. "América
       en la 'Colección de documentos inéditos para la his-
       toria de España: catálogo temático, geográfico y
       cronológico'." Anuario de estudios americanos, 27
       (1970), 641-732.

813   Griffin, Charles Carroll. Latin America: a guide to
       the historical literature. Austin: Published for the
       Conference on Latin American History by the Uni-
       versity of Texas Press, 1971. xx, 700 p. (Publi-
       cations, 4).

814   Historiografía y bibliografía americanistas. Sevilla:
       Escuela de Estudios Hispanoamericanos, 1971- .

815   Indice histórico español. Nendeln, Liechtenstein: Kraus
       Reprint, 197? 11 v. Reprint [in part] of 1953-
       1965.

816   International Mining Congress, 6th, Madrid, 1970. La
       minería hispana e iberoamericana. Contribución a su
       investigación histórica. Estudios, fuentes, biblio-
       grafía. León: Cátedra de San Isidoro, 1970. 7 v.

817   "Inventario de los estudios en ciencias sociales sobre
      América Latina: historia." Aportes. [Regular
      feature.]

818   Keniston, Hayward. List of works for the study of
      Hispanic-American history. New York: Kraus
      Reprint Corp., 1967. 451 p. Reprint of 1920 ed.

819   Lamberg, Vera B. de. "La guerrilla castrista en
      América Latina: bibliografía selecta, 1960-1970."
      Foro internacional, Mexico, 12:1 (jul./sep., 1971),
      95-111.

820   McGreevey, William Paul. A bibliography of Latin
      American economic history, 1760-1960. Berkeley:
      University of California Press, 1968. 60 p. (Cen-
      ter for Latin American Studies. Working papers).

821   Murra, John V. "Current research and prospects in
      Andean ethnohistory." Latin American research
      review, 5:1 (Spring, 1970), 3-36.

822   Naylor, Bernard. Accounts of nineteenth-century South
      America: an annotated checklist of works by British
      and United States observers. London: Athlone
      Press, 1969. vi, 80 p. (London. University.
      Institute of Latin American Studies. Monographs,
      2).

823   Norris, Robert E. "Estudios críticos sobre la his-
      toriografía latinoamericana: apuntes para una bib-
      liografía." Revista de historia de América, 61/62
      (1966), 245-393.

824   Russell, Charles A.; James A. Miller and Robert E.
      Hildner. "The urban guerrilla in Latin America: a
      select bibliography." Latin America research re-
      view, 9:1 (Spring, 1974), 37-79.

825   Sherman, William L. A. "Viceregal administration in
      the Spanish American colonies: some neglected
      sources." The Rocky Mountain social science jour-
      nal, 5:1 (1968), 143-151.

826   Steele, Colin. "A bibliography of English translations
      of Spanish, and Portuguese books on the Iberian
      New World, 1603-1726." In: his English

interpreters of the Iberian New World from Purchas
to Stevens: a bibliographical study, 1603-1726.
Oxford: Dolphin Book Co., 1975. pp. 169-196.

827 Wilgus, Alva Curtis. Latin America in the nineteenth
century; a selected bibliography of books of travel
and description published in English. Metuchen,
N.J.: Scarecrow Press, 1973. x, 174 p.

828 Zubatsky, David S. Doctoral dissertations in history
and the social sciences on Latin America and the
Caribbean accepted by Universities in the United
Kingdom, 1920-1972. London: University of London, Institute of Latin American Studies, [1973].
16 p.

ARGENTINA

829 Bibliografía argentina: historia. La Plata: Instituto
de Bibliografía, 197?- .

830 Buenos Aires. Universidad. Facultad de Derecho y
Ciencias Sociales. Catálogo de la exposición bibliográfica argentina de derecho y ciencias sociales;
homenaje a la Revolución de Mayo en su 150° aniversario, auspiciado por la Comisión Nacional del
Sesquicentenario de la Revolución de Mayo. Buenos
Aires, 1960. 180 p.

831 Caillet-Bois, Ricardo R. "Cuadernos de la Cátedra de
Historia Argentina de la Facultad de Filosofía y
Humanidades de la Universidad Nacional de Córdoba."
Boletín del Instituto de História Argentina "Doctor
Emilio Ravignani," 2a série, 12:20/21 (1969), 247-
249.

832 Feigin de Roca, Elisabeth and Alicia Gaer de Sabulsky.
Historiografía argentina, 1930-1970. Buenos Aires:
Librería Piloto, 1972. 2 v.

833 Fúrlong Cárdiff, Guillermo. "Bibliografía periodistica
del Sesquicentenario del Congreso de Tucumán,"
por Santiago Stella [seud]. Estudios, Buenos Aires,
575 (jul./ag., 1966), 331-334.

834 Geoghegan, Abel Rodolfo. "Bibliografía referente al

Congreso de Tucumán y los diputados." Fúrlong
Cárdiff, Guillermo. El Congreso de Tucumán.
Buenos Aires: Theoria, 1966. pp. 383-407.

835   Gutiérrez, Leandro. Recopilación bibliográfica y de
fuentes para el estudio de la historia y situación
actual de la clase obrera argentina. Buenos Aires:
Instituto Torcuato Di Tella, Centro de Investigaciones Sociales, 1969. 84 p. (Documentos de
trabajo, 63).

836   Guy, Donna J. "Fuentes tucumanas (1870-1890)."
Boletín del Instituto de Historia Argentina "Doctor
Emilio Ravignani," 2a série, 14/15:24/25 (1970/
1971), 137-157.

837   Indice historiográfico argentino. Buenos Aires: Instituto Bibliográfico "Antonio Zinny," 1973- .

838   Matijevic, Nicolás and Olga H. de Matijevic. Bibliografía patagónica y de las tierras australes. Bahia
Blanca, Argentina: Centro de Documentación Patagónica, Universidad Nacional del Sur Dr. Miguel
López Francés, 1973- . V. 1: Historia.

839   Russell, Charles A. and James F. Schenkel and James
A. Miller. "Urban guerrillas in Argentina: a select bibliography." Latin American research review, 9:3 (Fall, 1974), 53-89.

840   Villascuerna, Inés. Bibliografía para el estudio histórico de la marginalidad en el Noroeste de Argentina.
Buenos Aires: Instituto Torcuato Di Tella, Centro
de Investigaciones Sociales, 1970. 88 p. (Documentos de trabajo, 71).

BOLIVIA

841   Christman, Calvin Lee. "The Chaco War: a tentative
bibliography of its diplomacy." The Americas, 26:
1 (Jul. , 1969), 54-65.

842   Costa de la Torre, Arturo. El archivo histórico y la
biblioteca de Nicolás Acosta en Estados Unidos;
estudio histórico-biográfico. La Paz, 1970. 203 p.

843 _____. Bibliografía de la Revolución del 16 de
julio de 1809. La Paz, 1974. 128 p.

BRAZIL

844 Brazil. Arquivo Nacional. Ofícios dos vice-reis do
Brasil. Indice da correspondência dirigida à Corte
de Portugal de 1763 a 1808. 2a. ed., Rio de
Janeiro, 1970. 301 p. (Publicações, 2).

845 Brazil. Comissão de Estudo dos Textos de História
do Brasil. Bibliografia de história do Brasil. Rio
de Janeiro: Ministério das Relações Exteriores,
1969. 99 p.

846 _____. Bibliografia de história do Brasil: decênio
1959-1969. Rio de Janeiro: Imprensa Nacional,
1971. 214 p.

847 Brazil. Congresso. Câmara de Deputados. Centro
de Documentação e Informação. Ciclo da independencia (1808-1831); catálogo da exposição comemorativa do sesquicentenário da independência, abril a
setembro de 1972. Brasília, 1973. 114 p.

848 Camargo, Aureo de Almeida. "Roteiro de '32." Revista de história, São Paulo, 45:91 (julho/set.,
1972), 203-260.

849 Cardoso, Ney Eichler. "A FEB e a história militar."
Revista de história, São Paulo, 47:95 (julho/set.,
1973), 269-278.

850 Carvalho, Joaquim Barradas de. "O descobrimento do
Brasil através dos textos (edições críticas e comen-
tadas). I. A carta de Pero Vaz de Caminha.
1. A literatura portuguêsa de viagens na época dos
descobrimentos." Revista de história, São Paulo,
32:65 (jan./mar., 1966), 197-208.

851 Contier, Arnaldo. "O descobrimento do Brasil através
dos textos. I. A carta de Pero Vaz de Caminha.
3. Manuscritos, edições e traduções." Revista
de história, São Paulo, 33:67 (jul./set., 1966),
209-214.

852   Curran, Mark Joseph.   Selected bibliography of history
      and politics in Brasilian popular poetry.   Tempe,
      Arizona, 1971. 26 ℓ. (Arizona. State University
      at Tempe.   Center for Latin American Studies.
      Special study, 8).

853   Documents pour la préhistoire du Brésil mériodional,
      vol. 1: L'Etat de São Paulo, par N. Guidon et al.
      Paris: Mouton, 1973. 41 p.   (Cahiers d'archéolo-
      gie d'Amérique latine, 2).

854   "Genealogia e heráldica: bibliografia." Mensario do
      Arquivo Nacional, 4:2 (fev., 1973), 23-27.

854a Gordon, Eric; Michael M. Hall and Hobart A. Spalding.
      "A survey of Brazilian and Argentine materials at
      the Internationaal Instituut voor Sociale Geschiedenis
      in Amsterdam."   Latin American research review,
      8:3 (Fall, 1973), 27-77.

855   Horch, Rosemarie Erika.   "Viajantes estrangeiros no
      Brasil. Um ensaio bibliográfico." Revista de his-
      tória, São Paulo, 36:74 (abr./jul., 1968), 533-537.

856   Indiana University.   Lilly Library.   Brazil from dis-
      covery to independence: an exhibition commemorat-
      ing the 150th anniversary of the declaration of Bra-
      zilian independence on September 7, 1822.   Pre-
      pared by Mayellen Bresie.   Bloomington, 1972.
      48 p. (Publication, 16).

857   Memória da independência, 1808/1825. [Catálogo da]
      exposição histórica memória da independência no
      Museu Nacional de Belas Artes de 9.11.72 a 31.1.
      73.   Rio de Janeiro: Departamento de Assuntos
      Culturais do MEC, 1972. 1 v. unpaged.

858   "Revistas de institutos históricos." Mensario do Ar-
      quivo Nacional, Rio de Janeiro, 4:6 (jun., 1973),
      35.

859   Rio de Janeiro.   Biblioteca Nacional.   Exposição
      comemorativa.   Tricentenário da restauração per-
      nambucana: catálogo.   Pernambuco: Comissão
      Organizadora e Executiva, 1954. viii, 58 p.

860   _____. Independência do Brasil; sesquicentenário
      1822-1972.   Rio de Janeiro, 1972. 55 p.

861 _____. Ouro Preto; sesquicentenário da elevação de Vila Rica à categoria de imperial cidade de Ouro Preto, 1823-1973; catálogo da exposição. Rio de Janeiro, 1973. 78 p.

862 Salles, Gilka Vasconcelos F. de. "A pesquisa histórica em Goiás." Revista de história, São Paulo, 43:88 (out./dez., 1971), 453-491.

863 Silva, Genny da Costa e and Maria do Carmo Rodrigues. Bibliografia sôbre Goiana: aspectos históricos e geográficos. Recife: Commissão Organisadora e Executiva das Comemorações do IV Centenario do Povoamento de Goiana, 1972. 421 p.

864 Silva, Maria Beatriz Nizza da. "A livraria pública da Bahia em 1818: obras de história." Revista de história, São Paulo, 43:87 (jul./set., 1971), 225-239.

CARIBBEAN

865 Cortada, Rafael L. "A bibliography of comparative slave systems: the United States and the Greater West Indies." Current bibliography on African affairs, n. s., 2:9 (Sept., 1969), 9-21.

866 Cundall, Frank. Bibliography of the West Indies. New York: Johnson Reprint Corporation, 1971. 179 p. Reprint of 1909 ed.

867 Debien Gabriel. "Les Antilles françaises (1963-1967). Bibliographie des publications 1963-1967." Revue française d'histoire d'outre-mer, 53:192/193 (1966), 245-313.

868 _____. "Les Antilles françaises (1968 et 1969). " Revue française d'histoire d'outre-mer, 57:208 (1970), 299-354.

869 Handler, Jerome S. A guide to source materials for the study of Barbados history, 1627-1834. Carbondale: Southern Illinois University Press, 1971. xvi, 205 p.

870 Mathews, Thomas. "Los estudios sobre historia

111   HISTORY

económica del Caribe (1585-1910)." Historiografía
y bibliografía americanistas, 15:3 (dic., 1971),
445-476.

871 "Papiers privés sur l'histoire des Antilles." [par]
Marcel Châtillon et al. Revue française d'histoire
d'outre-mer, 59:216 (1972), 432-490.

872 Ragatz, Lowell Joseph. A guide for the study of British Caribbean history, 1763-1834, including the
abolition and emancipation movements. New York:
Da Capo Press, 1970. viii, 725 p. Reprint of
1932 ed.

CHILE

873 Aránguiz Donoso, Horacio. Bibliografía histórica
(1959-1967). Santiago de Chile: Universidad Católica de Chile, Instituto de Historia, 1970. 84 p.

874 Cooperation in Documentation & Communication. Bibliographical notes for understanding the military
coup in Chile. Edited by Mary Riesch and Harry
Strharsky. Washington: CoDoC International Secretariat, 1974. vii, 96 p. (Its Common catalogue, 1).

875 Felíu Cruz, Guillermo. Historia de las fuentes de la
bibliografía chilena; ensayo crítico. Santiago de
Chile, 1966-1969. 4 v.

876 "Fichero bibliográfico." Historia, Santiago de Chile.
[Regular feature.]

877 Santiago de Chile. Biblioteca Nacional. Exposición bibliográfica sobre la Guerra del Pacífico (1879-1884).
Santiago de Chile: Editorial Universitaria, 1961.
56 p.

878 Villalobos Rivera, Sergio. "La historiografía económica en Chile: sus comienzos." Historia, Santiago
de Chile, 10 (1971), 7-56.

COLOMBIA

879 Ocampo López, Javier. Historiografía y bibliografía

de la emancipación del Nuevo Reino de Granada.
Tunja: Universidad Pedagógica y Tecnológica de
Colombia, 1969. 555 p.

880 Ramsey, Russell W. "Critical Bibliography on La Violencia in Colombia." Latin American Research Review, 8:1 (Spring, 1973), 3-44.

881 Riaño, José Camilo. "Inventario del archivo del historiador José Manuel Restrepo." Archivos, Bogotá,
1:1 (ene./jun., 1967), 179-199.

CUBA

882 Abella, Rosa. "Bibliografía de la Guerra de los Diez
Años." Revista cubana, 1:1 (ene./jun., 1968), 239-
270.

883 Brünn. Krajská lidová knihovna. Kubánská revoluce:
bibliogr. a biografická pomucka. Brno: Knihovna
J. Mahena, 1974. 56 p.

884 Cuba. Ministerio de las Fuerzas Armadas. Dirección Política. Sección de Historia. Historia de
Cuba: bibliografía. La Habana, 1970. 480 p.

885 Pérez, Luis A. "The Cuban army, 1898-1958: a
bibliography." Southeastern Latin Americanist,
17:1 (June 1973), 4-7.

886 Smith, Harold F. "A bibliography of American travel-
lers' books about Cuba published before 1900." The
Americas, 22:4 (Apr., 1966), 404-412.

887 Somoshegyi-Szokol, Gaston. A bibliography of works
dealing with Cuban history and politics in the University Library at Berkeley. Berkeley, 1973. v,
133 p.

888 Trelles y Govin, Carlos. Bibliografía social cubana.
La Habana: Biblioteca Nacional José Martí, 1969.
1 v. (various pagings).

889 Valdes, Nelson P. and Edwin Lieuwen. The Cuban
revolution; a research-study guide (1959-1969). 1st
ed. Albuquerque: University of New Mexico Press,
1971. xii, 230 p.

ECUADOR

890 Ortiz Bilbao, Luis Alfonso. "Colección Vacas Galindo.
Cedulario. Indice general. Tomo II de oficios y
partes, 19 julio 1534-13 mayo 1538." Boletín de
la Academia Nacional de Historia, Quito, 49:107
(ene./jun., 1966), 49-92.

MEXICO

891 Avilés, René. Bibliografía de Benito Juárez. México:
Sociedad Mexicana de Geografía y Estadística, 1972.
345 p.

892 Azcue y Mancera, Luis. Códices indígenas. México:
Editorial Orión, 1966. 266 p.

893 Bibliografía histórica mexicana. [Compiled by Susana
Uribe de Fernández de Córdova] México: Colegio
de México, 1967- .

894 Cavazos Garza, Israel. "Fichas para una bibliohemerografía histórica de Nuevo León, 1960-1969."
Humanitas, 11 (1970), 361-387.

895 Cline, Howard Francis. Guide to ethnohistorical
sources. Austin: University of Texas Press, 1972-
1973. 2 v. (Handbook of Middle American Indians,
12-13).

896 Coker, William S. "Research in the Spanish Borderlands: bibliography." Latin American research review, 7:2 (Summer, 1972), 55-94.

897 Evans, G. Edward. "A guide to pre-1750 manuscripts
in the United States relating to Mexico and the South-
western United States, with emphasis on their value
to anthropologists." Ethnohistory, 17 (1970), 63-90.

898 _____ and Frank J. Morales. "Fuentes de la historia de México en archivos norteamericanos." Historia mexicana, 18:3 (ene./mar., 1969), 432-462.

899 Florescano, Enrique. "Bibliografía de la historia demo-
gráfica de México (época prehispanica-1910)." Historia mexicana, 21:3 (ene./mar., 1972), 525-537.

900 _____ and Alejandra Moreno Toscano. "Historia económica y social de México (época prehispanica-1910)." Historia mexicana, 15:2/3 (oct. 1965/mar. 1966), 310-378.

901 Fuentes para la historia de la ciudad de México, por Carlos Aguirre et al. Con una bibliografía sobre desarrollo urbano y regional preparada por Luís Unikel. México: Departamento de Investigaciones Históricas, Instituto Nacional de Antropología e Historia, 1972. 269 ℓ. (Colección científica. Serie: Catálogos y bibliografías, 2).

902 García Quintana, Josefina. "Bibliografía náhuatl: 1966-1969." Estudios de cultura náhuatl, 9 (1971), 273-293.

903 González-Polo, Ignacio. "Ensayo de una bibliografía de la colonización en México durante el siglo XIX." Boletín del Instituto de Investigaciones Bibliográficas, Mexico, 4 (1970), 179-191.

904 Gordillo Ortiz, Octavio. "Bibliografía del descubrimiento y conquista de México y Centroamérica." In: Congreso Mexicano-Centroamericano de Historia, 1st, Mexico City, 1972. Estudios indigenistas; memoria del primer ..., vol. 2: Exploraciones y conquista en México y Centroamérica. México: Sociedad Mexicana de Geografía y Estadística, 1972. pp. 249-262.

905 Grebinger, Ellen Marie. Topical index for some Spanish documents concerning the American Southwest, 1538-1700. Tucson, Arizona: University of Arizona, Dept. of Anthropology, 1971. 234 p.

906 Greenleaf, Richard E. and Michael C. Meyer. Research in Mexican history: topics, methodology, sources and a practical guide to field research. Lincoln: University of Nebraska Press, 1973. xiii, 226 p.

907 Guzmán y Raz Guzmán, Jesús. Bibliografía de la Reforma, la Intervención y el Imperio. New York: B. Franklin, 1973. 2 v. Reprint of 1930-31 ed.

908 Haferkorn, Henry Ernest. The war with Mexico,

1846-1848; a select bibliography on the causes, con-
duct, and the political aspect of the war together
with a select list of books and other printed material on the resources of Mexico and the characteris-
tics of the Mexican people, with annotations and an
index. New York: B. Franklin, 1970. 93 p.

909 Harkányi, Katalin. The Aztecs: bibliography. San
     Diego, California: State College, Library, 1971.
     30 ℓ.

910 Hedrick, Basil Calvin. Catálogo categorizado y crono-
     lógico del archivo parroquial de Parras, Coahuila,
     México. Cabondale, Ill.: University Museum,
     Southern Illinois University, 1969. 16 ℓ. (Meso-
     american studies, 1).

911 Holmes, Jack David Lazarus. A guide to Spanish
     Louisiana, 1762-1806. New Orleans, La.: [A. F.
     Laborde], 1970. 96 p. (Louisiana Collection series
     of books and documents on Colonial Louisiana, 2).

912 Kropfinger-von Kügelen, Helga. Europäischer Buchex-
     port von Sevilla nach Neuspanien im Jahre 1586/
     Libros del siglo xvi en la ciudad de Puebla de los
     Angeles. Wiesbaden: Franz Steiner Verlag GMBH,
     1973. 145 p. (Lauer, Wilhelm, ed. Dad Mexico-
     Projekt der Deutschen Forschungsgemeinschaft; eine
     deutsch-mexikanische Interdisziplinäre Regionalfor-
     schung im Becken von Puebla-Tlaxcala/El proyecto
     México de la Fundación Alemána para la Investiga-
     ción Científica; investigaciones regionales interdis-
     ciplinarias mexicano-alemánas realizadas en la
     cuenca de Puebla-Tlaxcala, 5). Includes "Bücher
     des 16. Jahrhunderts in Puebla de los Angeles/
     Libros del siglo xvi en la ciudad de Puebla de los
     Angeles," by Efraín Castro Morales.

913 Licea Ayala, Judith. "Una contribución a la bibliogra-
     fía sobre cultura náhuatl: índice de los artículos
     sobre esta disciplina publicados en los Anales del
     Museo Nacional y en los Anales del Instituto de
     Antropología e Historia." Boletín del Instituto de
     Investigaciones Bibliográficas, 1:1 (ene./jun., 1969),
     151-173.

914 Mateos Higuera, Salvador. "Colección de estudios

sumarios de los códices pictóricos indígenas."
Tlalocan, 1 (1943/1944) 235-242; 2 (1945/1948), 35-
36, 255-257, 374-376; 3 (1949/1957), 22-28.

915 Monroy Huitrón, Guadalupe. Archivo Histórico de
Matías Romero: catálogo descriptivo. México:
Banco de México, 1965- .

916 Reyes García, Cayetano. Indice y extractos de los
protocolos de la Notaría de Cholula (1590-1600).
México: Instituto Nacional de Antropología e Historia, 1973. 680 p. (Colección científica: Catálogos y bibliografías, 8).

917 Sierra, Carlos J. and Rogelio Martínez Vera. Bibliografía de la hacienda pública. México: Secretaría
de Hacienda y Crédito Público, 1972-1974. 4 v.

918 Steck, Francis Borgia. A tentative guide to historical
materials on the Spanish Borderlands. New York:
B. Franklin, 1971. 106 p. Reprint of 1943
ed.

919 Ulloa, Berta. "La historiografía de las relaciones
diplomáticas de México entre 1940 y 1969." In:
Reunión de Historiadores Mexicanos y Norteamericanos, 3d, Oaxtepec, 1969. Investigaciones contem-
poráneas sobre historia de México. México: Universidad Nacional Autónoma de México, 1971. pp.
566-601.

920 Uribe de Fernández de Córdoba, Susana. "Bibliografía
histórica méxicana." Historia méxicana, 16:1 (jul./
sept., 1966), 93-153.

921 Valle, Rafael Heliodoro. Bibliografía Maya. New
York: B. Franklin, [1971] 404 p. Reprint of 1937-
41 ed.

922 "Veinticinco años de investigación histórica en México."
Historia méxicana, 15:2/3 (oct., 1965/mar., 1966),
155-445; 15:4 (abr./jun., 1966), 453-782.

923 Wagner, Henry Raup. The Spanish Southwest, 1542-
1794; an annotated bibliography. New York: Arno
Press, 1967. 2 v. Reprint of 1937 ed.

NICARAGUA

924   Molina Argüello, Carlos.   "Bibliografía historiográfica
       de Nicaragua hasta 1954." Revista conservadora
       del pensamiento centroamericano, 21:102 (mar.,
       1969), 21-28.

PANAMA

925   Castillero, Ernesto J.   "Bibliografía nacional sobre el
       movimiento emancipador de la República de Panamá."
       Lotería, 212 (Sept., 1973), 78-80.

926   Lucena Salmoral, Manuel.   "Historiografía de Panamá:
       fichero bibliográfico, letras S, T. U. V, W y Z."
       Lotería, 12:145 (dic., 1967), 56-75.

927   Panama. Biblioteca Nacional. Departamento de Pro-
       cesos Técnicos. Bibliografía de libros sobre la
       historia de Panama. Panamá, 1971. 18 p.

PERU

928   Arequipa, Peru (City). Cabildo. Actas de sesiones y
       acuerdos, 1546-1556. Libro segundo. Indice, [por]
       Alejandro Málaga Medina et al. Arequipa: Im-
       prenta Editorial "El Sol," 1974. 87 p.

929   Barra, Felipe de la. Fichero bibliográfico histórico-
       militar peruano y antología de escritos del gral.
       EP Felipe de la Barra. Lima: Editorial Gráfica
       Industrial, 1970. 298 p.

930   Basadre, Jorge. Historia de la República del Perú,
       1822-1933. 6. ed. aum. y corr. vol. 17: Biblio-
       grafía general de la etapa republicana. Lima: Edi-
       torial Universitaria, 1970.

931   _____. Introducción a las bases documentales para
       la historia de la República del Perú con algunas re-
       flexiones. Lima: Ediciones P. L. Villanueva,
       1971-1972. 3 v.

932   "Bibliografía histórica peruana: 1965-1967" por Cris-
       tina Flores et al. Cuadernos del Seminario de

Historia, Pontificia Universidad Católica del Perú, Instituto Riva-Agüero, Lima, 7:9 (1968/1969), 83-116.

933   Campbell, Leon. "The historiography of the Peruvian guerrilla movement, 1960-1965." Latin American research review, 8:1 (1973), 45-70.

934   Friede, Juan. "Guía de los manuscritos relativos al Perú en la Universidad Indiana." Revista de Indias, 30:119/122 (1970), 239-270.

935   Herbold, Carl and Steve Stein. Guía bibliográfica para la historia social y política del Perú en el siglo XX (1895-1960). Lima: Instituto de Estudios Peruanos, 1971. 165 p.

936   Horkheimer, Hans. Identificación y bibliografía de importantes sitios pre-hispanicos del Perú. Pueblo Libre, Lima: Museo Nacional de Antropología y Arqueología, 1965. 51, 13 p. (Arqueológicos, 8).

937   Málaga Medina, Alejandro; Eusebio Quiroz Paz Soldán and Juan Alvarez Salas. Catálogo general del Archivo Municipal de Arequipa. Arequipa, Perú: Universidad Nacional de San Agustín, Departamento de Historia, Geografía y Antropología, 1974. 39 p.

938   Means, Philip Ainsworth. Biblioteca andina [pt. 1]: essays on the lives and works of the chroniclers, or, the writers of the sixteenth and seventeenth centuries who treated of the pre-Hispanic history and culture of the Andean countries. Detroit: Blaine Ethridge Books, 1973. 276-525 p. Reprint of 1928 ed.

VENEZUELA

939   Academia Nacional de la Historia, Caracas. Biblioteca. Exposición bibliográfica documental: historia colonial de Venezuela realizada con motivo del Primer Congreso Venezolano de Historia, 28 de junio al 3 de julio de 1971. Catálogo preparado por Rosa Elena de Valero. Caracas, 1971. 107 p.

940   Grases, Pedro. Libros y libertad. Caracas: Ediciones de la Presidencia de la República, 1974. xix, 263 p.

941 Lombardi, John V. "Venezuelan journals for histor-
     ians." Newsletter, Conference on Latin American
     History, 7:2 (Sept., 1971), 38-41.

942 Lovera De-Sola, R. J. "Bibliografía de historia vene-
     zolana durante 1971." Boletín histórico, Caracas,
     10:32 (mayo, 1973), 339-355.

943 Pérez Vila, Manuel. Ensayo sobre las fuentes para
     la historia de la diócesis de Guayana durante los
     períodos de la Colonia y la Independencia. Cara-
     cas: Archivo General de la Nación, 1969. 16 p.
     (Biblioteca venezolana de historia, 11).

944 Pi Sunyer, Carlos. "Algunas obras (inglesas) de in-
     terés histórico venezolano." Revista nacional de
     cultura, Caracas, 30:188 (abr./jun., 1969), 85-91.

945 Suárez, Santiago Gerardo. Las instituciones militares
     venezolanas del período hispanico en los archivos;
     índice sistemático documental. Caracas, 1969.
     lxxxiv, 633 p.

946 Venezuela. Universidad Central. Escuela de Biblio-
     teconomía y Archivos. Exposición de obras con-
     memorativas del sesquicentenario de nuestra inde-
     pendencia. Caracas, 1961. 21 p.

                         INDEXES

LA ABEJA ARGENTINA

947 Cutolo, Vicente Osvaldo. " 'La Abeja argentina' (1822);
     primera revista porteña." Investigaciones y en-
     sayos (Academia Nacional de la Historia, Buenos
     Aires), 6/7 (ene./dic., 1969), 259-275.

ABSIDE; REVISTA DE CULTURA MEJICANA

948 "Indice del último lustro de 'Abside': 1962 a 1966."
     Abside; revista de cultura mejicana, 30:4 (oct./dic.,
     1966), 478-495.

949 "Indice del último lustro de 'Abside': 1967 a 1971."

Abside; revista de cultura mejicana, 36:1 (ene./mar.,
1972), 106-125.

ACADEMIA CHILENA CORRESPONDIENTE DE LA REAL
ESPAÑOLA. BOLETIN.

950 Bocaz Concha, Arístides. "Discursos de incorporación
y recepción en el 'Boletín de la Academia Chilena
Correspondiente de la Real Academia Española.' "
Boletín de la Academia Chilena Correspondiente de
la Real Española, 59 (1970), 299-343.

ACADEMIA NACIONAL DE LA HISTORIA, CARACAS.
BOLETIN.

951 Academia Nacional de la Historia, Caracas. Boletín.
Indexes. Indice general del Boletín de la Academia
Nacional de la Historia, 1912-1964, nos. 1-888.
Caracas, 1966. 275 p.

AMERICA LATINA

952 América latina. Indexes. "Indice dos artigos publicados em América latina, Ano 6 n. 1 (1963)-Ano 8
n. 4 (1965)." América latina, 9:4 (out./dez., 1966),
146-150.

APOSTOLADO POSITIVISTA DO BRASIL. BOLETIM.

953 Apostolado Positivista do Brasil. Indice alfabético das
matérias contidas nos boletins em português do Apostolado Pozitivista do Brasil (1897-1905). Rio de
Janeiro, 1906. 8 p.

ARCHIVOS VENEZOLANOS DE FOLKLORE

954 "Indice analítico de Archivos venezolanos de folklore,
1-8 (ene./jun., 1952-1967)." In: Venezuela. Universidad Central. Escuela de Biblioteconomía y
Archivos. Catálogo bibliográfico de la Facultad de
Humanidades y Educación, 1948-1968. Caracas,
1969. pp. 188-248.

EL ARTISTA

955   Zubatsky, David S.   "Indice de la revista 'El Artista';
      I: índice alfabético de autores." Abside; revista
      de cultura mejicana, 33:2 (abr./jun., 1969), 225-
      232.

956   _____. "Indice de la revista 'El Artista' (Mejico
      1874-1875); II: índice por materias--III: traduc-
      ciones--IV: reseñas--V: ilustraciones." Abside;
      revista de cultura mejicana, 33:3 (jul./sept., 1969),
      344-357.

AZUL

957   Díaz Alejo, Ana Elena and Ernesto Prado Velázquez.
      Indice de la revista Azul (1894-1896) y estudio pre-
      liminar. México: Universidad Nacional Autónoma
      de México, Centro de Estudios Literarios, 1968.
      414 p.

BOLETIN INTERAMERICANO DE MUSICA

958   "Artículos publicados en el 'Boletín interamericano de
      música'." Boletín interamericano de música, 83
      (mar./jun., 1972), 86-119.

BULLETIN OF HISPANIC STUDIES

959   Bulletin of Hispanic studies. Indexes. [Index of
      volumes 1-50 (1923-1973)]. Bulletin of Hispanic
      studies, 50: Supplement (Dec., 1973), 433-583.

OS CADERNOS DE CULTURA

960   Cunha, Maria Emilia Melo e. "Catálogo e índice de
      'Os Cadernos de Cultura' 1952-1964." Revista do
      Livro, 13:41 (1970), 99-111.

CARACAS. UNIVERSIDAD CENTRAL. ESCUELA DE BIB-
   LIOTECONOMIA Y ARCHIVOS. ANUARIO

961   "Indice analítico del 'Anuario de la Escuela de

Biblioteconomía y Archivos,' 1-2, 1965-1966." In:
Venezuela. Universidad Central. Escuela de Biblioteconomía y Archivos. Catálogo bibliográfico de
la Facultad de Humanidades y Educación, 1948-1968.
Caracas, 1969. pp. 41-58.

CASA DE LAS AMERICAS; REVISTA

962 Casa de las Américas; revista. Indexes. Indice de
     "Casa de las Américas" no. 17-39 (mar. 1963 a dic.
     1966). n.p., n.d. 13 p.

963 _____. Indexes. Indice Casa de las Américas
     (1960-1967). Comp. por Aleida Domínguez y Luz
     Bertha Marín. La Habana: Biblioteca Nacional
     José Martí, 1969. 224 p.

964 "Indice de la revista 'Casa de las Américas,' números
     64-75, enero-diciembre 1971-1972." Casa de las
     Américas, 23 (nov./dic., 1972), 182-194.

CHIHUAHUA, MEXICO (STATE). PERIODICO OFICIAL

965 McClure, Charles R. Guide to the microfilm collec-
     tion of the Periódico oficial de Chihuahua. El
     Paso: Center for Inter-American Studies, Univer-
     sity of Texas at El Paso, 1974. ix, 37 p.

CLIO (Santo Domingo)

966 Cabral Mejía, Tobías E. Indice de Clio y del Boletín
     del Archivo General de la Nación. Santo Domingo:
     Editorial del Caribe, 1971. 288 p. (Academia
     Dominicana de la Historia. Publicaciones, 32).

CODEX; BOLETIN DE LA ESCUELA DE BIBLIOTECONOMIA
Y ARCHIVOS

967 "Indice analítico de 'Codex; boletín de la Escuela de
     Biblioteconomía y Archivos,' 1:1-4 (abr./jun., 1966-
     ene./mar., 1967." In: Venezuela. Universidad
     Central. Escuela de Biblioteconomía y Archivos.
     Catálogo bibliográfico de la Facultad de Humanidades

y Educación, 1948-1968.   Caracas, 1969.   pp. 59-90.

COLEÇÃO BRASILIANA

968   Fonseca, Edson Nery da.   "Indice de Coleção Brasili-
      ana." Revista do Livro, 12:38 (1969), 123-144.

COLECCION DE DOCUMENTOS INEDITOS PARA LA HIS-
TORIA DE ESPAÑA

969   Díaz-Trechuelo Spínola, María Lourdes. América en
      la "Colección de documentos inéditos para la his-
      toria de España": catálogo. Sevilla: Escuela de
      Estudios Hispano-Americanos, 1971. 104 p. (Pub-
      licaciones, 198).

COLOMBIA TODAY

970   Colombia today. Indexes. "Complete bibliography of
      Colombia today newsletter [1:1-8:4]." Colombia
      today, 8:4 (1973). unpaged.

CORDOBA, ARGENTINA.   UNIVERSIDAD NACIONAL.
REVISTA

971   Córdoba, Argentina. Universidad Nacional. Revista.
      Indexes. Indice de la "Revista de la Universidad
      de Córdoba," 1914-1970. Córdoba: Facultad de
      Filosofía y Humanidades, Escuela de Bibliotecarios,
      1973. 168 p.

COSMOPOLIS

972   Mayz, Carmen C. de. "Indice de la revista 'Cosmó-
      polis' (1894-1895)." Montalbán, 1 (1972), 527-539.

COSTA RICA.   UNIVERSIDAD.   REVISTA

973   Costa Rica. Universidad. Revista. Indexes. Indice
      de la Revista de la Universidad de Costa Rica, 1-
      25. San José: Biblioteca de la Universidad, 1968.
      47 p.

CUADERNOS AMERICANOS

974 Cuadernos americanos. Indexes. Indices de Cuadernos
americanos; materias y autores, 1942-1971, [por
Angel Flores]. México: Cuadernos Americanos,
1973. xliv, 409 p.

DESARROLLO ECONOMICO; REVISTA DE CIENCIAS SOCIALES

975 Desarrollo económico; revista de ciencias sociales:
índice de artículos, comunicaciones, notas y comen-
tarios, crítica de libros, conferencias y debates,
documentos e informaciones publicados en los volu-
menes 1 a 10 (números 1 a 40), abril 1961 a marzo
1971. Buenos Aires: Instituto de Desarrollo Económico y Social, 1972? unpaged.

DOCUMENTAL DEL PERU

976 Documental del Perú. Indexes. El pequeño diccionario peruano de Documental del Perú. Lima:
Ioppe S.A. Editores, s.d. 187 p. Indexes vols.
1-24.

DOS TEMAS

977 "Indice analítico de Dos temas, 1-6 (1962-dic. 1967)."
In: Venezuela. Universidad Central. Escuela de
Biblioteconomía y Archivos. Catálogo bibliográfíco
de la Facultad de Humanidades y Educación, 1948-
1968. Caracas, 1969. pp. 111-118.

LA EDUCACION

978 La educación. Indexes. "Indice general de 'La educación' No. 1 (1956) al No. 58 (1970)." La educación, 59 (ene./abr., 1971). 148 p.

EPISTEME

979 "Indice analítico de 'Episteme,' 1957-1961/1963." In:

Venezuela. Universidad Central. Escuela de Biblioteconomía y Archivos. Catálogo bibliográfico de la Facultad de Humanidades y Educación, 1948-1968. Caracas, 1969. pp. 289-295.

LA ESTRELLA DEL SUR

980 Musso Ambrosi, Luis Alberto. " 'La Estrella del Sur' ('The Southern Star'); índices analíticos para su estudio." Boletín histórico del Estado Mayor General del Ejército (Montevideo), 112/115 (1967), 241-262.

ESTUDIOS

981 Mendoza, Jaime and Tomás P. MacHale. Bibliografía de la revista "Estudios" (1932-1957). Santiago de Chile: Biblioteca Nacional, 1969. 171 p.

ESTUDIOS INTERNACIONALES

982 Aguirre Valdivieso, Ana María and Mara Magdalena Cox Baeza. "Estudios internacionales: índice general analítico de los números 1-20, 1967-1972." Estudios internacionales, 6:21 (ene./mar., 1973), 97-119.

FILOSOFIA Y LETRAS; REVISTA DE LA FACULTAD DE FILOSOFIA (Mexico)

983 Filosofía y letras; revista de la Facultad de Filosofía (México). Indexes. Indices de la revista filosofía y letras (1941-1958). México: Universidad Nacional Autónoma de México, 1974. 168 p. (Bibliografía filosófica mexicana, 1971).

FORO INTERNACIONAL

984 Foro internacional. Indexes. "Indice de los primeros cincuenta números, Julio, 1961-Octubre, 1972." Foro internacional, 13:2 (oct./dic., 1972). 43 p. Appended to issue.

HISPANIA (American Association of Teachers of Spanish and Portuguese)

985 Woodbridge, Hensley C. "Hispania: index for volumes XLI-L, 1958-1967." Hispania, 52 (Nov., 1969), 739-829.

HISTORIA MEXICANA

986 Historia mexicana. Indexes. Indice de los volúmenes I-XX (julio 1951-junio 1971), por Luis Muro. México: El Colegio de México, 1971. vi, 121 p.

HOY (Santiago de Chile)

987 Santiago de Chile. Biblioteca Nacional. Bibliografía literaria de la revista "Hoy" (1931-1943), [trabajo realizado por Justo Alarcón y María Iciar de Sasía, con la colaboración de María Elena Ruiz-Tagle y Juan Camilo Lorca]. Santiago de Chile: Ediciones de la Biblioteca Nacional, 1970. xi, 560 p.

IBERO-AMERICANA PRAGENSIA (Prague)

988 Ibero-Americana Pragensia. Indexes. "Bibliografía de Ibero-Americana Pragensia, 1-5 (1967-1971)." Ibero-Americana Pragensia, 5 (1971), 241-250.

INSTITUTO DE CULTURA PUERTORRIQUEÑA. REVISTA

989 Betancourt, José Antonio. Revista del Instituto de Cultura puertorriqueña: índice acumulativo, 1958-1970. New York: Centro de Estudios Puertorriqueños, 1974. 60 p.

INSTITUTO DO CEARA, FORTALEZA, BRASIL. REVISTA

990 Instituto do Ceará, Fortaleza, Brasil. Revista. Indexes. Indice anotado da Revista do Instituto do Ceará (do 1 tomo ao 68), [por] José Honório Rodrigues. Fortaleza: Imprensa Universitaria do Ceará, 1959. 391 p.

INSTITUTO GEOGRAFICO ARGENTINO, BUENOS AIRES.
BOLETIN

991 Goicoechea, Helga Nilda.   El Instituto Geográfico Argentino; historia e índice de su Boletín (1879-1911,
1926-1928).   Resistencia, Arg.: Universidad Nacional del Nordeste, Departamento de Historia, 1970.
96 p. (UNN. Departamento de Publicaciones e Im-
presiones [Publicaciones], 15).

INSTITUTO HISTORICO Y GEOGRAFICO DO RIO GRANDE
DO SUL. PORTO ALEGRE. REVISTA

992 Villas-Bôas, Pedro Leite.   Indice por autores e assuntos dos cento e vinte números da "Revista" do Instituto Histórico e Geográfico do Rio Grande do Sul.
Pôrto Alegre, 1963.

INSTITUTO PARAGUAYO, ASUNCION.   REVISTA

993 Díaz Melian, Mafalda Victoria.   Indice de la Revista
del Instituto Paraguayo, 1896-1909.   Parana: Instituto Nacional del Profesorado Secundario, Sección de
Historia, 1970.   35 p.

INTER-AMERICAN MUSIC BULLETIN

994 Organization of American States.   General Secretariat.
La OEA y la música.   Washington: OAS, 1972.
119 p.   Includes an index of the Inter-American
music bulletin, 1957-1971.

KOLLASUYO (La Paz)

995 Kollasuyo. Indexes.   Indice de la revista Kollasuyo,
1939-1973.   La Paz: Universidad Mayor de San
Andrés, 1974.   72 p.   "Elaborado por ... Victoria
Gestri de Suárez y ... Gregorio Calanis."

LEON PINELO, ANTONIO DE.   EPITOME DE LA BIBLIOTECA
ORIENTAL Y OCCIDENTAL, NAUTICA Y GEOGRAFICA

996 Quiñones Melgoza, José.   "Los cronistas de órdenes

religiosas mencionados en el epítome de León
Pinelo." Boletín de la Biblioteca Nacional,
Mexico, 17:3/4 (1966), 17-40.

LETRAS DE MEXICO (1937-1947)

997   Forster, Merlin H.   Letras de México (1937-1947):
      índice anotado. [Mexico: Universidad Iberoamer-
      icana, 1971]. 200 p.

LIMA.   MUSEO NACIONAL.   REVISTA

998   Lima. Museo Nacional. Revista. Indexes. "Indice
      acumulativo de los tomos xxxi-xl." Revista del
      Museo Nacional, 40 (1974), 471-481.

MAPOCHO

999 MacHale, Tomás P.   "Bibliografía de la revista
    'Mapocho'." Mapocho, 15:4 (1966), 317-338.

MARCHA

1000 Marcha. Indexes.   Indice de Marcha, periodo julio
      1967 a junio 1973, años 29-34, núm. 1360 al
      1649, por Javier Ubillos.   Montevideo, 1973.
      69 p.

MEDINA, JOSE TORIBIO.   HISTORIA Y BIBLIOGRAFIA DE
LA IMPRENTA EN EL ANTIGUO VIREINATO DEL RIO
DE LA PLATA

1001 MacDonald, Eric.   Analytical subject index to José
      Toribio Medina's 'Historia y bibliografía de la
      imprenta en el antiguo vireinato del Río de la
      Plata.' Los Angeles: School of Library Service,
      University of California, 1974.   48 p.

NORTE; PERIODICO LITERARIO

1002 Norte; periódico literario. Indexes. "Indice de

'Norte" (Números 1 al 12)." Norte, 1:12
(1936), 4.

NOSOTROS

1003   Ardissone, Elena and Nélida Salvador.   Bibliografía
       de la revista Nosotros, 1907-1943.   Buenos Aires:
       Fondo Nacional de las Artes, 1971.   700 p.   (Bib-
       liografía argentina de artes y letras.   Compila-
       ciones especiales, 39/42).

NOTICIA BIBLIOGRAFICA E HISTORICA

1004   Notícia bibliográfica e histórica.   Indexes.   "Indice
       dos números 1 a 62, [por] Odilon Nogueira de
       Matos."   Notícia bibliográfica e histórica, 63
       (1974), 459-560.

NUEVA REVISTA DE FILOLOGIA HISPANICA

1005   "Indice analítico de la 'Nueva revista de filología his-
       panica,' 16:1/2-17:1/2 (ene./jun., 1962-1963/1964)."
       In: Venezuela.   Universidad Central.   Escuela de
       Biblioteconomía y Archivos.   Catálogo bibliográfico
       de la Facultad de Humanidades y Educación, 1948-
       1968.   Caracas, 1969.   pp. 257-276.

PEDAGOGIA UNIVERSITARIA

1006   "Indice analítico de Pedagogía universitaria, 1-5
       (jun., 1963-abr., 1964)."   In: Venezuela.   Uni-
       versidad Central.   Escuela de Biblioteconomía y
       Archivos.   Catálogo bibliográfico de la Facultad
       de Humanidades y Educación, 1948-1968.   Caracas,
       1969.   pp. 119-124.

EL PLATA CIENTIFICO Y LITERARIO

1007   Auza, Néstor Tomás.   Estudio e índice general de
       El plata científico y literario, 1854-1855 y Atlan-
       tida, 1911-1913.   Buenos Aires: Facultad de His-
       toria y Letras, Universidad del Salvador, 1968.
       85 p.   (Colección indices y bibliografías, 3).

EL RENACIMIENTO, SEMINARIO LITERARIO MEXICANO

1008   Batis Martínez, Agustín Huberto.   Indices de "El
        renacimiento, seminario literario mexicano" (1869).
        México: Centro de Estudios Literarios, Universi-
        dad Nacional Autónoma de México, 1963.   328 p.
        (Publicaciones, 9).

REVISTA BIMESTRE CUBANA

1009   Havana.   Biblioteca Nacional José Martí.   Departa-
        mento Colección Cubana.   Indice analítico de la
        Revista bimestre cubana, por Araceli García-
        Carranza.   La Habana, 1968.   405 p.

REVISTA BRASILEIRA DE ESTUDOS POLITICOS

1010   Cerqueira, Sonio Pereira de.   Revista brasileira de
        estudos políticos: índice cumulativo 1956-69.
        Belo Horizonte, Minas Gerais: Edições da Re-
        vista..., Universidad Federal de Minas Gerais,
        1970.   64 p.

1011   Revista brasileira de estudos políticos; índice cumula-
        tivo, 1956-1973.   Organizado por Ana Maria Buf-
        falo Penna, Cláudia de Vasconcellos, Nara Maldon-
        ado de Carvalho.   Belo Horizonte, 1974.

REVISTA DE AVANCE

1012   Ripoll, Carlos.   Indice de la Revista de avance (Cuba,
        1927-1930).   New York: Las Américas Pub. Co.,
        1969.   162 p.

REVISTA DE FILOSOFIA DE LA UNIVERSIDAD DE COSTA RICA

1013   Revista de filosofía de la Universidad de Costa Rica.
        Indexes.   Indices de ... los veintisiete primeros
        números (1957-1970)....   s.l., s.n., s.d.   39 p.

REVISTA DE HISTORIA (Caracas)

1014   Revista de historia, Caracas. Indexes. "Indice
        analítico de la 'Revista de historia,' 1-8 (abr.
        1960-ag. 1961)." In: Venezuela. Universidad
        Central. Escuela de Biblioteconomía y Archivos.
        Catálogo bibliográfico de la Facultad de Humani-
        dades y Educación, 1948-1968. Caracas, 1969.
        pp. 328-351.

REVISTA DE INDIAS

1015   Revista de Indias. Indexes. Revista de Indias.
        Indices, núms. 51-114, 1953-1968. Madrid: In-
        stituto "G. Fernández Oviedo," [n.d.]. 138 p.

REVISTA DO LIVRO

1016   Revista do livro. Indexes. Indice da Revista do
        livro do número 1 ao 16. Rio de Janeiro: In-
        stituto Nacional do Livro, 1959. 25 p. Organi-
        zado por Augusto Sousa-Meyer e revisto e com-
        pletado por Heloisa Ramos.

REVISTA GEOGRAFICA

1017   Fatima, Maria de Fonseca Pereira da. Revista geo-
        gráfica: indice geral dos números 1 ao 63. Rio
        de Janeiro: Instituto Panamericano de Geografía e
        Historia, Comisión de Geografía, 1970. 116 p.

REVISTA MEXICANA DE CIENCIA POLITICA

1018   Revista mexicana de ciencia política. Indice analítico
        por autores, títulos y materias de los números 1
        (1955) al 60 (1970). México: Universidad Nacional
        Autónoma de México, Facultad de Ciencias Políti-
        cas y Sociales, 1971. 101 p.

REVISTA MEXICANA DE SOCIOLOGIA

1019   Martínez Ríos, Jorge. "Indice por materias y

autores de los artículos publicados en los cien
primeros números de la Revista mexicana de
sociología: 1939-1969." Revista mexicana de
sociología, 31:1 (ene./mar., 1969), 177-211.

REVISTA MUSICAL CHILENA

1020 Revista musical chilena. Indexes. "Indice de números
      publicados desde 1945 a 1974...." Revista musi-
      cal chilena, 29:129/130 (ene./jun., 1975), 17-105.

1021 _____. Indexes. "Revista musical chilena, 1945-
      1966 (1o. de Mayo de 1945 a Diciembre de 1966):
      índices." Revista musical chilena, 20:98 (oct./
      dic., 1966). Entire issue. Compiled by Magda-
      lena Vicuña.

S. A. L. A. L. M. FINAL REPORT AND WORKING PAPERS

1022 Kinard, Sammy R. Working papers of the Seminars
      on the Acquisition of Latin American Library Ma-
      terials: list and index. 2d revision. Washington:
      O. A. S., 1971. 31 p. (Cuadernos bibliotecológicos,
      22, Rev. 2).

S. A. L. A. L. M. COMMITTEE ON ACQUISITIONS. MICRO-FILMING PROJECTS NEWSLETTER

1023 Seminar on the Acquisition of Latin American Library
      Materials. Committee on Acquisitions. Micro-
      filming projects newsletter. Indexes. Microfilm-
      ing projects newsletter: index, numbers 1-10.
      Editor: Suzanne Hodgman. Compiled by Ellen
      Brow. Madison: University of Wisconsin, Memor-
      ial Library, s. d. 18 ℓ.

TEMAS BIBLIOTECONOMICOS

1024 "Indice analítico de 'Temas biblioteconomicos,' 1-5
      (jul., 1956-abr., 1963)." In: Venezuela. Uni-
      versidad Central. Escuela de Biblioteconomía y
      Archivos. Catálogo bibliográfico de la Facultad
      de Humanidades y Educación, 1948-1968. Caracas,
      1969. pp. 355-373.

UNIVERSITAS EMERITENSIS

1025 Hernández, Manuel. Indice general de Universitas
      Emeritensis. Mérida: Universidad de los Andes,
      Facultad de Humanidades y Educación, Escuela de
      Letras, 1971. iii, 68 p. (Centro de Investiga-
      ciones Literarias. Serie bibliográfica, 1).

VENEZUELA. MINISTERIO DE JUSTICIA. REVISTA

1025a Venezuela. Ministerio de Justicia. Revista. Indexes.
      Indice general 1952-1967, nos. 1-56. Caracas.

VENEZUELA. UNIVERSIDAD CENTRAL. CENTRO DE IN-
VESTIGACIONES PEDAGOGICAS. BOLETIN

1026 "Indice analítico del Boletín del Centro de Investiga-
      ciones Pedagógicas, 1-8 (abr. 1962-abr./sept.
      1967)." In: Venezuela. Universidad Central.
      Escuela de Biblioteconomía y Archivos. Catá-
      logo bibliográfico de la Facultad de Humani-
      dades y Educación, 1948-1968. Caracas, 1969.
      pp. 97-110.

VENEZUELA. UNIVERSIDAD CENTRAL. INSTITUTO DE
ANTROPOLOGIA E HISTORIA. ANUARIO

1027 "Indice analítico del Anuario del Instituto de Antro-
      pología e Historia, 1-2 (1964-1965)." In: Vene-
      zuela. Universidad Central. Escuela de Biblio-
      teconomía y Archivos. Catálogo bibliográfico de
      la Facultad de Humanidades y Educación, 1948-
      1968. Caracas, 1969. pp. 161-197.

ZULIA. ARCHIVO HISTORICO. BOLETIN

1028 Cardozo Galué, Germán. "Boletin del Archivo His-
      tórico del Zulia (Maracaibo, 1945); notas histórico-
      bibliográficas y extractos documentales." Boletín
      de la Biblioteca de la Universidad del Zulia, 8/9:
      13/14 (ag./jun., 1968/69), 95-167. Includes: In-
      dice de la "Colección Maracaibo" que reposa en el
      Acervo Histórico del Archivo General del Estado
      Zulia.

ZULIA.   CENTRO HISTORICO.   REVISTA

1029 Moreno Bustos, Lenny and Laura Apitz de Taborda.
      "Indice de los boletines del Centro Histórico del
      Zulia." Boletín de la Biblioteca General de la
      Universidad del Zulia, 10/11:17/18 (ag. 1970/jun.
      1971), 319-387.

INTERNATIONAL RELATIONS

1030 U.S. Air Force Academy. Library.   United States
      in the Caribbean.   Colorado Springs, 1970.   34 p.
      (Special bibliography series, 44).

1031 Venezuela.   Universidad Central, Caracas.   Instituto
      de Estudios Políticos.   Las relaciones, interna-
      cionales: guía bibliográfica básica.   Caracas,
      1972.

1032 Wolpin, Miles David.   United States intervention in
      Latin America; a selected and annotated bibliog-
      raphy.   New York: American Institute for Marx-
      ist Studies, 1971.   56 p.   (Bibliographical series,
      8).

LABOR AND LABORING CLASSES

1033 American Institute for Marxist Studies.   A bibliography
      of the history of the Latin American labor and
      trade union movements.   New York, 1967.   18 ℓ.
      (Bibliographical series, 1).

1034 Gutiérrez, Leandro.   Recopilación bibliográfica de
      fuentes para el estudio de la historia y situación
      actual de la clase obrera argentina.   Buenos
      Aires: Centro de Investigaciones Sociales, In-
      stituto Torcuato Di Tella, 1969.   iv, 84 p.   (Docu-
      mento de trabajo, 63).

1035 Rodríguez Escalonilla, Arturo.   Bibliografía sobre
      los problemas del trabajo en América Latina,
      1960-1970.   Ginebra, Suiza: Instituto Internacional
      de Estudios Laborales, 1971?   xii, 132 p.

LANGUAGE AND LITERATURE

GENERAL

1036   Anderson, Robert Roland. Spanish American modern-
       ism; a selected bibliography. Tucson: University
       of Arizona Press, 1970. xxii, 167 p.

1037   Bialik Huberman, Gisela. Mil obras de lingüística
       española e hispanoamericana: un ensayo de sín-
       tesis crítica. Madrid: Playor, 1973. 812 p.

1038   Bleznick, Donald W. A sourcebook for Hispanic
       literature and language; a selected annotated guide
       to Spanish American bibliography, literature,
       linguistics, journals, and other source materials.
       Philadelphia: Temple University Press, 1974.
       192 p.

1039   Bibliografia brasileira de livros infantís. No. 1- .
       1967- . Rio de Janeiro: Sindicato Nacional dos
       Editores de Livros. Annual.

1040   Coll, Edna. Indice informativo de la novela hispano-
       americana. Río Piedras: Editorial Universitaria,
       Universidad de Puerto Rico, 1974- .

1041   Contribución a una bibliografía de dialectología es-
       pañola y especialmente americana, por María R.
       Avellaneda et al. Madrid: Imprenta Aguirre,
       1967. 128 p. "Separata del Boletín de la Real
       Academia Española, tomos 46 y 47, cuadernos,
       178-181."

1042   Davis, Jack Emory. "The Spanish of Argentina and
       Uruguay: an annotated bibliography for 1940-1965."
       Orbis, 15 (1966), 160-189, 422-488; 17 (1968),
       232-277, 539-573; 20 (1970), 205-232.

1043   _____. "The Spanish of Mexico: an annotated bib-
       liography for 1940-1969." Hispania, 54 (Oct.,
       1971), 625-656.

1044   De la Portilla, Marta and Thomas Colchie. Textbooks
       in Spanish and Portuguese: a descriptive bibliog-
       raphy, 1939-1970. New York: Modern Language
       Association of America, 1972. vii, 120 p.

1045   Deyermond, A. D. "Portuguese studies: Language."
        In: Year's work in Modern Language Studies,
        29 (1968 for 1967), 240-245.

1046   Escudero, Alfonso M. Fuentes chilenas de informa-
        ción sobre letras hispanoamericanas. Primera
        entrega: de Bello a Omer Emeth. 2. ed. Santi-
        ago de Chile, s.n., 1969. 102 p.

1047   Flores, Angel. Bibliografía de escritores hispano-
        americanos. A bibliography of Spanish American
        writers, 1609-1974. New York: Gordian Press,
        1975. 318 p.

1048   Forster, Merlin H. "Spanish American literary bib-
        liography, 1967." Modern Language Journal, 53
        (1969), 87-89.

1049   Foster, David William. "Spanish American literary
        bibliography, 1968." Modern language journal, 53
        (1969), 550-554.

1050   _____ and Virginia Ramos Foster. Manual of His-
        panic bibliography. Seattle: University of Washing-
        ton Press, 1970. x, 206 p.

1051   Frey, Herschel J. Teaching Spanish: a critical bib-
        liographic survey. Rowley, Mass.: Newbury
        House Publishers, 1974. 184 p.

1052   Glass, Elliot. "Video tape in language instruction:
        a brief survey and annotated bibliography of Span-
        ish and bilingual video tapes." The Bilingual re-
        view/La Revista bilingüe, 1:1 (Apr., 1974), 124-
        136.

1053   Grismer, Raymond Leonard. A reference index to
        twelve thousand Spanish American authors: a
        guide to the literature of Spanish America. New
        York: Burt Franklin, 1970. xvi, 150 p. Re-
        print of the 1939 ed.

1054   Hoge, Henry W. Portuguese language teaching mater-
        ials. Milwaukee: Distributed by the Language and
        Area Center for Latin America, University of Wis-
        consin, 1966. 14 ℓ.

1055 Horn-Monvel, Madeleine. Répertoire bibliographique
      des traductions et adaptations françaises du théâtre
      étranger du XVe siècle à nos jours. Paris:
      Centre Nationale de la Recherche Scientifique,
      1958- . Tome IV: Théâtre espagnol; Théâtre
      de l'Amérique latine; Théâtre portuguaise.

1056 Johnson, Harvey L. "Spanish American literary bib-
      liography: 1970 and 1971." Modern Language
      Journal, 56:6 (Oct., 1972), 365-373.

1057 Jones, Willis Knapp. Latin American writers in
      English translation: a classified bibliography.
      Detroit: Blaine Ethridge Books, 1972. vi, 140 p.
      Reprint of 1944 ed.

1058 Levine, Suzanne Jill. Latin America: fiction and
      poetry in translation. New York: Center for
      Inter-American Relations, 1970. 71 p.

1059 Nueva revista de filología hispánica. México. Regu-
      larly features an excellent bibliography of recent
      research on the language and literature of the Por-
      tuguese and Spanish speaking worlds.

1060 Ocampo de Gómez, Aurora Maura. Novelistas ibero-
      americanos contemporáneos; obras y bibliografía
      crítica. México: Universidad Nacional Autónoma
      de México, Centro de Estudios Literarios, 1971- .
      (Cuadernos, 2).

1061 Reichardt, Dieter. Lateinamerikanische Autoren:
      Literaturlexikon und Bibliographie der deutschen
      Übersetzungen. [Hrsg. vom Institut für Ibero-
      amerika-Kunde]. Hamburg, Tübingen: H. Erd-
      mann, 1972. 718 p.

1062 Rela, Walter. Guía bibliográfica de la literatura
      hispanoamericana desde el siglo XIX hasta 1970.
      Buenos Aires: Casa Pardo, 1971. 613 p.

1063 Revista de filología española. Madrid. Regularly
      features an extensive bibliography of articles and
      books.

1064 United Nations Educational, Scientific and Cultural
      Organization. Bibliografía general de la literatura

latinoamericana, por Guillermo Lohmann et al.
Paris: Unesco, 1972. 187 p.

1065 The year's work in modern language studies. London:
Modern Humanities Research Association.

1066 Zubatsky, David S. "An international bibliography of
cumulative indexes to journals publishing articles
on Hispanic languages and literatures." Hispania,
58:1 (March, 1975), 75-101.

ARGENTINA

1067 Bertodatti, Juan Domingo. Diccionario de poetas argentinos, [por] Vanber (Juan Domingo Bertodatti).
Rosario: Lira, 1972. 110 p.

1068 Fernández, Belisario. Bibliografía del español de la
Argentina. Buenos Aires: Consejo Nacional de
Educación, 1967. 127 p.

1069 Foster, David William and Virginia Ramos Foster.
"Fuentes interamericanas para el estudio de la
literatura argentina: una bibliografía anotada de
obras principales." La Torre, 18:68 (abr./jun.,
1970), 159-174; 18:69 (jul./sept., 1970), 172-186.

1070 _____ and _____. Research guide to Argentine
literature. Metuchen, N.J.: Scarecrow Press,
1970. 146 p.

1071 Gobello, José. Nueva antología Lunfarda (Autores
argentinos). Buenos Aires: Plus Ultra, 1972.
238 p.

1072 Lafleur, Héctor René and Sergio D. Provenzano.
Las revistas literarias argentinas, 1893-1967.
Buenos Aires: Centro Editor de América Latina,
1968. 351 p.

1073 Museo Americanista. II exposición de libros de escritores lomenses, 15 al 30 de diciembre de
1972. Lomas de Zamora, Argentina, 1973?
62 p.

139   LANGUAGE/LITERATURE

BOLIVIA

1074   Ortega, José.   Letras bolivianas de hoy: Renato
       Prada y Pedro Shimose.   Manual de bibliografía
       de la literatura boliviana.   Buenos Aires: García
       Cambeiro, 1973.   115 p.   (Colección estudios
       latinoamericanos, 5).

BRAZIL

1075   Curran, Mark Joseph.   Selected bibliography of his-
       tory and politics in Brazilian popular poetry.
       Tempe: Arizona State University, Center for
       Latin American Studies, 1971.   26 ℓ.   (Special
       study, 8).

1076   Gorog, Ralph P. de.   "Bibliografia de estudos do
       vocabulario português."   Luso-Brasilian review,
       4:1 (1967), 83-110; 4:2 (1967), 95-110.

1077   Hoge, Henry W.   A selective bibliography of Luso-
       Brasilian linguistics.   Milwaukee: Distributed by
       the Language and Area Center for Latin America,
       University of Wisconsin, 1966.   70 ℓ.

1078   Leite, Ligia Chiappini Moraes.   Modernismo no Rio
       Grande do Sul; materiales para o seu estudo.
       São Paulo: Instituto de Estudos Brasileiros,
       U.S.P., 1972.   358 p.   (Publicações, 20).

1079   "Livros para crianças, 1969."   Revista do livro,
       12:40 (1970), 129-147.

1080   Moraes, Jomar.   Bibliografia crítica da literatura
       maranhense.   São Luís: Departamento de Cultura
       do Maranhão, 1972.   xix, 122 p.

1081   Parker, John M.   "Latin American Studies: Brazilian
       language and literature."   In: Year's Work in
       Modern Language Studies, 29 (1968 for 1967),
       290-303.

1082   Rio de Janeiro.   Biblioteca Nacional.   O romance
       brasileiro; catálogo da exposição.   Rio de Janeiro,
       1974.   86 p.

1083   Sociedade Brasileira de Autores Teatrais.   Catálogo
de peças teatrais; agôsto, 1962.   Rio de Janeiro:
Serviço de Reembôlso Postal da SBAT, 1962.
20, [1]p.

CARIBBEAN

1084   Engber, Marjorie.   Caribbean: fiction and poetry.
New York: Center for Inter-American Relations,
1970. 86 p.

1085   Merriman, Stella E. and Joan Christiani.   Commonwealth Caribbean writers; a bibliography.   Georgetown, Guyana: Public Library, 1970.   iv, 98 p.

CHILE

1086   Godoy, Gallardo, Eduardo.   "Indice crítico-bibliográ-
fico del premio Eugenio Nadal: 1944-1968."
Mapocho, 22 (1970), 109-136.

1087   Referencias críticas sobre autores chilenos.   Santiago
de Chile: Biblioteca Nacional.

1088   Zamorano y Caperan.   Bibliografía de novelistas y
cuentistas chilenos.   Santiago de Chile: Zamorano
y Caperan, 1969.   39 p.

COLOMBIA

1089   Hudson, Gertrude.   "Síntese de la literatura colombiana; índice de los autores y de sus obras representantes (1566-1966)."   Boletín cultural y bibliográfico, 9:7 (1966), 1415-1424.

1090   Orjuela, Héctor H.   Bibliografía de la poesia colombiana.   Bogotá: Instituto Caro y Cuervo, 1971.
xxvii, 486 p.   (Serie bibliográfica, 9).

1091   Peña Gutiérrez, Isaias.   La generación del bloqueo y
del estado de sitio.   Bogotá: Punto Rojo, 1973.
253 p.

1092   Pérez Silva, Vicente.   "Papeletas bibliográficas:

141   LANGUAGE/LITERATURE

diccionarios de autores colombianos." Boletín
cultural y bibliográfico, 9:3 (1966), 511-520.

1093   Romero Castañeda, Rafael.   Autores magdalenses.
Bogotá, 1968.   115, 5 p.

CUBA

1094   Abella, Rosa.   "Bibliografía de la novela publicada
en Cuba, y en el extrangero por cubanos, desde
1959 hasta 1965."   Revista iberoamericana, 32:62
(jul./dic., 1966), 307-311.

1095   _____.   "Bibliografía de la novela reimpresa en
Cuba desde 1959 hasta 1965."   Revista iberoamericana, 32:62 (jul./dic., 1966), 313-318.

1096   Casal, Lourdes.   "A bibliography of Cuban creative
literature: 1958-1971."   Cuban Studies Newsletter,
2:2 (June, 1972), 1-29.

1097   _____.   "The Cuban novel, 1959-1969: an annotated
bibliography."   Abraxas, 1:1 (Fall, 1970), 77-92.

1098   Ford, Jeremiah Denis Matthais and Maxwell Isaac
Raphael.   A bibliography of Cuban belles-lettres.
New York: Russell and Russell, 1970.   204 p.
Reprint of 1933 ed.

1099   Hernández-Myares, Julio.   "The Cuban short story in
exile: a selected bibliography."   Hispania, 54:2
(May, 1971), 384-385.

1100   Montes Huidobro, Matías and Yara González.   Bibliografía crítica de la poesía cubana; (exilio: 1959-
1971).   New York: Plaza Mayor, 1972.   136 p.
(Colección Scholar, 15).

1101   Muriedas, Mercedes.   Bibliografía de la literatura
infantil cubana, siglo XIX.   La Habana: Departamento Juvenil, Biblioteca Nacional José Martí,
1969- .

DOMINICAN REPUBLIC

1102   Alfau Durán, Vetilio.   "Apuntes para la bibliografía

poética dominicana." Clio, 33 (1965), 34-60; 36
(1968), 107-119; 37 (1969), 53-69; 38 (1970), 50-77.

MEXICO

1103 Estrada, José T. "Periódicos y escritores del siglo
XIX: gacetas de literatura de México (1831-1898)."
Boletín bibliográfico de la Secretaría de Hacienda
y Crédito Público, Mexico, 12:353 (1966), 14-16.

1104 Moore, Ernest Richard. Bibliografía de novelistas de
la Revolución Mexicana. New York: B. Franklin,
1972. 189 p. (Burt Franklin bibliography & reference series, 460. Selected essays & texts in
literature & criticism, 184). Reprint of 1941 ed.

1105 Rutherford, John David. An annotated bibliography of
the novels of the Mexican Revolution of 1910-1917
in English and Spanish. Troy, N.Y.: Whitston
Publishing Company, 1972. 180 p.

PANAMA

1106 Panama (City). Biblioteca Nacional. Departamento
de Procesos Técnicos. Bibliografía de obras
panameñas escritas por mujeres y sobre ellas.
Panamá: Ministerio de Educación, 1970. 55, 3 ℓ.

PERU

1107 Carrión Ordóñez, Enrique and Tilbert Diego Stegmann.
Bibliografía del español en el Perú. Tübingen:
Niemeyer, 1973. xiii, 274 p. (Schriftenreihe
des Sonderforschungsbereichs 14. Iberoromanis-
tik, Band 1).

1108 Pinto Gamboa, Willy. Contribución a la bibliografía
de la literatura peruana en la prensa española.
Lima: Universidad Nacional de San Marcos, 1965.
170 p. (Repertorio bibliográfico de la literatura
latinoamericana. Serie B: 1).

PUERTO RICO

1109   Biblioteca José M. Lázaro.   Puerto Rican literature:
       translations into English.   Literatura puertor-
       riqueña: traducciones al inglés.   Río Piedras,
       1974.   viii, 38 ℓ.

1110   Mohr, Eugene V.   "Fifty years of Puerto Rican litera-
       ture in English, 1923-1973:   an annotated bibliog-
       raphy."   Revista interamericana; a journal of the
       Inter American University of Puerto Rico, 3:3
       (Fall, 1973), 290-298.

TRINIDAD AND TOBAGO

1111   Pantin, Maritza and Diane Hunte.   Creative writers
       in Trinidad and Tobago: a bibliography.   St.
       Augustine: University of the West Indies Library,
       1970.   34 ℓ.

VENEZUELA

1112   Cardozo, Lubio.   Bibliografía de la literatura meri-
       deña.   Mérida, Venezuela: Centro de Investiga-
       ciones Literarias, Universidad de los Andes,
       Facultad de Humanidades y Educación, 1967 [i.e.,
       1968].   91 p.

1113   _____.   "Contribución a la bibliografía de poetas
       merideños."   Boletín (Zulia.   Universidad.   Bib-
       lioteca), 9/10:15/16 (jul. 1969/jul. 1970), 49-130.

1114   Mérida, Venezuela.   Universidad de los Andes.   Cen-
       tro de Investigaciones Literarias.   Diccionario
       general de la literatura venezolana (autores).
       Mérida, 1974.   xiv, 829 p.

1115   Querales, Juan H.   Bibliografía de la poesía caroreña.
       Carora: Casa de la Cultura, 1972.   23 p.

LAW

1116   American Association of Law Libraries.   Committee

on Foreign and International Law.   Union list of
basic Latin American legal materials.   Editor:
Kate Wallach.   South Hackensack, N.J.:   published
for American Association of Law Libraries by
F. B. Rothman, 1971.   viii, 64 p.   (AALL publications series, 10).

1117   Argentina.   Congreso.   Biblioteca.   Amnistía.
Buenos Aires, 1973.   7 ℓ.

1118   Arismendi A., Alfredo.   Contribución a la bibliografía del derecho constitucional y su historia.   Caracas: Instituto de Derecho Público, Facultad de
Derecho, Universidad Central de Venezuela, 1972.
200 p.

1119   Bibliografia brasileira de direito.   v. 1- .   1966/
1968- .   Rio de Janeiro: Instituto Brasileiro de
Bibliografia e Documentaçâo, 1970- .

1120   "Bibliografía sobre el derecho de asilo."   Boletín del
Centro de Relaciones Internacionales, Universidad
Nacional Autónoma de México, 27 (feb., 1973),
93-97.

1121   "Bibliografia sôbre infrações e penalidades tributárias."
Revista de política e administraçâo fiscal, 2:4/5
(jul./out., 1970), 293-309.

1122   Carrillo León, Omaida and Eolida Sánchez Pulido.
"Indice cronológico y analítico de leyes, decretos
ejecutivos, decretos presidenciales, resoluciones
y reglamentos publicados en la Gaceta oficial de
la República (10 de enero de 1972-31 de diciembre de 1972)."   Anuario de la Facultad de Derecho, Universidad de los Andes, 4 (1974), 389-519.

1123   Clagett, Helen (Lord) and David M. Valderrama.   A
revised guide to the law and legal literature of
Mexico.   Washington: Library of Congress, 1973.
xii, 463 p.   (Latin American series, 38).   Revi-
sion of the 1945 edition by John T. Vance and
Helen L. Clagett.

1124   Costa, Moacyr Lobo da.   Breve notícia histórica do
direito processual civil brasileiro e de sua literatura.   Sâo Paulo: Editora Revista dos Tribunais,

1970.   206 p.   Includes: "Bibliografia brasileira de direito processual civil."--pp. 133-206.

1125   Echeverría y Reyes, Aníbal.   La bibliografía jurídica chilena.   Santiago de Chile: Zamorano y Caperán, 1969?   16 p.

1126   Fitzgibbon, Russell Humke.   Latin American constitutions: textual citations.   Tempe: Center for Latin American Studies, Arizona State University, 1974. 18 p.

1127   Galindo Guarneros, Gustavo.   Certificados de participación; expectativas y frustraciones: bibliografía sobre el fideicomiso.   México: Universidad Nacional Autónoma de México, 1972.   80 p.

1128   García Iturbe, Arnoldo.   Bibliografía venezolana sobre derecho penal.   Caracas: Sociedad Venezolana de Derecho Penal y Criminología, 1972.   70 p.

1129   "Indice analítico y cronológico de los trabajos doctrinales y jurisprudenciales publicados en la Revista y Anuario de la Facultad de Derecho." Anuario de la Facultad de Derecho, Universidad de los Andes, 4 (1974), 587-604.

1130   Larrea Olguín, Juan Ignacio.   Bibliografía jurídica del Ecuador.   Quito: Casa de la Cultura Ecuatoriana, 1970.   178 p.

1131   "Leyes y reglamentos cuyos textos han aparecido en la Revista y Anuario de la Facultad de Derecho." Anuario de la Facultad de Derecho, Universidad de los Andes, 4 (1974), 520.

1132   Ortega Torres, Jorge.   "Bibliografía jurídica colombiana."   Boletín cultural y bibliográfico.   [Regular feature.]

1133   Patchett, Keith and Valerie Jenkins.   A bibliographical guide to law in the Commonwealth Caribbean. Mona, Jamaica: University of the West Indies, Institute of Social and Economic Research and Faculty, 1973.   xvi, 80 p.

1134   "Registro bibliográfico de obras y artículos sobre

ciencias jurídicas y sociales publicadas en el país durante el período 1967/1969. la. parte." Boletín bibliográfico de la Facultad de Ciencias Jurídicas y Sociales, Universidad Nacional de la Plata, 21 (1970). Continued in subsequent issues.

1135 Ribeiro Júnior, José. "Extracto da legislação para o Brasil durante o reinado de D. José I, 1750-1777." Anais de historia, Faculdade de Filosofia, Assis, 1 (1968/1969), 77-130.

1136 Sánchez Quintanar, Andrea. "Bibliografía selectiva del Artículo 3.o de la Constitución Política Mexicana de 1917." Boletín del Instituto de Investigaciones Bibliográficas, México, 2:1 (ene./jun., 1970), 153-169.

1137 São Paulo, Brazil (State). Tribunal de Alcada Criminal. Biblioteca. Catálogo. São Paulo, 1970?- .

1138 Thomé, Joseph R. Bibliografía temática sobre aspectos jurídicos institucionales del proceso de reforma agraria en América Latina con énfasis en el proceso chileno de 1965-1970. Version preliminar. Santiago de Chile, 1972. iii, 24 ℓ.

1139 U.S. Library of Congress. Hispanic Law Division. Hispanic Foundation. Index to Latin American legislation. First supplement, 1961-1965. Boston: G. K. Hall, 1970. 2 v.

1140 _____. _____. Second supplement, 1966-1970. Boston: G. K. Hall, 1973. 1, 230 p.

1141 Villalón-Galdamés, Alberto. Bibliografía jurídica de América Latina, 1810-1965. Santiago de Chile: Editorial Jurídica, 1969- .

LIBRARIES AND ARCHIVES

GENERAL

1142 Bartley, Russell H. and Stuart L. Wagner. Latin America in basic historical collections: a working guide. Stanford, Calif.: Hoover Institution Press,

1972.   xviii, 217 p.   (Stanford University.   Hoover
Institution on War, Revolution and Peace.   Bibliographical series, 51).

1143 Congreso Bolivariano de Archiveros, 1st, Caracas,
1967. Primer Congreso Bolivariano de Archiveros,
Caracas, diciembre, 1967: actas, discursos,
ponencias. Caracas: Archivo General de la Nación, 1968. 646 p.

1144 Muñoz, Esther A. de and Sada Zalba. "Bibliografía
sobre bibliotecas escolares e infantiles." Boletín
bibliográfico, Biblioteca Pública, La Plata, 20
(1969), 19-32.

1145 "A preliminary listing of published materials relating
to the archives and manuscript collections in Latin
America." News from the Center for the Coordination of Foreign Manuscript Copying, Library of
Congress, Manuscript Division, 7 (Spring, 1970),
28-46.

1146 Valcarcel, Carlos Daniel. Fuentes documentales para
la historia de la independencia de América. Mi-
sión de investigación en los archivos europeos.
Caracas, 1974. 457 p. (Pan American Institute
of Geography and History. Commission on History. Publications, 19).

ARGENTINA

1147 Archivo Histórico de la Provincia de Buenos Aires
Dr. Ricardo Levene. Catálogo del Archivo de la
Real Audiencia y Cámara de Apelación de Buenos
Aires. La Plata: Provincia de Buenos Aires,
Ministerio de Educación, Subsecretaria de Cultura,
1974- . (Catálogos e índices de los documentos
del Archivo, 4).

1148 _____. Catálogo del Tribunal de Cuentas y Conta-
duría de la Provincia. La Plata, 1967. 41 p.
(Catálogos e índices de documentos del Archivo,
1).

1149 _____. Indice de la Cámara de Diputados de la
Provincia de Buenos Aires, 1853-1882. La Plata,

1973.   321 p.   (Catálogos de los documentos del Archivo, 6).

1150 _____. Indice de la Cámara de Senadores de la Provincia de Buenos Aires, 1854-1882. La Plata, 1971. xii, 216 p. (Catálogos e índices de los documentos del Archivo, 5).

1151 _____. Indice de la Sala de Representantes de la Provincia de Buenos Aires, 1821-1852. La Plata, 1970. 211 p. (Catálogos e índices de los documentos del Archivo, 3).

1152 _____. Indice de mapas, planos y fotografías de la Sección Ministerio de Obras Públicas, 1885-1910. La Plata: El Archivo, 1969. xii, 149 p. (Catálogo de los documentos del Archivo, 2).

1153 Argentina. Congreso. Biblioteca. Servicio de Referencia. Serie bibliográfica. no. 1- . 1973- . Buenos Aires.

1154 Banco Central de la República Argentina. Biblioteca. Boletín bibliográfico. Buenos Aires.

1155 Buenos Aires. Universidad. Facultad de Ciencias Exactas y Naturales. Biblioteca. Catálogo-guía de la sección arquitectura. Buenos Aires, 1934. iii-viii, 75 p.

1156 Buenos Aires. Universidad. Facultad de Filosofía y Letras. Biblioteca. ... Catálogo de la Biblioteca. Buenos Aires: Compañía sud-americana de billetes de Banco, 1912. 167 p.

1157 Buenos Aires. Universidad. Instituto Bibliotecológico. Catálogo de la biblioteca. Buenos Aires, 1964-66. 2 v.

1158 _____. Catálogo de la biblioteca; publicaciones periodicas. Buenos Aires, 1967. xiii, 48 p. (Publicación, 24).

1159 _____. Catálogo de la biblioteca. Suplemento. Buenos Aires, 1966- .

1160 _____. Guía de las bibliotecas de la Universidad de Buenos Aires. Buenos Aires, 1966. 64 p.

1161 "Catálogo de los borradores de las Actas del Congreso Nacional de las Provincias Unidas del Río de la Plata, 1816-1818." Revista del Archivo General de la Nación, 1:1 (1971), 81-94.

1162 Córdoba, Argentina. Universidad Nacional. Biblioteca Mayor. Los incunables de la Biblioteca Mayor..., por Graciela Bringas Aguiar. Córdoba, 1973. 56 ℓ.

1163 Tanodi, Aurelio Z. Guía de los archivos de Córdoba. Córdoba: Universidad Nacional de Córdoba, 1968. xxv, 168 p. (Collectanea archivística, 3).

1164 Tucumán, Argentina (Province). Arquivo Histórico. Indices documentales. Sección protocolos. Años 1588-1610. Tucumán, 1970. 56 p. (Indices documentales, 1).

1165 Zuretti, Juan Carlos. "Documentos sobre historia eclesiástica existentes en el Archivo General de la Nación (de Buenos Aires): Sala IX; desde 3-2/8 hasta 31-9-6." Archivum; Revista de la Junta de Historia Eclesiástica Argentina, 10 (1968), 233-266.

BARBADOS

1166 Wellum, Jessica. Caribbeana in the University Centre Library, Antigua. Cave Hill, Barbados, 1970. 28 ℓ.

BELGIUM

1167 Liagre-De Sturler, Leone and Jean Baerten. Guide des sources de l'histoire d'Amérique latine conservées en Belgique. Bruxelles: Archives Générales du Royaume, 1967. 132 p. (Guide de sources de l'histoire de nations. A: Amérique latine, 3).

BOLIVIA

1168 René-Moreno, Gabriel. Catálogo del Archivo de Mojos

y Chiquitos.   2. ed. , con estudio preliminar y
notas adicionales de Hernando Sanabria Fernández.
La Paz: Editorial "Juventud," 1973.   583 p.

BRAZIL

1169 "Antigos jornais mineiros na Biblioteca do Arquivo."
Mensario do Arquivo Nacional, 5:8 (ag. , 1974),
24-27.

1170 Baptista, Francisco Nivaldo de. "Os cartórios no
Município de Marília." Revista de história, São
Paulo, 44:89 (jan./mar. , 1972), 269-284.

1171 _____. "As fontes primárias do Município de
Alvinlândia." Revista de história, São Paulo,
40:82 (abr./jun. , 1970), 451-462.

1172 Bellotto, Manoel Lelo. "Arrolamento das fontes históricas do município de São Pedro do Turvo e
região circunvizinha." Revista de história, São
Paulo, 34:69 (jan./mar. , 1967), 187-201.

1173 Bibliografia de obras de referencias da Biblioteca
Pública do Estado, pelas alunas do 3o. ano da
Escola de Biblioteconomia e Documentação, Uni-
versidade Federal do Rio Grande do Sul. . . .
Porto Alegre: Departamento de Educação e Cul-
tura, 1968.   34 ℓ.

1174 Biblioteca Municipal Mario de Andrade. Boletím bibliográfico. São Paulo: Prefeitura do Município
de São Paulo. Continues: São Paulo, Brazil
(City) Biblioteca Pública Municipal. Boletím bibliográfico.

1175 _____. Catálogo de obras raras. . . . São Paulo:
Prefeitura do Município de São Paulo, Secretaria
de Educação e Cultura, Departamento de Cultura,
1969.   viii, 537 p.

1176 Brazil.   Arquivo Nacional. Relação de algumas
cartas das sesmarias concedidas em território da
Capitania do Rio de Janeiro, 1714-1800. Rio de
Janeiro, 1968.   74 p. (Its Publicações, la série,
61).

1177 Brazil. Arquivo Nacional. Biblioteca. Catálogo da
Biblioteca do Archivo Público Nacional. Rio de
Janeiro: Imprensa Nacional, 1901. 90 p.

1178 Brazil. Arquivo Nacional. Serviço de Registro e
Assistência. Catálogo coletivo dos arquivos brasileiros; contribuição preliminar de repertório
referente à Independência do Brasil. Rio de
Janeiro, 1972. 73 p. (Série Instrumentos de
trabalho, 24).

1179 Brazil. Ministério das Relações Exteriores. Arquivo
Histórico do Itamaraty. Arquivo particular do
Barão do Rio Branco. Rio de Janeiro, 1967.
136 p. (Its Publicações, Parte III - 34:6).

1180 Brazil. Ministerio das Relações Exteriores. Biblioteca. Lista dos periódicos existentes na Biblioteca do Itamaraty. Rio de Janeiro, 1966. 202 ℓ.

1181 Brazil. Superintendência do Desenvolvimento da
Região Sul. Divisão de Documentação. Bibliografia de educação e assuntos correlatos; material
bibliográfico existente na Divisão.... Pôrto Alegre,
1970. 36 ℓ.

1182 Brazil. Superintendência do Desenvolvimento do Nordeste. Biblioteca. Catálogo de periódicos da
Biblioteca da SUDENE. Recife, 1972. 158 p.

1183 Camargo, Ana Maria de Almeida. "A hemeroteca
'Júlio de Mesquita' do Instituto Histórico e Geográ-
fico de São Paulo." Revista de história (São
Paulo), 43:88 (out./dez., 1971), 511-516.

1184 Camargo, Antônio Euler Lopes. "Arrolamento das
fontes históricas do município de Tupã (SP)."
Revista de história, São Paulo, 43:88 (out./dez.,
1971), 549-570.

1185 Cardoso, Clotilde de Santa Clara Medina. "Arrolamento das fontes históricas do município de Bata-
tais." Revista de história, São Paulo, 37:76 (out./
dez., 1968), 447-459.

1186 Cardoso, Jayme Antônio. "Nota prévia sôbre o levantamento de fontes primárias existentes no Arquivo

da Câmara Municipal de Curitiba." Revista de história, São Paulo, 36:73 (jan./mar., 1968), 257-266.

1187 Casalecchi, José Enio. "Arrolamento das fontes históricas do município de Andradas (estado de Minas Gerais)." Revista de história, São Paulo, 42:85 (jan./mar., 1971), 227-240.

1188 Castro, Jeanne Berrance de and José Sebastião Witter. "Arrolamento das fontes primárias de Rio Claro." Revista de história, São Paulo, 28:58 (abr./jun., 1964), 427-453.

1189 "Catálogo da Coleção Antônio P. Rebouças." Anais da Biblioteca Nacional, Rio de Janeiro, 88 (1968), 189-203.

1190 Centro de Pesquisas do Cacau, Itabuna. Catálogo de periódicos da Biblioteca do CEPEC. Itabuna, 1969. 138 p.

1191 Córdoba, Argentine Republic. Universidad Nacional. Biblioteca Mayor. Catálogo de los impresos porteños anteriores a 1831 existentes en la Biblioteca Mayor de la Universidad Nacional de Córdoba, [excepto los de Niños Expósitos, por] Ana María Manera de Roldán. Córdoba, 1973. 58 ℓ.

1192 Costa, Odah Regina Guimarães and Maria Ignês Mancini de Boni. Arquivo da Paróquia de Campo Largo da Piedade. Curitiba: Universidade Federal do Paraná, Instituto de Ciências Humanas, Departamento de História, 1972. 56 p. (Boletim, 17).

1193 Exposição comemorativa do centenario do termino da Guerra do Paraguai, 1870-1970: acervo da Biblioteca Rio-Grandense, Coleção José Arthur Montenegro. Rio Grande do Sul?: Serviço de Docmentação Geral da Marinha, 1970. 41 p.

1194 Instituto Hans Staden, São Paulo, Brazil. Catalog of holdings of newspapers, journals and annuals. São Paulo, 1967.

1195 Instituto Histórico e Geográfico Brasileiro. "Arquivo do Barão de Cotegipe." Revista do Instituto

Histórico e Geográfico Brasileiro, 290 (jan./mar.,
1971), 163-402.

1196 Kiemen, Mathias C. "A summary index of ecclesias-
tical papers in the Archive of the Papal Nunciature
of Rio de Janeiro for the period of 1808-1891."
The Americas, 28:1 (July, 1971), 99-112.

1197 Museu Imperial do Brasil, Petrópolis. Arquivo His-
tórico. Inventario analítico do Arquivo da Casa
Imperial do Brasil, 1807-1816. Petrópolis: Min-
isterio da Educação e Cultura, Departamento de
Assuntos Culturais, Museu Imperial, 1974. 311 p.
(Série Arquivo Histórico do Museu Imperial, 2).

1198 _____. Inventario do Arquivo Leitão da Cunha,
Barão de Mamoré. Petrópolis: Ministério da
Educação e Cultura, Departamento de Assuntos
Culturais, Museu Imperial, 1972. 109 p. (Série
O Arquivo Histórico do Museu Imperial, 1).

1199 Paraná, Brazil (State). Universidade Federal. Departamento de Historia. Arquivos da cidade de
Castro. Curitiba, 1972. 129 p. (Its Boletim,
16).

1200 Paula, Maria Regina Cunha Rodrigues Simões de.
"As fontes primárias existentes no Arquivo da
Cúria Metropolitana de São Paulo (capital)." Revista de história, São Paulo, 32:66 (abr./jun.,
1966), 437-493.

1201 Placer, Xavier. Publicações da Biblioteca Nacional.
Catálogo: 1973-1974. Rio de Janeiro: Biblioteca
Nacional, 1975. 128 p.

1202 Reis, Josué Callander dos. "Arrolamento das fontes
históricas de Feijó (Acre)." Revista de história,
São Paulo, 48:98 (abr./jun., 1974), 541-561.

1203 Ramos, Dulce Helena Alvares Pessoa and Raquel Gle-
zer. "Notícia sôbre a documentação do Museu
das Bandeiras, Goiás." Revista de história, São
Paulo, 76 (1968), 461-483.

1204 Rio de Janeiro. Biblioteca Nacional. Amazônia brasileira; catálogo da exposição. Rio de Janeiro, 1969.
91 p.

1205 _____. Catálogo de incunáblos.... [Preparado por Rosemarie Erika Horch]. Rio de Janeiro: Ministério da Educação e Cultura, 1956. 377 p.

1206 _____. 4 séculos do Rio de Janeiro; exposição comemorativa do iv centenário da fundação da cidade do Rio de Janeiro, 1565-1965. Rio de Janeiro, 1965. 49 p.

1207 _____. Exposição Coleção Barbosa Machado. Rio de Janeiro, 1967.

1208 _____. O livro raro em seus diversos aspectos; catálogo. Organizado pela Bibliotecária Iracema Celeste Rodrigues Monteiro. Rio de Janeiro, 1972. 58 p.

1209 _____. Ouro Preto; sesquicentario da elevação de Vila Rica à categoria de Imperial Cidade de Ouro Preto, 1823-1973: catálogo da exposição. Rio de Janeiro, 1973. 77 p.

1210 Rocha, Maria Helena Degani. "Arrolamento das fontes históricas de Itatiba." Revista de história, São Paulo, 34:69 (jan./mar., 1967), 203-210.

1211 _____. "Arrolamento das fontes históricas de Jundiaí." Revista de história, São Paulo, 34:70 (abr./jun., 1967), 555-567.

1212 Santos, Corcino Medeiros dos. "Arrolamento das fontes históricas do Município de Lucélia." Revista de história, São Paulo, 40:81 (jan./mar., 1970), 205-220.

1213 Silva, Pedro Alberto C. "Indice dos documentos da Coleção Studart." Revista do Instituto do Ceara, 85 (jan./dez., 1967), 312-313.

1214 Sousa, José Bonifácio de. "Indice dos documentos da Coleção Studart." Revista do Instituto de Ceará, 72 (1958), 257-271.

1215 Vilar, Ana Terêsa Ferrari and Marlene Aparecida Guiselini. "Arrolamento das fontes primárias de Limeira." Revista de história, São Paulo, 39:79 (jul./set., 1969), 221-238.

CHILE

1216   Casassas Cantó, José María. "Inventario de los
        archivos del Arzobispado de Antofagasta, de la
        Prelatura de Calamas y sus respectivas parró-
        quias." Anales de la Universidad del Norte, Anto-
        fagasta, Chile, 8 (1970), 141-303.

1217   Dougnac Rodríguez, Antonio. "Indice del Archivo de
        Escribanos de Valparaiso 1660-1700." Historia,
        Santiago de Chile, 7 (1968), 227-282.

1218   Tovar Pinzón, Hermes. "Las haciendas jesuitas de
        México; índice de documentos existentes en el
        Archivo Nacional de Chile." Historia mexicana,
        20:4 (abr./jun., 1971), 563-617; 21:1 (jul./sep.,
        1971), 135-189.

COLOMBIA

1219   Academia Colombiana de Historia. "Indices de la
        Sección de Archivos y Microfilmes de la Academia
        Colombiana de Historia." Archivos, Bogotá, 1:1
        (ene./jun., 1967), 201-219; 1:2 (jul./dic., 1967),
        471-487; 3:4 (ene./dic., 1971), 255-268.

1220   _____. "Inventario del archivo del historiador
        José Manuel Restrepo." Archivos, Bogotá, 1:1
        (ene./jun., 1967), 179-199.

1221   Arboleda Llorente, José María. Catálogo general
        del Archivo Central del Cauca. Epoca de la
        Independencia. Popayán: Editorial Universidad
        del Cauca, 1969-1973. 4 v.

1222   Archivo Central del Cauca. Archivo histórico de
        Popayán (época de la Independencia); [catálogo
        general detallado del Archivo Central del Cauca,
        formado por José María Arboleda Llorente.
        Popayán: Universidad del Cauca], 1944- .

1223   Banco Central Hipotecario, Bogotá. Catálogo general
        de la Biblioteca y Hemeroteca. Bogotá: Editorial
        Ponce de León.

1224   Colombia. Departamento Nacional de Planeación.

Biblioteca.   Divulgación bibliográfica.   Bogotá,
1972. v, 505 p.

1225   Corporación Autónoma Regional de los Valles del
Magdalena y del Sinú.   Catálogo general de la
Biblioteca.   Bogotá: División de Información
Básica, Departamento de Ingeniería, 1968- .

1226   Gómez, Carmen.   Catálogo de los periódicos conservados en la Hemeroteca de la Universidad de
Antioquia.   Medellín: Universidad de Antioquia,
Escuela Interamericana de Bibliotecología, 1967.
66 p.

1227   Graff, Gary Wendell.   "Inventario de algunos archivos
locales de Colombia en los Departamentos de Santander, Norte de Santander, Antioquia y Cundina-
marca."   Anuario colombiano de historia social y
de la cultura, 5 (1970), 219-229.

1228   Horna, Hernán.   Colombian archival sources on colonial Peru.   Washington: Pan American Institute
of Geography and History, U.S. National Section,
1971.   39 p.   (Special publication, 5).

1229   Instituto Colombiano de Comercio Exterior.   Centro
de Documentación.   Catálogo del Centro de Documentación, INCOMEX: publicaciones registradas
en el periodo 1 agosto 1973-30 abril 1974..., por
José Ignacio Bohórquez C.   s.l.: s.n., 1974.
415 ℓ.

1230   Lopez Lema, Frederico.   "Inventario del Archivo
Diocesano de Santa Marta."   Archivos, Bogotá,
2:3 (ene., 1968/dic., 1970), 171-320.

1231   Medellín, Colombia.   Universidad de Antioquia.   Escuela Interamericana de Bibliotecología.   Biblioteca.   Boletín de adquisiciones.   Medellín.

1232   Riaño, Camilo.   "Inventario de los documentos corres-
pondientes al laudo arbitral en la cuestión de
límites entre Colombia y Venezuela."   Archivos,
Bogotá, 3:4 (ene./dic., 1971), 109-210.

1233   "Ultimas adquisiciones de libros extrangeros."   Boletín cultural y bibliográfico.   [Regular feature.]

CUBA

1234   Havana.   Biblioteca Nacional "José Martí."   Movi-
       miento editorial en Cuba, 1959-1960; exposición de
       libros, folletos y revistas.   La Havana, 1961.
       44 p.

1235   Lozano, Eduardo.   Cuban periodicals in the University
       of Pittsburgh Libraries.   Pittsburgh: University
       of Pittsburgh Libraries, 1971.   unpaged.

ECUADOR

1236   Ortiz Bilbao, Luis Alfonso.   "Colección 'Vacas
       Galindo.'   Cedulario.   Indice general."   Boletín
       de la Academia Nacional de la Historia, Quito,
       49:107 (ene./jun., 1966), 49-92.

EL SALVADOR

1236a "Indice de documentos del Archivo General de la
       Nación."   Repositorio, seg. época, 2:2 (nov.,
       1972), 170-187.

1236b "Indice de documentos del Archivo Histórico Nacional."
       Repositorio, seg. época, 2:2 (nov., 1972), 91-169.
       Originally appeared in the Diario oficial, 82:69 (23
       de marzo de 1917)-85:246 (30 de oct. de 1918).

FRANCE

1237   France.   Ministère de la France d'Outre-mer.   Ser-
       vice des Archives.   Inventaire de la série colonies
       C8A Martinique (correspondance a l'arrivée), par
       Etienne Taillemite.   Paris: Impr. Nationale,
       1967.   654 p.

1238   Meyer, Jean.   "Le Méxique dans les archives diplo-
       matiques et consulaires de France."   Caravelle,
       13 (1969), 109-116.

1239   Ozanam, Didier.   Les sources de l'histoire de l'Amér-
       ique Latine: guide du chercheur dans les archives
       françaises.   1.   Les Affaires étrangères.   Paris,

1963. 110 p. (Cahiers de l'Institut des Hautes
Etudes de l'Amérique Latine, 4, pt. 1).

GERMANY, EAST

1240 Germany (Democratic Republic). Staatliche Archiv-
verwaltung. Ubersicht über quellen zur geschichte
lateinamerikas in archiven der deutschen demo-
kratischen republik. Potsdam: Staatliche Archiv-
verwaltung, 1971. 122 p. (Ubersicht über quellen
zur Geschichte de Nationen. A: Lateinamerika).

GERMANY, WEST

1241 Hauschild-Thiessen, Renate and Elfriede Bachmann.
Führer durch die Quellen zur Geschichte Latein-
amerikas in der Bundesrepublik Deutschland.
Bremen: Carl Schünemann Verlag, 1972. 437 p.
(Veröffentlichungen aus dem Staatsarchiv der
Freien Hansestadt Bremen, 38).

GREAT BRITAIN

1242 Goldsmith, V. F. A short title catalogue of Spanish
and Portuguese books, 1601-1700, in the Library
of The British Museum (The British Library -
Reference Division). Folkestone: Dawsons of
Pall Mall, 1974. vi, 250 p.

1243 A Guide to manuscript sources for the history of
Latin America and the Caribbean in the British
Isles. [Edited by] Peter Walne; with a foreword
by R. A. Humphreys. London: Oxford Univer-
sity Press [for] the Institute of Latin American
Studies, University of London, 1973. xx, 580 p.

1244 Hispanic and Luso-Brazilian Councils. Canning
House Library. Canning House Library, Hispanic
Council, London: author and subject catalogue.
First supplement. Boston: G. K. Hall, 1973.
627 p.

1245 _____. Canning House Library, Luso-Brazilian
Council, London: author and subject catalogue.

First supplement. Boston: G. K. Hall, 1973.
288 p.

1246 Latin American periodicals; a union list of the li-
      braries of six British universities. London: In-
      stitute of Latin American Studies, University of
      London, 1970. 62 p. (British union catalogue of
      Latin Americana. New Latin American titles.
      Supplement 1).

1247 Oxford. University. Bodleian Library. Independent
      Mexico; a collection of Mexican pamphlets in the
      Bodleian Library. Edited by Colin Steele and
      Michael P. Costeloe. [London]: Mansell, 1973.
      xxxviii, 92 p.

1248 Vittorino, Antonio. "Documentos sobre la historia
      de Colombia existentes en el Museu Británico de
      Londres. Primera parte." Anuario colombiano
      de historia social y de la cultura, 6/7 (1971/1972),
      157-222.

GUATEMALA

1249 Guatemala (City). Museo del Libro Antiguo. Catá-
      logo del Museo del Libro Antiguo: impresos gua-
      tamaltecos de la época colonial. Guatemala:
      Editorial José Ibarra, 1971. 165 p.

GUYANA

1250 Guyana. Public Free Library. Select bibliography of
      the works of Guyanese and on Guyana, on the oc-
      casion of Guyana Week, 19-25 February 1967.
      Georgetown, 1967. 51 p.

1251 University of Guyana. Library. Catalogue of the
      A.W.B. Long Collection. Comp. by Carol Col-
      lins, Alleyne Riley and John Shinebourne. George-
      town, 1970. 12 ℓ. (Library series, 2).

1252 _____. A catalogue of the Roth collection in the
      University of Guyana Library. Compiled by Carol
      Collins. Georgetown, 1971. ii, 32 ℓ. (Library
      series, 4).

LIBRARIES/ARCHIVES   160

1253 _____. Selection of documents on Guyana. [Comp.
by Yvonne V. Stephenson]. Georgetown, 1969?
17 ℓ.

1254 _____. _____. Comp. by Claire Collins and
Yvonne V. Stephenson. Georgetown, 1969. 24 p.

ITALY

1255 Guzman, Eulalia. Manuscritos sobre México en archivos de Italia. México: [Sociedad Mexicana de
Geografía y Estadística], 1964. 428 p. (Colección de materiales para la historiografía de México, 1).

JAMAICA

1256 Mona, Jamaica. University of the West Indies. Library. Quarterly accessions list of materials relating to the West Indies. Mona, Jamaica.

JAPAN

1257 Kobe Daigaku. Keizai Keiei Kenkyujo. Catalogue of
the Latin American books. Kobe, Japan, 1970.
191 p. (Tokushu bunko mokuroku, 5).

MEXICO

1258 Banco de México. Biblioteca. Boletín mensual de
obras recibidas y catalogadas. México.

1259 Biblioteca Nacional de Antropología e Historia. Catá-
logos de la..., México. Catalogs of the National
Library of Anthropology and History, Mexico.
Boston: G. K. Hall, 1972. 10 v.

1260 Cavazos Garza, Israel. "Algunos impresos jaliscienses del siglo xix existentes en el Archivo General
del Estado de Neuvo León." Boletín del Instituto
de Investigaciones Bibliográficas, México, 4 (jul./
dic., 1970), 73-83.

1261 _____. Catálogo y síntesis de los protocolos del
Archivo Municipal de Monterrey, 1700-1725. Monterrey: Universidad Autónoma de Nuevo León,
1973. 269 p.

1262 _____. "Guía del Ramo Militar del Archivo General del Estado de Nuevo León, 1797-1850." Humanitas, 12 (1971), 227-246.

1263 Centro Intercultural de Documentación. Archivos.
Catálogo de adquisiciones. Cuernavaca, 1967- .
Issued in its Cuadernos series.

1264 Colín, Mario. Indice de documentos relativos a los
pueblos del Estado de México: ramo de Indios del
Archivo General de la Nación. México, 1968.
xv, 530 p. (Biblioteca enciclopédica del Estado
de México, 14).

1265 Galarza, Joaquín. "Un index de manuscrits picto-
graphiques mexicains: Colección de Códices del
Museo Nacional de Antropología de México."
Journal of Social Anthropology, 59 (1970), 91-105.

1266 Grajales Ramos, Gloria. Guía de documentos para
la historia de México en archivos ingleses (siglo
XIX). México: Universidad Nacional Autónoma de
México, 1969. xix, 455 p. (Instituto de Investi-
gaciones Bibliográficas. Publicaciones, 13.
Guías, 1).

1267 _____. Guía de documentos para la historia de
México existentes en la Public Record Office de
Londres (1827-1830). México: Instituto Panameri-
cano de Geografía e Historia, 1967. 50 p.

1268 Greenleaf, Richard E. and Michael C. Meyer. Research in Mexican history: topics, methodology,
sources and a practical guide to field research.
Lincoln: University of Nebraska Press, 1973.
xiii, 226 p.

1269 "Guía del ramo de cárceles y presidios." Boletín
del Archivo General de la Nación, Mexico, 2d ser.,
12:1/2 (1971), 253-262.

1270 Hutchinson, C. Alan. "Bibliographical guide to

archival collections in the Mexican states." In:
Greenleaf, Richard E. and Michael C. Meyer.
Research in Mexican history: topics, methodology,
sources, and a practical guide to field research.
Lincoln: University of Nebraska Press, 1973.
pp. 193-196.

1271 "Indice del ramo de Provincias Internas." Boletín
del Archivo General de la Nación, México, 2d
ser., 7:1/2 (1966), 813-826. A continuation; continued in subsequent issues.

1272 "Indice del ramo de reales cédulas." Boletín del
Archivo General de la Nación, México, 2d ser.,
7:1/2 (1966), 513-524.

1273 "Indice del ramo de tierras." Boletín del Archivo
General de la Nación, México, 2d ser., 7:1/2
(1966), 527-536. A continuation; continued in subsequent issues.

1274 "Información bibliográfica mensual de la Biblioteca
Abelardo L. Rodríguez, Nacional Financiera,
S.A. ..." El Mercado de valores.

1275 Lamadrid Lusarreta, Alberto A. "Guías de foras-
teros y calendarios mexicanos de los siglos XVIII
y XIX, existentes en la Biblioteca Nacional de
México." Boletín del Instituto de Investigaciones
Bibliográficas, México, 6 (1971), 9-135.

1276 López Jiménez, Eucario. Cedulario de la Nueva
Galicia. Guadalajara, Jalisco: Editorial Lex,
1971. xx, 217 ℓ.

1277 Mantecón Navasal, José Ignacio. "Inventario del
Archivo del Comisario General de las Provincias
Franciscanas de Nueva España y Filipinas, 1698."
Boletín del Instituto de Investigaciones Bibliográ-
ficas, México, 4 (jul., 1970), 263-288.

1278 Mexico (City). Ayuntamiento. Archivo. Catálogo
general del Archivo del Ayuntamiento de la Ciudad
de México, [por] Miguel Mendoza López. [Méx-
ico: Instituto Nacional de Antropología e Historia,
Seminario de Historia Urbana], 1972. 65 ℓ.
(Publicaciones, 1).

1279   Monterrey, Mexico. Instituto Tecnológico y de Estudios Superiores. Biblioteca. Catálogo abreviado de libros y folletos manuscritos en el ..., por María del Socorro del Hoyo Briones. Monterrey, 1971. viii, 64 p. (Publicaciones. Serie: Catálogos de Biblioteca, 4).

1280   Moreno, Roberto. "Guía de las obras en lenguas indígenas existentes en la Biblioteca Nacional." Boletín de la Biblioteca Nacional, México, 18: 1/2 (ene./jun., 1966), 21-210.

1281   Ongay Muza, Danilo. Indice de nombres de la Guía del Archivo de la Antigua Academia de San Carlos, 1781-1800. México, 1971. 23 p. (Anales del Instituto de Investigaciones Estéticas, UNAM, 40. Suplemento 2). Index of Guía del Archivo ..., by Justino Fernández.

1282   Palacio, Lucas de. Archivo diplomático "Lucas de Palacio" en la Biblioteca del Instituto Tecnológico y de Estudios Superiores de Monterrey, editado por Eugenio del Hoyo. Monterrey, 1968. xxix, 164 p. (Publicaciones. Serie: Catálogos de Biblioteca, 2).

1283   Parral, Mexico. Archivo. English translation of the Index to el Archivo de Hidalgo del Parral, 1631-1821. Translated by Consuelo P. Boyd. Tucson: Arizona Silhouettes, [1971]. xxxv, [2], 493 p.

1284   Río Ch., Ignacio del. "Documentos sobre las Californias que se encuentran en el Archivo Franciscano de la Biblioteca Nacional." Boletín del Instituto de Investigaciones Bibliográficas, México, 2:1 (ene./jun., 1970), 9-22.

1285   Sánchez, Andrea. "Exposición de incunables de la Biblioteca Nacional." Boletín del Instituto de Investigaciones Bibliográficas, México, 6 (1971), 201-208.

NETHERLANDS

1286   Gordon, Eric; Michael M. Hall and Hobart A. Spalding. "A survey of Brazilian and Argentine

materials at the Internationaal Instituut Voor So-
ciale Geschiedenis in Amsterdam." Latin American Research Review, 8:3 (Fall, 1973), 27-77.

1287 Meilink-Roelofz, Marie Antoinette Petronella. A survey of archives in the Netherlands pertaining to
the history of the Netherlands Antilles. The
Hague: G. P. O. , 1968. 53 p.

1288 Roessingh, M. P. H. Guide to the sources in the
Netherlands for the history of Latin America.
The Hague: Government Printing Office, 1968.
232 p. (Guide to the sources of the history of
the nations. A. Latin America, III, 2).

PARAGUAY

1289 "Documentación paraguaya." Revista paraguaya de
sociología. Regular feature listing Paraguayan
imprints acquired by the Library of the Centro
Paraguayo de Documentación Social.

PERU

1290 "Certificados de depósito de publicaciones y documentos recibidos en la Biblioteca Nacional." Boletín
de la Biblioteca Nacional, Lima. [Regular feature.]

1291 "Documentos referentes a la Biblioteca Nacional: 1822-
25, 1829." Boletín de la Biblioteca Nacional,
Lima, 25/26:59/60 (1971), 5-11.

1292 Esparaza Castillo, Norka and Alejandro Tumba Ortega.
"Selección de artículos publicados en revistas y
periódicos nacionales llegados a la Biblioteca de
enero a diciembre de 1966." Boletín de la Biblioteca Central de la Universidad Nacional Mayor
de San Marcos, 39:1/4 (1966), 131-348.

1293 Heras, Julián. "Fuentes para la historia del Convento
de Ocopa (1725-1967)." Revista histórica, Lima,
29 (1966), 137-172.

1294 Malaga Medina, Alejandro; Eusebio Quiroz Paz Soldan

and Juan Alvarez Salas. Catálogo general del
Archivo Municipal de Arequipa. Arequipa, Peru:
Universidad Nacional de San Agustin, Departamento
de Historia, Geografía y Antropología, 1974.
39 p.

1295   "Obras de reciente adquisición." Boletín de la Biblioteca Nacional, Lima. [Regular feature.]

1296   Orezzoli, Rosa Yolanda. "Catálogo unido; libros in-
gresados a las bibliotecas de la Universidad Nacional Mayor de San Marcos, de enero a diciembre de 1967." Boletín bibliográfico de la Biblioteca Central ..., 39:1/4 (1966), 359-544.

1297   Rivera Serna, Raúl. "Indice de manuscritos existentes
en la Biblioteca Nacional (15)." Boletin de la Biblioteca Nacional, Lima, 20:37/38 (1966), 22-39.
Continued in subsequent issues.

PORTUGAL

1298   Coimbra. Universidade. Biblioteca. Catálogo dos
manuscritos ... relativos ao Brasil, extractos do
catálogo de manuscritos ..., por Francisco Mor-
ais. Coimbra, 1941. 127 p.

1299   Ferreira, Carlos Alberto. Indice dos documentos
relativos à América do Sul existentes na Biblioteca da Ajuda. Rio de Janeiro: Arquivo Nacional, 1968. 153 p.

1300   _____. Inventario dos manuscritos da Biblioteca
da Ajuda referentes à América do Sul. Coimbra,
1946. 682 p.

1301   Guerra, Flávio. Alguns documentos de arquivos por-
tuguêses de interêsse para a história de Pernambuco. Indice analítico do prof. Gilberto Osório de
Andrade. Recife: Arquivo Público Estadual,
1969. 309 p.

1302   Iria, Alberto. "Inventario geral dos códices do Ar-
quivo Histórico Ultramarino apenas referentes ao
Brasil: fontes para a história luso-brasileira."
Studia, Lisbon, 18 (ago., 1966), 41-191.

1303   Souza, Antonio de.   Manuscritos do Brasil nos arqui-
       vos de Portugal e da Espanha.   Rio de Janeiro:
       Imprensa do Exército, 1969. 67 p.

PUERTO RICO

1304/6   Puerto Rico. University. Library. Publicaciones
         latinoamericanas y del Caribe incorporadas a la
         colección de la Biblioteca General. Rio Piedras,
         1971- . Bimonthly.

SPAIN

1307   Madrid. Museo Naval.   Catálogo de los documentos
       referentes a la independencia de Colombia exis-
       tentes en el Museo Naval y Archivo de Marina
       "Bazán." Madrid: Consejo Superior de Investi-
       gaciones Científicas, Instituto Histórico de Marina,
       1969. xvii, 223 p.

1308   Martínez Ortiz, José.   Documentos manuscritos y
       obras varias impresas referentes a la historia del
       Brasil, existentes en Valencia, España.   Valencia:
       Instituto de Estudios Americanistas, Institución Al-
       fonso el Magnánimo, 1969. 65 p.

1309   Melo Neto, João Cabral de.   O Arquivo das Indias
       e o Brasil; documentos para a história do Brasil
       existentes no Arquivo das Indias de Sevilha. [Rio
       de Janeiro]: Ministerio das Relações Exteriores,
       1966. 779 p.

1310   Morales Padrón, Francisco.   "Fondos relativos a las
       Antillas Menores en el Archivo de Indias, Sevilla,
       España." Caribbean studies, 6:1 (Apr., 1966),
       41-56.

1311   Nectario María, Brother.   Catálogo de los documentos
       referentes a la antigua provincia de Maracaibo,
       existentes en el Archivo General de Indias de Se-
       villa. Caracas: Instituto de Investigaciones His-
       tóricas, Universidad Católica "Andrés Bello,"
       1973. 399 p.

1312   Real Díaz, José Joaquin.   Catálogo de las cartas y

peticiones del Cabildo de San Juan Bautista de
Puerto Rico en el Archivo General de Indias:
siglos XVI-XVIII.   San Juan: Instituto de Cultura
Puertorriqueña [and] Municipio de San Juan, 1968.
311 p.

1313   Spain.   Archivo General de Indias, Sevilla.   Catálogo
de documentos del Archivo General de Indias, Sección V, Gobierno.   Audiencia de Santo Domingo
sobre la época española de Luisiana, por José de
la Peña y Cámara [et al.].   Madrid and New Or-
leans: Dirección General de Archivos y Bibliotecas de España y Loyola University, 1968.   2 v.

1314   _____.   Inventarios.   Sevilla, 1971?- .   (Direc-
ción General de Archivos y Bibliotecas.   Servicio
Nacional de Microfilm.   Publicaciones en Microfilm/
Microficha, 2-5).

1315   Spain.   Archivo Histórico Nacional, Madrid.   Inventario de la série de Gobierno de Puerto Rico,
[preparada] bajo la dirección de María Teresa de
la Peña Marazuela.   [Madrid, 1972].   294 p.
(Archivo Histórico Nacional.   Sección de Ultramar.
[Fondos] 1).

1316   _____.   Inventario de la série Fomento de Puerto
Rico, [preparado] bajo la dirección de María
Teresa de la Peña Marazuela.   [Madrid, 1972].
xi, 224 p.   (Archivo Histórico Nacional.   Sección
de Ultramar.   [Fondos] 2).

1317   Spain.   Dirección General de Archivos y Bibliotecas.
Guía de fuentes para la historia de Ibero-América
conservados en España.   Madrid: Obra publicada
bajo los auspicios de la UNESCO y del Consejo
Internacional de Archivos, 1966-1969.   2 v.   (Guía
de fuentes para la historia de las naciones.   A.
América Latina.   4.   Fuentes conservadas en España, fasc. 1, 2).

1318   Vázquez Machicado, José.   Catálogo de documentos
referentes a Potosí en el Archivo de Indias de
Sevilla.   [Potosí: Editorial "Potosí"], 1964.
xxiii, 66 p.

SCANDINAVIA

1319   Ibero-Americana; research news and principal acquisi-
       tions of documentation on Latin America in Den-
       mark, Finland, Norway and Sweden. Stockholm:
       Institute of Latin American Studies, 1971- .

1320   Mörner, Magnus. Fuentes para la historia de Ibero-
       América conservadas en Suecia; guía. Stockholm:
       Riksarkivet, 1968. 105 p.

UNITED STATES

1321   Alabama. University. Library. A catalog of the
       Yucatan Collection on microfilm in the University
       of Alabama Libraries, prepared by Marie Ballew
       Bingham. University, Ala.: University of Ala-
       bama Press, 1972. 100 p.

1322   Bingaman, Joseph W. Latin America: a survey of
       holdings at the Hoover Institution on War, Revolu-
       tion and Peace. Stanford: Hoover Institution,
       1972. vii, 96 p. (Hoover Institution survey of
       holdings, 5).

1323   Boston. Public Library. Ticknor Collection. Cata-
       logue of the Spanish library and of the Portuguese
       books bequeathed by George Ticknor to the Boston
       Public Library. Boston: G. K. Hall, 1970. xv,
       550 p. Reprint of the 1879 ed. with an appendix
       listing material acquired subsequently.

1324   Burrus, Ernest J. "Mexican historical documents in
       the Central Jesuit Archives." Manuscripta, 12:3
       (Nov., 1968), 133-161.

1325   California. State Library, Sacramento. Sutro Branch,
       San Francisco. Catalogue of Mexican pamphlets in
       the Sutro Collection, 1623-1888, with supplements,
       1605-1687. New York: Kraus Reprint Co., 1971.
       963, 290, 65 p. Reprint of the 1939-1941 ed.

1326   California. University, Berkeley. Bancroft Library.
       A guide to the manuscript collections of the Ban-
       croft Library, vol. 2: Manuscripts relating chiefly
       to Mexico and Central America, edited by George

169   LIBRARIES/ARCHIVES

P. Hammond. Berkeley: University of California
Press, 1972. ix, 294 p.

1327 California. University, Berkeley. Library. List of
Latin American acquisitions, July-Sept. 1972.
Compiled by Gaston Somoshegyi-Szokol. Berkeley,
1972. 1 v., various pagings.

1328 California. University, Riverside. Bibliography of
Ibero-American bibliographies; holdings of the
University of California at Riverside. By Betty
Jean Dunham and Diana K. Moody. Riverside,
1968. 29 ℓ.

1329 Estep, Raymond. A Latin American bibliography.
[Maxwell Air Force Base, Ala.]: Documentary
Research Division, Aerospace Studies Institute,
Air University, 1969. v, 170 p. (Documentary
research study, AU-203-66-ASI).

1330 Florida. University, Gainesville. Libraries. Catalog of the Latin American collection. Boston:
G. K. Hall, 1973. 13 v. "To be kept current
by supplements."

1331 García Zamor, Jean Claude and Gary R. Welles. A
bibliography of Latin American bibliographies related to political science in the Libraries of the
University of Texas at Austin. Austin: University
of Texas Department of Government, 1970. 13 ℓ.

1332/3 Garner, Jane. "Significant acquisitions of Latin American materials by U.S. and Canadian libraries."
In: Seminar on the Acquisition of Latin American
Library Materials, 15th, Toronto, 1971. Final
report and working papers. Washington: O.A.S.,
1971. v. 1, pp. 225-248.

1334 _____. "Significant acquisitions of Latin American
materials: decennial cumulation 1961/62-1970/71."
In: Seminar on the Acquisition of Latin American
Library Materials, 16th, Puebla, Mexico, 1971.
Final report and working papers. Washington:
O.A.S., 1973. v. 1, pp. 163-307.

1335 Garner, Richard Lyle and Donald C. Henderson.
Columbus and related family papers, 1451 to 1902:

an inventory of the Boal Collection. University
Park: The Pennsylvania State University Press,
1974. 96 p. (Pennsylvania State University
studies, 37).

1336 Geographical Association. Library. The Americas:
a list of works added to the Geographical Association Library, 1958-1968. Sheffield: Geographical
Association, 1968. 32 p. Forms a supplement
to the catalogue, North and Latin America, published in 1958.

1337 "The Goerge C. A. Boehrer Collection." Books and
libraries at the University of Kansas, 6:1 (Sept.,
1968), 1-5.

1338 Gillett, Theresa and Helen McIntyre. Catalog of
Luso-Brazilian material in the University of New
Mexico Libraries. Metuchen, N.J.: Scarecrow
Press, 1970. xiv, 961 p.

1339 Harkányi, Katalin. The Aztecs; bibliography. San
Diego, Calif., 1971. 30 ℓ.

1340 Harvard University. Library. Latin American literature; classification schedule, classified listing by
call number, author and title listing, chronological
listing. Cambridge: Distributed by Harvard University Press, 1969. 498 p. (Widener Library
shelflist, 21).

1341 Hispanic Society of America, New York. Library.
Catalogue. First supplement. Boston: G. K.
Hall, 1970. 4 v.

1342 Hodgman, Suzanne. "Microfilm projects newsletter."
In: Seminar on the Acquisition of Latin American
Library Materials. Final report and working
papers. [Regular feature; also available separ-
ately.]

1343 Indiana. University. Lilly Library. A guide to selected Latin American manuscripts in the Lilly
Library ..., by Rebecca Campbell Mirza. Bloomington, Ind.: Latin American Studies Program,
Indiana University, 1974. 58 p. (Working papers,
5).

1344 _____. Manuscritos latinoamericanos en la Biblioteca Lilly. Compilacion de Elfrieda Lang. Bloomington, Ind., 1970. 55 ℓ.

1345 _____. Mexicana en la Biblioteca Lilly (1544-1821), por Miguel de J. Solís. Bloomington, Ind.: Latin American Studies Program, 1974. 33 p. (Working papers, 6).

1346 Indiana. University. School of Music. Latin-American Music Center. Music of Latin America available at Indiana University: scores, tapes and records. Edited by Juan A. Orrego-Salas. Bloomington, 1971. vi, 412 p.

1347 Lozano, Eduardo. Cuban periodicals in the University of Pittsburgh Libraries. Pittsburgh: University of Pittsburgh Libraries, 1971. unpaged.

1348 Lujan, Herman D. A Central American bibliography of works available at the University of Kansas. Lawrence, Kansas: Program Coordination Office, Ford Cooperative Research Grant, University of Kansas, 1970. 157 ℓ.

1349 Mesa, Rosa Quintero. Argentina. New York: Bowker, 1971. xxxii, 693 p. (Latin American serial documents, 5).

1350 _____. Bolivia. New York: R. R. Bowker, 1972. xxxiii, 156 p. (Latin American serial documents, 6).

1351 _____. Brazil. Ann Arbor: University Microfilms, 1968. viii, 2, 343, 12 p. (Latin American serial documents, 2).

1352 _____. Chile. Ann Arbor, Mich.: Xerox University Microfilms, 1973. xxxii, 327 p. (Latin American serial documents, 7).

1353 _____. Colombia. Ann Arbor, Mich.: University Microfilms, 1968. xv, 137 p. (Latin American serial documents, .1).

1354 _____. Cuba. Ann Arbor: University Microfilms, 1969. xvi, 207 p. (Latin American serial documents, 3).

1355 _____. Ecuador. Ann Arbor, Mich.: Xerox University Microfilms, 1973. xxxii, 142 p. (Latin American serial documents, 8).

1356 _____. Mexico. Ann Arbor, Mich.: University Microfilms, 1970. xxi, 351 p. (Latin American serial documents, 4).

1357 _____. Paraguay. Ann Arbor, Mich.: Xerox University Microfilms, 1973. xxxii, 61 p. (Latin American serial documents, 9).

1358 _____. Peru. Ann Arbor, Mich.: Xerox University Microfilms, 1973. xxxiv, 273 p. (Latin American serial documents, 10).

1359 _____. Uruguay. Ann Arbor: Xerox University Microfilms, 1973. xxxiii, 169 p. (Latin American serial documents, 11).

1360 New Mexico. State Records Center and Archives. Guide to the microfilm of the Spanish archives of New Mexico, 1621-1821: in the Historical Services Division of the State of New Mexico Records Center and Archives, ...; Myra Ellen Jenkins, project director and editor. 2d ed. Santa Fe, 1975. 13 p.

1361 New York. Public Library. Reference Department. Dictionary catalog of the history of the Americas. First supplement. Boston: G. K. Hall, 1973. 9 v.

1362 Newberry Library, Chicago. A catalogue of the Greenlee Collection. Boston: G. K. Hall, 1970. 2 v.

1363 Oliveira Lima Library. Catalog ..., the Catholic University of America. Boston: G. K. Hall, 1970. 2 v.

1364 Pittsburgh. University. Library. Recent acquisitions in Latin American studies. Compiled by Eduardo Lozano. Pittsburgh, 197?- .

1365 Santos, Richard G. "Documentos para la historia de México en los archivos de San Antonio, Texas."

Revista de historia de América, 63/64 (1967), 143-149.

1366 Silveira de Braganza, Ronald Louis and Charlotte Oakes. The Hill Collection of Pacific voyages. San Diego: Library, University of California, 1974. 333 p.

1367 Somoshegyi-Szokol, Gaston. A selected list of reference sources for students of Latin American studies. Berkeley: Library, University of California, 1971. 38 ℓ.

1368 Spell, Lota May (Harrigan). Research materials for the study of Latin America at the University of Texas. Westport, Conn.: Greenwood Press, 1970. ix, 107 p. Reprint of 1954 ed.

1369 Syracuse University. Library. Hispanic and Luso-Brazilian serials and newspapers in Syracuse University Libraries: a checklist. Syracuse, N.Y., 1971. 74 ℓ.

1370 Texas. University at Austin. Institute of Latin American Studies. Catálogo de los manuscritos del Archivo de don Valentin Gómez Farías; obrantes en la Universidad de Texas, Colección latinoamericana. Preparado por Pablo Max Ynsfrán. México: Editorial Jus, 1968. xii, 566 p.

1371 Texas. University at Austin. Library. Latin American Collection. Catalog of the Latin American Collection. Boston: G. K. Hall, 1969. 31 v.

1372 _____ . _____ . First Supplement. Boston: G. K. Hall, 1971. 5 v.

1373 _____ . _____ . Second supplement. Boston: G. K. Hall, 1973. 3 v.

1374 _____ . Recent acquisitions for Cuba.... Nos. 1-2, 1962/March, 1967-1966/March, 1970. Austin, 1968-1971.

1375 _____ . Recent acquisitions for the Caribbean Islands (excluding Cuba) and Guyana, French Guiana and Surinam.... No. 1, 1962/March, 1967. Austin, 1968.

1376   Texas. University at Austin. Library. Latin
        American Collection. Recent acquisitions for
        Uruguay.... Nos. 1-2, 1962/March, 1967-
        April, 1968/March, 1970. Austin, 1969-1971.

1377   _____. Recent acquisitions of books etc. from
        Central America.... Nos. 1-2, 1962/1965-1966/
        March, 1970. Austin, 1967-1970.

1378   _____. Recent Argentine acquisitions.... Nos. 1-
        4, 1962/April, 1964-January, 1969/March, 1970.
        Austin, 196?-1971.

1379   _____. Recent Bolivian acquisitions.... Nos. 1-
        2, 1962/July, 1965-August, 1966/March, 1970.
        Austin, 1967-1971.

1380   _____. Recent Brazilian acquisitions.... Nos. 1-
        4, 1961/April, 1963-January, 1969/March, 1971.
        Austin, 1963-1971.

1381   _____. Recent Chilean acquisitions.... Nos. 1-
        3, 1962/1964-August, 1967/March, 1970. Austin,
        196?-1971.

1382   _____. Recent Colombian acquisitions.... Nos.
        1-3, 1962/1964-January, 1969/March, 1970. Aus-
        tin, 196?-1971.

1383   _____. Recent Ecuadorian acquisitions.... Nos.
        1-2, 1962/December, 1968-January, 1969/March,
        1970. Austin, 1970-1971.

1384   _____. Recent Mexican acquisitions.... Nos. 1-
        5, 1962/April, 1964-January, 1969/March, 1970.
        Austin, 196?-1971.

1385   _____. Recent Paraguayan acquisitions.... Nos.
        1-2, 1962/March, 1967-April, 1967/March, 1970.
        Austin, 1968-1971.

1386   _____. Recent Peruvian acquisitions.... Nos. 1-
        3, 1962/April, 1964-January, 1969/March, 1970.
        Austin, 196?-1970.

1387   _____. Recent Venezuelan acquisitions.... Nos.
        1-2, 1962/1964-August, 1965/December, 1968.
        Austin, 196?-1970.

1388 _____ . A tentative list of Mexican journals in the
field of humanities in the Latin American Collection of.... Clarice G. Neal, compiler. Austin,
1968. 136 p.

1389 Tulane University of Louisiana. Library. Catalog of
the Latin American Library. Boston: G. K. Hall,
1970. 9 v.

1390 _____ . _____ . First supplement. Boston:
G. K. Hall, 1973. 2 v.

1391 U.S. Library of Congress. Manuscript Division.
The Harkness Collection in the Library of Con-
gress; manuscripts concerning Mexico: a guide.
With selected transcriptions and translations by
J. Benedict Warren. Washington: Library of
Congress, 1974. xi, 315 p.

1392 U.S. National Archives. Materials in the National
Archives of the United States relating to the in-
dependence of Latin American nations. Washington, 1968. 19 p. (Its Publication, 68-12; Reference information papers, 45).

1393 U.S. National Archives and Records Service. Guide
to materials on Latin America in the National
Archives of the United States, by George S. Ulibarri and John P. Harrison. Washington, 1974.
xii, 489 p. "Supersedes the Guide to materials
on Latin America in the National Archives (vol.
1, 1961), compiled by John P. Harrison."

1394 _____ . Records of the Department of State relating to internal affairs of Brazil, 1910-1929. Washington, 1972. 19 p.

1395 _____ . Records of the Department of State relating to internal affairs of El Salvador, 1910-1929.
Washington, 1968. 11 p.

1396 _____ . Records of the Department of State relating to internal affairs of Peru, 1910-1929. Washington, 1969. 10 p.

1397 _____ . Records of the Department of State relating to political relations between Panama and other
states, 1910-1929. Washington, 1972. 4 p.

1398   . Records of the State Department relating to political relations between the United States and Guatemala and between Guatemala and other states, 1910-1929. Washington, 1973. 13 p.

1399 Washington University, St. Louis. Library. Research sources for Ibero-American studies: a union list of serials in the fields of humanities and social sciences held by Washington University Libraries, compiled by David S. Zubatsky. St. Louis, 1970? iii, 202 p. (Library studies, 4).

1400   .   . Supplement one: September 1969-June 1971. St. Louis, 1971. 32 p. (Library studies, 8).

1401 Wisconsin. University. Land Tenure Center. Library. Agrarian reform in Brazil; a bibliography.... Madison, 1972. 2 v. (Training and methods series, 18-19).

1402   . Bolivia: agricultura, economía y política; a bibliography, compiled by Teresa J. Anderson. Madison, 1968. 21 p. (Training and methods series, 7).

1403   .   . Supplement 1: a bibliography of materials dealing with Bolivia in the Library.... Madison, 1970. 9 p. (Training and methods series, 7, Supplement 1).

1404   .   . Supplement 2.... Madison, 1972. 10 p. (Training and methods series, 7, Supplement 2).

1405   . Chile's agricultural economy; a bibliography.... Madison, 1970. 65 p. (Training and methods series, 12).

1406   .   . Supplement. Madison, 1971. 20 p. (Training and methods series, 12, Supplement).

1407   . Colombia: background and trends; a bibliography.... Madison, 1969. 56 p. (Training and methods series, 9).

1408   Wisconsin.   University.   Land Tenure Center.   Library.   Colombia: background and trends; a bibliography....   Supplement.   Madison, 1971.   34 p. (Training and methods series, 9, Supplement).

1409   _____.   Economic aspects of agricultural development in Ecuador; a bibliography....   Madison, 1972.   28 p.   (Training and methods series, 21).

1410   _____.   Land tenure and agrarian reform in Mexico; a bibliography....   Madison, 1970.   51 p. (Training and methods series, 10).

1411   _____.   _____.   Supplement.   Madison, 1971. 18 p.   (Training and methods series, 10, Supplement).

1412   _____.   Peru: land and people; a bibliography.... Madison, 1971.   71 p.   (Training and methods series, 15).

1413   _____.   _____.   Supplement.   Madison, 1972. 20 p.   (Training and methods series, 15, Supplement).

1414   _____.   Rural development in Venezuela and the Guianas; a bibliography.   Madison, 1972.   67 p. (Training and methods series, 20).

1415   _____.   Sources for legal and social science research on Latin America: land tenure and agrarian reform, compiled by Teresa J. Anderson. Madison, 1970.   34 p.   (Training and methods series, 11).

URUGUAY

1416   Montevideo.   Universidad de la República.   Catálogo colectivo de publicaciones periódicas existentes en las bibliotecas universitarias del Uruguay.   Montevideo, 1970.   2 v.

1417   Uruguay.   Archivo General de la Nación.   Inventario de los fondos documentales del Archivo General de la Nación.   Montevideo, 1965-1966.   2 v.

VATICAN

1418   Bandelier, Adolph Francis Alphonse.   A history of the
       Southwest; a study of the civilization and conversion
       of the Indians in Southwestern United States and
       Northwestern Mexico from earliest times to 1700.
       Edited by Ernest J. Burrus.   Volume 1: A cata-
       logue of the Bandelier Collection in the Vatican
       Library.   Rome: Jesuit Historical Institute; St.
       Louis: St. Louis University, 1969.

1419   Pasztor, Lajos.   Guida delle fonti per la storia dell'
       America latina negli archivi della santa sede e
       negli archivi ecclesiastici d'Italia.   Citta del Va-
       ticano: Archivio Vaticano, 1970.   vi, 665 p.
       (Collectanea, 2).

VENEZUELA

1420   Academia Nacional de la Historia, Caracas.   Biblio-
       teca.   Catálogo razonado de los libros de los sig-
       los xv, xvi y xvii de la ..., por Agustín Millares
       Carlo.   Prólogo por Mario Briceño Perozo.   Cara-
       cas, 1969.   xiv, 181 p.

1421   Alvarez González, Margarita.   "Catálogo de la exposi-
       ción de obras referentes a bibliotecología y otros
       temas conexos presentada por la Biblioteca General
       de la Universidad del Zulia con motiva del dia de
       Bibliotecologo."   Boletín de la Biblioteca General
       de la Universidad del Zulia, 10/11:17/18 (ag. 1970/
       jun., 1971), 397-428.

1422   "Bibliografía de la Biblioteca Nacional [Caracas]."
       Bibliografía venezolana, 1:3 (jul./sept., 1970),
       41-46.

1423   Bibliografía venezolana.   Año 1, núm. 1- .   Caracas:
       Biblioteca Nacional, 1970- .

1424   Briceño Perozo, Mario.   El Archivo de la Academia
       Nacional de la Historia, Caracas.   Caracas: El
       Cojo, 1966.   43 p.

1425   Bruni Celli, Blas.   "El archivo de Manuel Felipe
       Tovar."   Boletín de la Academia Nacional de la

Historia, Caracas, 51: 203 (jul./sept., 1968), 416-436.

1426 Caracas. Casa Natal de Simón Bolívar. Archivo. Indice de la reproducción [en microfilm del Archivo]. Caracas, 1961. 23 p.

1427 Cumaná, Venezuela. Universidad de Oriente. Nucleo de Sucre. Biblioteca. Catálogo de publicaciones periódicas (existentes hasta enero de 1971). Cumaná, 1971. 138 p.

1428 Fundación La Salle de Ciencias Naturales, Caracas. Biblioteca. Sección de Antropología. Catálogo de revistas y publicaciones seriadas. Caracas, 1972.

1429 Fundación para el Desarrollo de la Comunidad y Fomento Municipal, Caracas. Biblioteca. Catálogo general. Caracas, 1971- .

1430 "Indice de la Colección Maracaibo." Boletín de la Biblioteca de la Universidad de Zulia, Maracaibo, 8/9:13/14 (ago./jun., 1968/1969), 95-167.

1431 "Indice de la reproducción en microfilme del Archivo del Libertador." Revista de la Sociedad Bolivariana de Venezuela, 28:95 (24 de jul., 1968), 279-308.

1432 "Indices [del Archivo General de la Nación, Caracas]." Boletín del Archivo General de la Nación, 56:210 (ene./jun., 1966), 84-195. [Regular feature.]

1433 Maracaibo. Consejo. Archivo del Consejo de Maracaibo. Expedientes diversos I-II. Prólogo, índice y extractos por Agustín Millares Carlo. Maracaibo, Venezuela: Centro de Historia del Estado Zulia, 1968. 196 p.

1434 Marco Dorta, Enrique. Materiales para la historia de la cultura en Venezuela, 1523-1828: documentos del Archivo General de Indias de Sevilla. Caracas: Fundación John Boulton, 1967. 547 p.

1435 Millares Carlo, Agustín. Estudio bibliográfico de los archivos venezolanos y extranjeros de interés

para la historia de Venezuela.   Caracas: Archivo
General de la Nación, 1971.   367 p.   (Biblioteca
venezolana de historia, 12).

WEST INDIES

1436   Baker, Edward Cecil.   A guide to records in the
Windward Islands.   Oxford, England: published
by the University of the West Indies by Blackwell,
1968.   xii, 95 p.

1437   British Development Division in the Caribbean.   A
catalogue of West Indian publications available in
the Library.   Bridgetown, Barbados, 1970.   147 p.

1438   Central Library of Trinidad and Tobago.   West Indian
Reference Section.   Bibliography: annual accessions.   Port-of-Spain.

1439   St. Augustine, Trinidad.   University of the West Indies.   The Library.   Recent acquisitions of Trinidad and Tobago imprints.   No. 1- .   Apr.
1973- .   St. Augustine.

LIBRARY SCIENCE

1440   Abella, Rosa; Amelia Mederos and Haydée Piedracueva.   Index to the SALALM Progress Reports,
1956-1970.   Amherst, Mass.:   SALALM Secretariat, 1975.   vii, 163 p.

1441   Bibliografía bibliotecológica argentina.   Bahia Blanca:
Centro de Documentación Bibliotecológica, Universidad Nacional del Sur.   A continuation of Bibliografía bibliotecólogica argentina by Nicolás Matijevic.

1442   Bibliografía sobre documentación e información, compilada por Romalinda Ambruster et al. ... La
Habana: Departamento de Publicaciones, Biblioteca
Nacional José Martí, 1970.   v, 35 ℓ.   (Folletos
de divulgación técnica y científica, 33).

1443   Buenos Aires.   Universidad.   Grupo de Documentación

181   LIBRARY SCIENCE

Mecanizada. Bibliografía de informática. Buenos
Aires: Instituto Bibliotecológico, 1969. 16 ℓ.
(Publicación, 34/69).

1444 Buenos Aires. Universidad. Instituto Bibliotecológico.
Bibliografía: Seminario de Introducción al Procesamiento de Datos Aplicado a la Bibliotecología
y Documentación. Buenos Aires, 1971. 11 ℓ.

1445 _____. Catálogo de la Biblioteca: publicaciones
periódicas. Buenos Aires, 1967. xiii, 48 p.
(Publicación, 24).

1446 _____. Contribución a la bibliografía sobre planeamiento de los servicios bibliotecarios. Buenos
Aires, 1967. 10 ℓ.

1447 Carvalho, Maria de Lourdes Borges de; Maria Helena
de Andrade Magalhães and Maria Luiza Alphonsus
de Guimaraens Ferreira. "Ensino da ciência de
informação; bibliografia analítica." Revista da
Escola de Biblioteconomia da Universidade Federal
de Minas Gerais, 3:1 (mar., 1974), 107-130.

1448 Dardón Córdova, Gonzalo. Bibliografía sobre métodos
y tecnicas de investigación. 4. ed. aumentada.
Guatemala: Biblioteca Central, Universidad de San
Carlos de Guatemala, 1973. ii, 44 ℓ. (Guía bibliográfica, 2).

1449 Florén Lozano, Luis. Bibliografía bibliotecológica
bibliográfica y de obras de referencia colombianas
publicadas en 1971. Medellín: Universidad de Antioquia, Escuela Interamericana de Bibliotecología,
1972. 33 ℓ.

1450 _____. Bibliografía bibliotecológica bibliográfica y
de obras de referencia colombianas publicadas en
1972. Medellín: Universidad de Antioquia, Escuela Interamericana de Bibliotecología, 1974.
39 ℓ.

1451 Kinard, Sammy Rebecca. Working papers of the
Seminars on the Acquisition of Latin American
Library Materials: list and index. 2d rev.
Washington: O.A.S., 1971. 31 p. (Cuadernos
bibliotecológicos, 22, rev. 2).

1452 Lozano Rivera, Uriel. Resúmenes de tesis presenta-
      das por los candidatos al título de licenciado en
      bibliotecología de 1960-1970. Medellín: Colombia,
      Editorial Universidad de Antioquia, 1972. xiii,
      126 ℓ. (Escuela Interamericana de Bibliotecología.
      Publicaciones. Bibliografías, 19).

1453 Matijevic, Nicolás. Bibliografía bibliotecológica argen-
      tina (hasta 1967). Bahía Blanca, Arg.: Centro
      de Documentación Bibliotecológica, Universidad Na-
      cional del Sur, 1969. xii, 354 p.

1454 Musso Ambrosi, Luis Alberto. Bibliografía biblio-
      tecológica y bibliográfica del Uruguay, 1964-1969.
      Montevideo: Centro de Estudios del Pasado Uru-
      guayo, 1970. 49 p. Updates the author's Biblio-
      grafía de bibliografías uruguayas (1964) and Biblio-
      grafía bibliotecológica del Uruguay (1964).

1455 Peralta, Atilio. Bibliografía bibliotecológica argentina,
      1968-1969. Bahía Blanca, Argentina: Universidad
      Nacional del Sur, 1971. 50 p.

1456 Seminario de Introducción al Procesamiento de Datos
      Aplicados a la Bibliotecología y Documentación, 2d,
      Buenos Aires, 1971. Bibliografía para el Semin-
      ario de Introducción al Procesamiento de Datos Ap-
      licados a la Bibliotecología y Documentación.
      Buenos Aires: Universidad, Instituto Bibliotecoló-
      gico, 1971. 11 ℓ.

                           MAPS

1457 Antioquia, Colombia (Dept.). Departamento Adminis-
      trativo de Planeación. Indice cartográfico: ori-
      ginales, copias, mapas. Medellín, 1969. 37 ℓ.

1458 Bernson, Alexander. "Panama: a bibliography of 20th
      century general maps and atlases of the Republic of
      Panama in the Library of Congress." Bulletin
      (Special Libraries Association, Geography and Map
      Division), 75 (Mar., 1969), 21-25.

1459 Calderón Quijano, José Antonio. "Nueva cartografía
      de los puertos de Acapulco, Campeche y Veracruz."

Estudios de historia novohispana, 4 (1971), 59-
103.

1460 _____. Nueva cartografía de los puertos de Aca-
pulco, Campeche y Veracruz. Sevilla: Escuela de
Estudios Hispanoamericanos, 1969. 49 p. (Publicaciones, 194; Colección Anuario, 171).

1461 Chile. Instituto Geográfico Militar. Catálogo de
mapas y cartas para la venta. Santiago de Chile.

1462 Culebra de Soberanes, Cecilia. Catálogo de mapas
existentes en la Biblioteca de El Colegio de México. México: El Colegio de México, 1972.
39 ℓ. (Apuntes para el estudiante, 7).

1463 Drenikoff, Ivan. Mapas antiguos de Venezuela, graba-
dos e impresos antes de 1800 con la reproducción
del primer mapa impreso en Venezuela y de mapas
antiguos. Caracas: Ediciones del Congreso de la
República, 1971. 57 p.

1464 Estación Experimental Agropecuaria Pergamino. Centro Documental. Catálogo de la colección cartográ-
fica del Centro Documental. Pergamino, Arg.,
1970. 268 p. (Serie bibliográfica, 52).

1465 González, Julio. Catálogo de mapas y planos de Santo
Domingo. Madrid: Dirección General de Archivos
y Bibliotecas, 1973. 447 p.

1466 Jáuregui O., Ernesto. Mapas y planos contemporán-
eos de México. México: Universidad Nacional
Autónoma de México, Instituto de Investigaciones
Sociales, 1968. 132 p.

1467 Kapp, Kit S. The early maps of Panama up to 1865.
North Bend, Ohio: K. S. Kapp Publications, 1971.
31 p.

1468 _____. The early maps of Colombia up to 1850.
London: Map Collectors' Circle, 1971. 32 p.
(Map Collectors' series, 8th vol., no. 77).

1469 _____. The printed maps of Jamaica up to 1825.
Kingston, Jamaica: Bolívar Press, 1968. 36 p.

1470 Koeman, Cornelis. Bibliography of printed maps of Surinam, 1671-1971. Amsterdam: Theatrum Orbis Terrarum, 1973. 156 p.

1471 Monteiro, Palmyra V. M. A catalogue of Latin American flat maps, 1926-1964. Austin: Institute of Latin American Studies, University of Texas, 1967-1969. 2v. (Guides and bibliographies series, 2).

1472 Spain. Archivo General de Indias, Seville. Catálogo de mapas y planos de Venezuela. Compilado por Julio González. Madrid: Dirección General de Archivos y Bibliotecas, 1968. 157 p.

1473 Turco Greco, Carlos A. Catálogo cartográfico de la República Argentina. Buenos Aires: Consejo Nacional de Investigaciones Científicas y Técnicas, Editorial Universitaria de Buenos Aires, 1967. 262 ℓ.

1474 Valderrama G., Lucila. "Breve catálogo do mapas del Perú y América existentes en algunas bibliotecas de Madrid." Boletín de la Biblioteca Nacional, Peru, 23:49/50 (1969), 23-36.

MASS MEDIA

1475 Aidar, Ivete; M. Christina Barbosa de Almeida and Walter Graeber. Indices de periódicos correntes em comunicações e artes. v. 1- . Out. 1970- . São Paulo: Escola de Comunicações e Artes.

1476 Alba Robayo, Vicente and Hernán Rincón Rincón. Latinoamérica y la comunicación social; inventario bibliográfico. Bogotá, 1971. 25 p.

1477 Brazil. Serviço de Estatística da Educação e Cultura, Imprensa periódica, 1967. Brasília, 1967. iii, 109 ℓ.

1478 Exposição da Imprensa Universitária, 1st., São Paulo, 1972. Primeira exposição da imprensa universitária 1972. Brasília: Ministerio da Educação e Cultura, Instituto Nacional do Livro, 1972. 202 p.

1479 Feuereisen, Fritz and Ernst Schmacke. Die Presse in Lateinamerika: ein Handbuch für Wirtschaft und Werbung. The Press in Latin America: a hand-

book for Economics and advertising. 2. Aufl.
München: Verlag Dokumentation, 1973. 268 p.

1480 Gardner, Mary A. The press of Latin America: a
tentative and selected bibliography in Spanish and
Portuguese. Austin: Institute of Latin American
Studies, University of Texas, 1973. viii, 34 p.
(Guides and bibliographies, 4).

1481 "Indice analítico del Boletín del Instituto de Investiga-
ciones de Prensa, 1 (1967)." In: Venezuela.
Universidad Central, Caracas. Escuela de Bibliote-
conomía y Archivos. Catálogo bibliográfico de la
Facultad de Humanidades y Educación, 1948-1968.
Caracas, 1969. pp. 301-303.

1482 Indice corrente de comunicações. Set. 1970- . São
Paulo: Universidade de São Paulo, Departamento
de Biblioteconomia e Documentação.

1483 Melo, José Marques de. "Bibliografia brasileira de
editoração." Revista de comunicação social, 1:2
(1971), 45-52.

1484 _____. Bibliografia brasileira de pesquisa em comunicação. São Paulo: Universidade de São
Paulo, Departamento de Journalismo, 1969. 45 ℓ.

1485 Pereira, Godofredo. "Comunicação: roteiro bibliográfico." Revista de comunicação social, 1:1
(1971), 75-95.

1486 Ramírez Vargas, María Teresa. Documentación per-
iodística de Bogotá. Bogotá: Fundación Universidad de América, Escuela de Ciencias de la Comunicación Social, 1973. xiv, 129 ℓ.

1487 Rio de Janeiro. Biblioteca Nacional. Hipólito José de
Costa e a imprensa no Brasil: Catálogo da exposição
organizada pela Seção da Exposições e inaugurada
em 1974. Rio de Janeiro: Biblioteca Nacional, Divisão de Publicações e Divulgação, 1974. 41 p.

1488 São Paulo, Brazil (City). Universidade. Departamento de Biblioteconomia e Documentação. Disciplina Referência e Bibliografia. Bibliografia
sôbre censura e liberdade de imprensa para II Semana de Estudos de Jornalismo, do Departamento

de Jornalismo e Editoração da Escola de Comunicações e Artes da USP. São Paulo: Departamento de Jornalismo e Editoração, 1970. 10 ℓ. (Série Biblioteconomia e documentação, 1).

1489 Universidad Centroamericana, Managua. Instituto de Historia. Catálogo de la exposición "Treinta años de periodismo en Nicaragua, 1830-1860." Managua, 1971. 264 p.

MUSIC

1490 Aretz, Isabel. "Bibliografía final del artículo de ... 'La etnomusicología en Venezuela' (Publicado en este mismo 'Boletín' en el Num. 55 de septiembre de 1966)." Boletín interamericano de música, 56 (nov., 1966), 3-34.

1491 "Bibliografía reciente venezolana sobre etnomusicología y folklore." Boletín bibliográfico de antropología americana, 31 (1968), 56-57.

1492 U.S. Library of Congress. Music Division. Bibliography of Latin American folk music. Compiled by Gilbert Chase. New York: AMS Press, 1972. ix, 141 p. Reprint of 1942 ed.

PERIODICALS

1493 Aliaga de Vizcarra, Irma. Guía de publicaciones periódicas agrícolas y conexas de Bolivia. La Paz: Sociedad de Ingenieros Agrónomos de Bolivia, 1968. 2, 11 ℓ. (Boletín bibliográfico, 8).

1494 Amaral, Antônio Barreto do. "Nossas revistas de cultura; ensaio histórico-literário." Revista do Arquivo Municipal (São Paulo), 174 (jul./set., 1968), 127-175.

1495 Arboleda Sepúlveda, O. and A. Alvear. Catálogo de publicaciones periódicas de la Biblioteca Conmemorativa Orton. 2a. ed. rev. Turrialba, Costa Rica: Instituto Interamericano de Ciencias Agrícolas, Biblioteca y Servicio de Documentación, 1970. 285 p. (IICA. Bibliotecología y documentación, 6).

1496 Azevedo, Aroldo de. "Jornais de Lorena (1870-1960)."
Revista de história (São Paulo), 40:81 (jan./mar.,
1970), 199-204.

1497 Birkos, Alexander S. and Lewis A. Tambs. Latin
American studies. Kent, Ohio: Kent State University Press, 1971. 359 p. (Academic writer's
guide to periodicals, 1).

1498 Cáceres Ramos, Hugo. Publicaciones periódicas y
seriadas agrícolas de América Latina; una guía
corriente. Turrialba, Costa Rica: Instituto Interamericano de Ciencias Agrícolas, Centro Interamericano de Documentación e Información Agrícola, 1971. 69 p. (IICA. Bibliotecología y documentación, 19).

1499 Camargo, Aureo de Almeida. "Imprensa amparense:
jornais, revistas, almanaques, poliantéias de
1871 a nossos dias." Revista de história (São
Paulo), 36:74 (abr./jun., 1968), 475-532.

1500 Centro Internacional de Agricultura Tropical. Catálogo do publicaciones periódicas de la Biblioteca
del CIAT. Cali, 1974. 125 p.

1501 Centro Nacional de Información y Documentación.
Catálogo colectivo nacional de publicaciones periódicas. Santiago, Chile: CENID, 1968.

1502 Cerutti, Franco. "Apuntes sobre el periodismo antiguo en Nicaragua; otras adiciones al fichero
Meléndez Chaverry." Revista conservadora del
pensamiento centroamericano, 137 (abr., 1971),
57-64.

1503 _____. "Contribución a un fichero de la prensa
periódica nicaragüense." Revista del pensamiento
centroamericano, 29:143 (ag., 1972), 1-56 [i.e.
43-98].

1504 Colombia. Departamento Administrativo Nacional de
Estadística. División de Información, Publica-
ciones y Biblioteca. Publicaciones periódicas en
Colombia. Bogotá, 19??- .

1505 Cordeiro, Daniel Raposo. "A checklist of newsletters

pertaining to Latin American and Iberian studies in the United States." Latin American Research Review, 7:2 (Summer, 1972), 143-147.

1506 "Cuban periodicals." Cuban studies newsletter, 2:1 (Nov., 1971), 26-28.

1507 "Cuban periodicals, 1959-1970." Cuban studies newsletter, 1:2 (May, 1971), 2-12.

1508 Dávila, Mauro. Arqueo hemerográfico de la Mérida (Siglo XIX). Mérida, Venezuela: Centro de Investigaciones Literárias, Universidad de los Andes, 1972. vii, 214 p. (Serie bibliográfica, 4).

1509 Fernández Esquivel, Rosa María. Las publicaciones oficiales de México; guía de publicaciones periódicas y seriadas, 1937-1967. México, 1967. 269 p. (UNAM Seminario de Investigaciones Bibliográficas. Publicaciones. Serie B: Bibliografía, 4).

1510 Ferreira Sobral, Eduardo F. Publicaciones periódicas argentinas, 1781-1969. Buenos Aires: Ministerio de Agricultura y Ganadería de la Nación, 1971- .

1511 Foster, David William and Virginia Ramos Foster. "Bibliografía anotada de revistas de actualidad dentro del campo de la literatura y de interés para los hispanistas." La Torre, 18:67 (ene./mar., 1970), 125-147.

1512 Havana. Biblioteca Nacional José Martí. Departamento de Hemeroteca e Información de Humanidades. Indices de las revistas cubanas. Bajo la responsabilidad de Aleida Domínguez Alfonso et al. La Habana, 1969- . V. 1: Verbum; Espuela de plata; Nadie parecía; Clavileño; Poeta; Orígenes; Ciclón.

1513 Hernández de Caldas, Angela and Zoila Guayasamín de López. Publicaciones periódicas bioagrícolas latinoamericanas. 3. ed. Pasto, Colombia, 1968. 118 ℓ. (Universidad de Nariño. Instituto Tecnológico Agrícola. Biblioteca. Serie bibliográfica, 5).

1514 Indice general de publicaciones periódicas cubanas.
      La Habana: Biblioteca Nacional José Martí,
      1970?- .

1515 Inter-American Institute of Agricultural Sciences.
      Orton Memorial Library. Catálogo de publica-
      ciones periódicas de la Biblioteca Conmemorativa
      Orton. 2. ed. rev. Turrialba, Costa Rica:
      IICA, 1971. 285 p. (Colección Biblioteca y docu-
      mentación, 6).

1516 Lombardi, Mary. Brazilian serial documents: a se-
      lective and annotated guide. Bloomington: Indiana
      University Press, 1974. xxxvii, 445 p.

1517 Márquez M., Orfila and B. Gutiérrez. Guía de pub-
      licaciones periódicas agrícolas de Venezuela.
      Maracay: Oficina de Comunicaciones Agrícolas y
      Fondo Nacional de Investigaciones Agropecuarias,
      1972. 34 p.

1518 Maison des sciences de l'homme, Paris. Service
      d'echange d'informations scientifiques. Liste mon-
      diale des périodiques spécialisés. Amérique
      latine. Paris: Mouton, 1974. 186 p. (Its Pub-
      lications. Série C: Catalogues et inventaires,
      5).

1519 Menotti Spósito, Emilio. La prensa en el estado
      Mérida. Centenario del periodismo merideño;
      nómina de las revistas y periódicos que vieron a
      la luz en el estado Mérida, desde 1840 hasta
      1950. Mérida, 1951. 44 p. (Publicaciones de la
      Dirección de Cultura de la Universidad de los
      Andes, 12).

1520 Montiel Argüello, Alejandro. "Adiciones al 'Fichero
      del periodismo antiguo de Nicaragua' del Lic.
      Carlos Meléndez Chaverry." Revista conservadora
      del pensamiento centroamericano, 127 (abr., 1971),
      53-54.

1521 Pallais Lacayo, Mauricio. "Correcciones y ampliaci-
      ones al 'Fichero del periodismo antiguo de Nicara-
      gua' del Lic. Carlos Meléndez Chaverry." Re-
      vista conservadora del pensamiento centroameri-
      cano, 127 (abr., 1971), 44-56.

1522 Pasto, Colombia. Universidad de Nariño. Instituto
      Tecnológico Agrícola. Biblioteca. Hemeroteca.
      Publicaciones periódicas recibidas en la Hemero-
      teca del Instituto Tecnológico Agrícola por Zoila
      Guayasamín de López. Pasto, 1968. 142 ℓ.
      (Serie Bibliográfica, 6).

1523 Pons Espinosa, Olga and Marcia Oviedo P. Catálogo
      colectivo de publicaciones periódicas existentes en
      las bibliotecas agrícolas del Ecuador. Quito:
      Asociación Interamericana de Bibliotecarios y
      Documentalistas Agrícolas, Filial del Ecuador,
      1973. 285 p.

1524 Publicaciones periodicas argentinas. Publicaciones de
      Buenos Aires. 1- . 1971- . Buenos Aires:
      F. García Cambeiro.

1525 Quiros, Bernabe. "Bibliografía de periódicos costar-
      ricenses." Memoria de la Secretaría de Instruc-
      ción Pública (1897), 145-156.

1526 Rosinha, Raul C. Periódicos brasileiros de agricul-
      tura, Brasília: Departamento Nacional de Pes-
      quisa Agropecuária, 1973. 48 p.

1527 Sant'Anna, Eurydice Pires de. Catálogo coletivo re-
      gional de periódicos da Bahia. Salvador: Univer-
      sidade Federal e Fundação Gonçalo Moniz, 1969.
      427 p.

1528 São Paulo, Brazil (City). Universidade. Biblioteca
      Central. Catálogo das publicações periódicas da
      Universidade de São Paulo. Compilado por Maria
      de Lourdes Cintra de Camargo. São Paulo: Bib-
      lioteca Central, 1968- .

1529 Silva Montañés, Ismael. Algunos papeles periódicos
      venezolanos, 1808-1830. Caracas: Amazonas
      Artes Gráficas, 1971. 134 p.

1530 Vega Bolaños, Andrés. "Adiciones al 'Fichero del
      periodismo antiguo de Nicaragua' del Lic. Carlos
      Meléndez Chaverry." Revista conservadora del
      pensamiento centroamericano, 133 (oct., 1971),
      33-41.

191 PERIODICALS

1531 Zubatsky, David S. "A bibliography of cumulative indexes of Latin American journals of the XIX and XX
centuries. Humanities and social sciences." Revista de historia de América, 70 (jul./dic., 1970),
421-469.

1532 _____. "A bibliography of cumulative indexes to
Hispanic American language and literary reviews
of the 19th and 20th centuries." Inter-American
review of bibliography, 20:1 (Jan./Mar., 1970),
28-57.

PHILOSOPHY

1533 Battistella, Ernesto. "Bibliografía didáctica sobre
lógica simbólica." Boletín de la Biblioteca General de la Universidad del Zulia, 9/10:15/16 (jul.,
1969/jul., 1970), 229-237.

1534 Bibliografía filosófica mexicana. año 1- . 1968- .
México: Instituto de Investigaciones Bibliográficas
with the Instituto de Investigaciones Filosóficas,
Universidad Autónoma de México, 1968- .

1535 Buenos Aires. Universidad. Instituto Bibliotecológico.
Bibliografía filosófica del siglo XX; catálogo de la
exposición bibliográfica internacional de la filosofía del siglo XX. Buenos Aires: Ediciones Peu-
ser, 1952. 465 p.

1536 Redmond, Walter Bernard. Bibliography of the philosophy in the Iberian colonies of America. The
Hague: Nijhoff, 1972. xiv, 175 p. (International
archives of the history of ideas, 51).

POLITICAL SCIENCE

GENERAL

1537 Bibliografía de "Relaciones iglesia-estado en América
Latina." Madrid: Ciudad Universitaria, Centro
de Información y Sociología de la OCSHA, n.d.
17 p. (Boletín bibliográfico iberoamericano).

1538 Bibliografía sobre "Los militares en América Latina."
      Madrid: Ciudad Universitaria, Centro de Informa-
      ción y Sociología de la OCSHA, n.d. 17 p.
      (Boletín bibliográfico iberoamericano).

1539 Chilcote, Ronald H. Revolution and structural change
      in Latin America; a bibliography on ideology, de-
      velopment, and the radical left (1930-1965). Stan-
      ford, Calif.: Hoover Institution on War, Revolu-
      tion and Peace, Stanford University, 1970. 2 v.
      (Hoover Institution bibliographical series, 40).

1540 Childs, James Bennett. "Forty years of Latin Ameri-
      can document bibliography." Herald of Library
      Science, 7:2 (Apr., 1968), 71-78.

1541 Cuban guerrilla training centers and Radio Havana: a
      selected bibliography, by Jon D. Cozean et al.
      Washington: American University, Center for Re-
      search in Social Systems, 1968. iv, 36 p.

1542 Einaudi, Luigi R. and Herbert Goldhamer. "An an-
      notated bibliography of Latin American military
      journals." Latin American research review, 2:2
      (Spring, 1967), 95-122.

1543 Hernández de Caldas, Angela and Susan Casement.
      Bibliografía sobre política tecnológica. Bogotá:
      Cámara de Comercio de Bogotá, Centro de Infor-
      matica Económica, Departamento de Documenta-
      ción, 1974. 100 ℓ.

1544 "Inventario de los estudios en ciencias sociales sobre
      América Latina. Política." Aportes. [Regular
      feature.]

1545 La Riva, Hernán. Politología: guía bibliográfica
      básica. Caracas: Universidad Central de Venezue-
      la, Instituto de Estudios Políticos, 1972.

1546 Lindenberg, Klaus. Fuerzas armadas y política en
      América Latina: bibliografía selecta. Santiago
      de Chile: Instituto Latinoamericano de Investiga-
      ciones Sociales, 1972. 199 p.

1547 Mesa, Rosa Quintero. "Bibliography of organization
      manuals and other sources of information on

governmental organizations of the countries of
Latin America." In: Seminar on the Acquisition
of Latin American Library Materials, 15th,
Toronto, 1970. Final report and working papers.
Washington: O. A. S., 1971. v. 2, pp. 257-276.

1548 Nunn, Frederick M. "The Latin American military
establishment: some thoughts on the origins of
its socio-political role and an illustrative bibliographical essay." The Americas; a quarterly review of Inter-American cultural history, 28:2
(Oct., 1971), 135-151.

1549 Pastorales de los obispos latinoamericanos sobre
cuestiones político-sociales. Madrid: Ciudad
Universitaria, Centro de Información y Sociología
de la OCSHA, n. d. (Boletín bibliográfico iberoamericano).

1550 Russell, Charles A.; James A. Miller and Robert E.
Hildner. "The urban guerrilla in Latin America:
a select bibliography." Latin American Research
Review, 9:1 (Spring, 1974), 37-79.

1551 Staropolsky, Frida and Guillermo Boils. "Bibliografía sobre el militarismo en América Latina."
Revista mexicana de ciencia política, 16:59 (ene./
mar., 1970), 85-121.

1552 Velasco, Gustavo R. Bibliografía de la libertad. 2.
ed. México: Instituto de Investigaciones Sociales
y Económicas, 1972.

ARGENTINA

1553 Bibliografía sobre el peronismo. Buenos Aires:
Cultura Popular, 1972. 15, v ℓ.

1554 Ferrari, Gustavo. "Bibliografía de base sobre política exterior argentina." Boletín del Instituto de
Historia Argentina "Doctor Emilio Ravignani," 2a.
serie, 14/15:24/25 (1970/1971), 74-97.

1555 Russell, Charles A.; James F. Schenkel and James
A. Miller. "Urban guerrillas in Argentina: a
select bibliography." Latin American Research
Review, 9:3 (Fall, 1974), 53-89.

BOLIVIA

1556 Siles Guevara, Juan. "Cambios en Bolivia; bibliografía selecta de ciencias sociales." Aportes, 17 (jul., 1970), 121-132.

BRAZIL

1557 Cooperation in Documentation and Communication. Bibliographical notes for understanding the Brazilian model: political repression and economic expansion. Edited by Mary Riesch and Harry Strharsky. Washington: CoDoC International Secretariat, 1974. vi, 72 p. (Common catalogue, 2).

CHILE

1558 Bibliografía sobre "Chile y el socialismo." Madrid: Ciudad Universitaria, Centro de Información y Sociología de la OCSHA, n.d., 17 p. (Boletín bibliográfico iberoamericano).

1559 Chile. Centro Nacional de Información y Documentación. Bibliografía de política científica. Santiago de Chile, 1972. 81 p. (Serie Bibliográfica, 1).

1560 "Chile: the coup d'état; political refugees." IDOC bulletin, 15/16 (Jan./Feb., 1974), 16-19.

COLOMBIA

1561 Bibliografía oficial colombiana. no. 1- . 1964- . Medellín: Escuela Interamericana de Bibliotecología.

1562 Ramsey, Russell W. "Critical bibliography on 'La Violencia en Colombia'; insurrection, rebellion, riots, and revolutionary actions, 1956-1965. Latin American research review, 8:1 (Spring, 1973), 3-44.

CUBA

1563 Montenegro González, Augusto. "La revolución cubana; recopilación bibliográfica." Universitas humanística, Bogotá, 1 (may., 1971), 283-299.

195   POLITICAL SCIENCE

1564 Pérez, Luis A. "The Cuban Army, 1898-1958: a bibliography." South Eastern Latin Americanist, 17:1 (Jun., 1973), 4-7.

DOMINICAN REPUBLIC

1565 Grabendorff, Wolf. Bibliographie zu Politik und Gesellschaft der Dominikanischen Republik: Neuere Studien 1961-1971. [München]: Weltforum-Verlag, 1973. 103 p. (Materialien zu Entwicklung und Politik, 3).

1566 Wiarda, Howard J. Materials for the study of politics and government in the Dominican Republic, 1930-1966. Santiago de los Caballeros: Universidad Católica Madre y Maestra, 1968. 142 p. (Colección estudios, 5).

ECUADOR

1567 Johnson, James B. Bibliography on party politics in Ecuador, 1950-1962. Evanston, Ill.: Northwestern University, International Comparative Political Parties Project, 1968. 15 p. (ICPP Bibliography series, 3, I).

GUYANA

1568 Cummings, Leslie P. Bibliography on boundaries; boundary problems in the Guianas. Georgetown? Guyana, 1968? 7 ℓ.

PARAGUAY

1569 "Bibliografía y documentos sobre la política en el Paraguay." Revista paraguaya de sociología, 5:13 (dic., 1968), 155-159.

1570 Ferraro, Oscar and Sofía Mareski. Bibliografía para el estudio de los mensajes presidenciales del Paraguay. Asunción: Centro Paraguayo de Documentación Social, 1974. 19 ℓ.

URUGUAY

1571   Melogno, Wellington and Fernando Ainsa.   Bibliogra-
       fía para el estudio de los partidos políticos uru-
       guayos.   París: Instituto Latinoamericano de Rela-
       ciones Internacionales, n. d.   44 ℓ.

WEST INDIES

1572   Institute of Jamaica, Kingston.   West India Reference
       Library.   Jamaican government publications: a
       bibliography.   [Prepared by Suzette Hinds].   Kings-
       ton, 1971.   13 ℓ.

1573   Stephenson, Yvonne.   A bibliography on the West In-
       dian Federation.   Georgetown: University of Gu-
       yana Library, 1972.   34 p.

1574   _____.   Official publications in the English-speaking
       Commonwealth Caribbean Territories.   Turkeyen?,
       Guyana, 19??   16 p.

PRINTING

1575   Millares Carlo, Agustín.   Ensayo de una bibliografía
       de la imprenta y el periodismo en Venezuela.
       Washington: O. A. S., 1971.   91 p.   (Bibliografías
       básicas, 8).

1576   Montoya R. del V., Isabel.   "Imprentas volantes en la
       emancipación."   Boletín de la Biblioteca Nacional,
       Lima, 26:61/62 (1972), 3-12.

1577   Passos, Alexandre.   Um século de imprensa universi-
       tária (1831-1931).   Rio de Janeiro: Editora Pon-
       getti, 1971.   101 p.

PUBLIC ADMINISTRATION

1578   Bahia, Brazil (State) Universidade Federal.   Centro
       de Administração Pública.   Publicações do Centro
       de Administração Pública-ISP, 1964-1972.   Salva-
       dor, 1972.   12 ℓ.

1579   Escola Interamericana de Administração Pública. Reforma administrativa; bibliografia seleccionada. Rio de Janeiro, 1973? 81 ℓ. "Atualização da bibliografia analítica que a EIAP publicou em Resumos selecionados, no ano de 1972."

1580   Goldsmith, William W.; Pierre Clavel and Deborah Roth. "A bibliography on public planning in Puerto Rico." Latin American research review, 9:2 (Summer, 1974), 143-169.

1581   Instituto Centroamericano de Administración Pública. Bibliografía sobre adiestramiento. San José, Costa Rica: ICAP, 1971. 125 p. (Colección Series misceláneas, 909).

1582   Instituto Centroamericano de Administración Pública. Catálogo de publicaciones. San José, Costa Rica, 1971. 34 p. (Catálogo de publicaciones, 7).

1583   Instituto de Estudios Supeiiores de Administración. Bibliografía preliminar socio-económica-política de Venezuela con atención especial al campo de la administración. Compiled by Richard L. Duncan. [Caracas?], 1968. 86 ℓ.

1584   Lima. Escuela de Administración de Negocios para Graduados. Catálogo de publicaciones periódicas. Edición revisada y aumentada. Lima, 1973. i, 91 p.

1585   Mexico (City) Universidad Nacional. Comisión de Estudios Administrativos. Guía bibliográfica de administración. México, 1972. vii, 398 p.

1586   Moraes, Suzana and Maria Lúcia Gudolle. Bibliografia. Pôrto Alegre: Centro de Estudios e Pesquisas em Administração, 1971. 14 p.

1587   Rebello, Lêda. Catálogo geral da documentação. Salvador: Universidade Federal da Bahia, Centro de Administração Pública.

1588   Verner, Joel G. "Material útil para el estudio de recursos humanos en el sistema administrativo de Guatemala." Revista mexicana de ciencia política, 16:60 (1970), 247-264.

PUBLISHERS

1589   Apostolado pozitivista do Brasil. Catálogo das publi-
        cações. Rio de Janeiro: Na Sêde Central da
        Igreja Positivista do Brasil, 1932.   64 p.

1590   Argentina. Ministerio de Cultura y Educación. De-
        partamento de Estadística Educativa. Catálogo de
        publicaciones. Buenos Aires, 1972.

1591   Brazil. Ministério do Planejamento e Coordenação
        Geral. Catálogo das publicações do MINIPLAN.
        Rio de Janeiro, 1968- .

1592   Brazil. Superintendência do Desenvolvimento da Ama-
        zonia. Publicações editadas. Belèm: Pará,
        1972. 14 ℓ.

1593   Brazil. Superintendência do Desenvolvimento do Nor-
        deste. Departamento de Administração Geral.
        Biblioteca. Catálogo das publicações editadas pela
        SUDENE (1959-1969). Recife, 1969. 133 p.

1594   Brazil. Superintendência do Desenvolvimento do Nor-
        deste. Departamento de Recursos Humanos.
        Catálogo das publicações editadas pelo DRH/
        SUDENE, 1962-1970. Recife, 1970. 187 p.

1595   Belo Horizonte, Brazil. Universidade de Minas
        Gerais. Boletim bibliográfico. Ano I, núm.
        1- . jul., 1962- . Belo Horizonte.

1596   Buenos Aires. Universidad. Museo Etnográfico.
        Publicaciones del Museo etnográfico. Buenos
        Aires, 1939. 22 p., 1 ℓ.

1597   Castillo, Stella. "Indice de los documentos publicados
        entre 1967-1974 por las distintas unidades que inte-
        gran el Departamento Nacional de Planeación:
        primera parte." Revista de planeación y desa-
        rrollo, 6:2 (abr./sept., 1974), 75-129.

1598   Centro Interamericano de Investigación y Documenta-
        ción sobre Formación Profesional. Catálogo de
        publicaciones CINTERFOR, 1964-1971. Monte-
        video, 1971. 92 p.

1599 Centro Intercultural de Documentación, Cuernavaca, México. Catálogo de publicaciones. Cuernavaca, México.

1600 "Centro Latinoamericano de Investigaciones en Ciencias Sociales: diez años de actividades." Revista mexicana de sociología, 31:2 (abr./jun., 1969), 457-482.

1601 Colombia. Imprenta Nacional. Catálogo. Bogotá, 1966. 23 p.

1602 Comas, Juan. Cien años de Congresos Internacionales de Americanistas. México Instituto de Investigaciones Históricas, UNAM, 1974. Includes: "Volúmenes publicados por los Congresos ... efectuados entre 1875 y 1972" and "Indice de los trabajos publicados en los volúmenes de los Congresos ... (1875-1972)." --pp. 117-136 and 137-439 respectively.

1603 Costa Rica. Instituto Geográfico Nacional. Publicaciones del Instituto Geográfico Nacional, (1954-1972); índice bibliográfico. San José, 1973. 24 p.

1604 _____. Publicaciones del Instituto Geográfico Nacional: XV aniversario, 1954-1969; índice bibliográfico, preparado por Eduardo Protti Martinelli. San José, Costa Rica, 1970. 16 p.

1605 Editorial Universitaria, Guatemala. XXV aniversario de la autonomía universitaria labor Editorial. Guatemala: Universidad de San Carlos de Guatemala, 1969. 30 p.

1606 Estación Experimental Agropecuaria Anguil. Catálogo de publicaciones editadas por la.... La Pampa, Anguil, Argentina, 1968. 12 ℓ.

1607 Fundação Casa de Rui Barbosa, Rio de Janeiro. Lista de suas publicações. Rio de Janeiro, 1974. [21 p.]

1608 Fundación para la Educación Superior y el Desarrollo. Biblioteca. FEDESARROLLO; Bibliografía de publicaciones; materias y autores. Bogotá, 1974. 28 p.

1609   Havana. Biblioteca Nacional "José Martí." Catálogo
       de publicaciones de la Biblioteca Nacional, 1959-
       1969. La Habana, 1969. 54 p.

1610   Hispanic Society of America. List of publications:
       library subjects. New York, 1974. 8 p.

1611   _____. List of publications: museum subjects.
       New York, 1974. 11 p.

1612   Huertas, Maritza and M. D. Malugani. Contribuciones
       del IICA a la literatura de las ciencias agrícolas.
       Turrialba, Costa Rica: Instituto Interamericano de
       Documentación e Información Agrícola, 1972.
       164 p. (Bibliotecología y documentación, 12).

1613   Instituto Indigenista Peruano. Bibliografía de los es-
       tudios y publicaciones del Instituto Indigenista
       Peruano, 1961-1969. Lima, 1970. (Serie biblio-
       gráfica, 2).

1614   Malugani, María Dolores and Maritza Huertas. Con-
       tribuciones del Instituto Interamericano de Ciencias
       Agrícolas a la literatura de las ciencias agrícolas.
       Ed. preliminar. Turrialba: Instituto Interameri-
       cano de Ciencias Agrícolas, Biblioteca y Servicio
       de Documentación, 1968. ix, 187 p. (Bibliote-
       cología y documentación, 12).

1615   Marino Flores, Anselmo. "Bibliografía del Instituto
       de Antropología e Historia, 1966-1968 (México)."
       Boletín bibliográfico de antropología americana,
       31 (1968), 33-52.

1616   _____. "Bibliografía del Instituto Nacional de An-
       tropología e Historia (México), 1968-1969." Bole-
       tín bibliográfico de antropología americana, 33/34
       (1970/71), 155-166.

1617   Matos Moctezuma, Eduardo. "Contribución a la bib-
       liografía del Instituto Nacional de Antropología e
       Historia." Boletín bibliográfico de antropología
       americana, 29/30 (1966/1967), 5-429.

1618   Mexico (City) Universidad Nacional. Instituto de Geo-
       grafía. Catálogo de publicaciones, 1965-1973 [i. e.
       1974]. México, 1974. 26 p. Includes contents of
       the Institute's Boletín (nos. 1-5).

201   PUBLISHERS

1619 Pan American Institute of Geography and History.
      Commission on History. Catálogo de publicaciones.
      México, 1969. 92 p.

1620 Pérez de la Dehesa, Rafael. "La Editorial Sempere
      en Hispanoamérica y España." Revista ibero-
      americana, 35:69 (sept./dic., 1969), 551-555.

1621 Peru. Oficina Nacional de Desarrollo Cooperativo.
      Biblioteca. Catálogo de publicaciones de la
      ONDECOOP, 1965-1971. Compilación de Alicia
      Ibáñez. Lima, 1972. ii, 52 p. (Serie biblio-
      gráfica, 5).

1622 Placer, Xavier and Nellie Figueira. Publicações da
      Biblioteca Nacional; catálogo, 1873-1974. Rio de
      Janeiro: Biblioteca Nacional, 1975. 128 p.
      (Coleção Rodolfo Garcia. Sér. B: Catálogos e
      bibliografias).

1623 "Publicaciones de la Dirección de Bibliotecas Archivos
      y Museos." Mapocho, 23 (primavera, 1970), 327-
      328.

1624 Ramírez Vargas, María Teresa and Susan Casement.
      La Cámara de Comercio de Bogotá y sus publica-
      ciones. s.l., s.n., 1974. 115 ℓ.

1625 Recife, Brazil. Universidade Federal de Pernambuco.
      Catálogo de publicações da Imprensa Universitária,
      1967. Recife, 1969. 32 p.

1626 _____. Catálogo de publicações da Imprensa Uni-
      versitária, 1969-1970. Recife: Biblioteca Central,
      1971. 43 p.

1627 Rodón, Montserrat Leonor. Catálogo de los impresos
      de Niños existentes en la Biblioteca Mayor de la
      Universidad Nacional de Córdoba. Córdoba: Bib-
      lioteca Mayor, 1972. 51 ℓ.

1628 Ruiz Larré, Alcira. Lista de las publicaciones de la
      Facultad de Humanidades y Educación. Caracas:
      Universidad Central de Venezuela, 1961. 28 p.

1629 United Nations. Economic Commission for Latin
      America. Bibliografía de la CEPAL, 1948-1972.
      Santiago de Chile, 1973. xi, 165 p.

1630 Venezuela. Presidencia. Secretaría General. Catá-
      logo de publicaciones de la Presidencia de la Re-
      pública (1969-1973). Caracas, 1973. 66 p.

1631 Venezuela. Universidad Central. Escuela de Biblio-
      teconomía y Archivos. Catálogo bibliográfico de
      la Facultad de Humanidades y Educación, 1948-
      1968. Caracas, 1969. 498 p. (Indice de publica-
      ciones oficiales de la Universidad Central de Vene-
      zuela, 1).

1632 Wisconsin. University. Land Tenure Center. Avail-
      able publications list. Madison.

                        RELIGION

1633 Abib, Jamil. "Subsidios para a história das institui-
      ções religiosas em Rio Claro." Anais do Museu
      Paulista, 24 (1970), 103-164.

1634 Ariza S., Alberto E. Bibliografía de la provincia
      dominicana de Colombia. Bogotá, 1967. 119 p.

1635 Associação de Seminários Teológicos Evangélicos,
      São Paulo. Resenha bibliográfica. São Paulo,
      1970. 24 p.

1636 Caracas (Archdiocese). Archivo. Catálogo general
      del Archivo Arquidiocesano de Caracas, por Jaime
      Suría. Madrid: Escuelas Profesionales "Sagrado
      Corazón de Jesús," 1964. 79 p.

1637 Centro de Estudios para el Desarrollo e Integración
      de América Latina. Desarrollo y revolución, Igle-
      sia y liberación; bibliografía. Bogotá, 1973. 2 v.

1638 Kieman, Mathias C. "A summary index of ecclesias-
      tical papers in the archive of the Papal nunciature
      of Rio de Janeiro for the period of 1808-1891."
      The Americas, 28:1 (July, 1971), 99-112.

1639 López, Eucario. "Compendio de los libros de actas
      del venerable Cabildo de la Santa Iglesia Catedral
      de Guadalajara." Boletín del Instituto de Investi-
      gaciones Bibliográficas, México, 5 (ene./jun., 1971),
      119-361.

1640   Maldonado Barrios, Alberto. La iglesia y el control
        de la natalidad; bibliografía sobre 'Humanae Vitae.'
        Buenos Aires: Paidós, 1970. xv, 93 p.

1641   Mantecón Navasal, José Ignacio. "Inventario del Ar-
        chivo del Comisario General de las Provincias
        Franciscanas de Nueva España y Filipinas, 1698."
        Boletín del Instituto de Investigaciones Bibliográ-
        ficas, México, 4 (jul./dic., 1970), [263]-288.

1642   Minnich, Emil; Willard H. Smith and Wilmar Stahl.
        "Mennonites in Latin America; an annotated bib-
        liography, 1912-1971." Mennonite Quarterly Re-
        view, 46 (Apr., 1972), 177-235.

1643   Olivas, Luis and Oscar Delgado. "Bibliografía sobre
        la iglesia y el cambio social en América Latina."
        Anuario de sociología de los pueblos ibéricos, 5
        (1969), 52-109.

1644   Oliveira, P. A. Ribeiro de. "Le catholicisme populaire
        en Amérique Latine." Social compass, 19:4 (1972),
        567-584.

1645   Ortega, Benjamin. Repertorio para el estudio de las
        iglesias en la sociedad de América Latina, 1960-
        1969. Colaboración especial de Carlos Condamines.
        Cuernavaca, México: Centro Intercultural de Docu-
        mentación, 1970. 7, 208 p. (CIDOC Cuadernos,
        52).

1646   Rey Fajardo, José del. Bio-bibliografía de los Jesui-
        tas en la Venezuela colonial. Caracas: Universi-
        dad Católica Andrés Bello, Instituto de Investiga-
        ciones Históricas, 1974. 590 p. (Série histórica,
        27).

1647   _____. "Notas bio-bibliográficas. Los jesuitas
        extranjeros que trabajaron en las misiones venezo-
        lanas." Boletín de la Academia Nacional de la
        Historia, Caracas, 53:209 (ene./mar., 1970), 91-
        125.

1648   Rio de Janeiro. Biblioteca Nacional. Sermões im-
        pressos dos autos de fé: bibliografia, por Rose-
        marie Erika Horch. Rio de Janeiro: Divisão de
        Publicações e Divulgação, 1969. 115 p. (Coleção

Rodolfo Garcia. Serie B: Catálogos e bibliografias).

1649 Silva, Emilio. La Orden de la Merced en el Brasil y fichas para una bibliografía mercedaria. Rio de Janeiro: Departamento de Imprensa Nacional, 1973. 145 p.

1650 Vekemans, Roger. "Antecedentes para el estudio de la teología de la liberación; comentario bibliográfico." Tierra nueva, 1:2 (jul., 1972), 5-23; 1:3 (oct., 1972), 5-20; 2:4 (abr., 1973), 15-34.

1651 Weber, Francis J. A select bibliography: the California missions, 1765-1972. Los Angeles: Dawson's Book Shop, [1972]. 86 p.

SOCIAL SCIENCES

GENERAL

1652 Abruch L., Miguel. Bibliografía: selección de libros y publicaciones sobre relevantes temas judíos. México: Comité Judío Americano, Instituto de Relaciones Humanas, 1971. 56 ℓ.

1653 Acosta Saignes, Miguel. "Introducción al estudio de los repositorios documentales sobre los africanos y sus descendientes en América: bibliografía." América indígena, 29:3 (jul., 1969), 780-786.

1654 Almeida, Maria Lêda Rodrigues de. Família e desenvolvimento: uma análise bibliográfica (relatório final). Rio de Janeiro: Centro Latino-Americano de Pesquisas em Ciências Sociais, 1971. 28, 39 ℓ. (CLAPCS Grupo de Estudos sobre Família. Documento, 2).

1655 Bibliografía de demografía en lengua española. v. 1- . 1969- . Buenos Aires: Fundación Interamericana de Bibliotecología Franklin.

1656 Briceño, Liliana. Guía bibliográfica sobre población y familia; selección de artículos de revistas afines al tema y memorias y tesis de grado en el período

comprendido entre 1959-1969. Santiago de Chile:
Centro para el Desarrollo Económico y Social de
América Latina, 1970. 96 ℓ.

1657 Bruun, Stanley D. Urbanization in developing countries;
an international bibliography. East Lansing: Latin
American Studies Center, Michigan State University,
1971. xviii, 693 p. (Research report, 8).

1658 Centro Latinoamericano de Pesquisas em Ciências Sociais. Bibliografía. Rio de Janeiro: Centro Latinoamericano de Pesquisas em Ciências Sociais,
1962-

1659 Centro Latinoamericano de Pesquisas em Ciências
Sociais. Serviço de Documentação. Bibliografia
sobre juventude na América Latina (problemas sociais, psicológicos, estudiantís e aspirações). Rio
de Janeiro, 1969. 22 ℓ.

1660 _____. Levantamento das pesquisas sociais em
curso na América Latina (resultados provisórios).
Rio de Janeiro, 1969. 59 ℓ.

1661 Centro para el Desarrollo Económico y Social de América Latina. Guía de investigaciones. 2. ed. Santiago de Chile, 1970. 28 p.

1662 Chardon de Ferrer, Francisco. Bibliografía anotada
de artículos acerca de la juventud. Río Piedras,
Puerto Rico: Universidad de Puerto Rico, Centro
de Investigaciones Pedagógicas, 1971. 143 p.
(Monografías. Serie A. Bibliografía, 1).

1663 Conference of Latin American Geographers. Population
dynamics of Latin America; a review and a bibliography. Edited by Robert N. Thomas. East Lansing, Michigan, 1973. 200 p. (Publication series,
2).

1664 Culebra de Soberanes, Cecilia. "Bibliografías latinoamericanas: ciencias sociales." Foro internacional,
12:2 (oct./dic., 1971), 229-269.

1665 "Demografía y población." Biblioboletín, Universidad
de Los Andes, Centro de Estudios sobre Desarrollo
Económico (ene., 1971), 45-76.

SOCIAL SCIENCES   206

1666   Fernández Robaina, Tomás. Bibliografía sobre estu-
       dios afro-americanos. La Habana: Biblioteca Na-
       cional José Martí, Departamento de Hemeroteca e
       Información de Humanidades, 1968. ix, 96 p.

1667   Friberg, Justin C. Migraciones hacia la ciudad y las
       consequencias de la urbanización en latinoamerica;
       una bibliografía preliminar. Bucaramanga: Uni-
       versidad Industrial de Santander, División de Inves-
       tigaciones, 1971. 69 p.

1668   Gleaves, Edwin Sheffield. Guía de fuentes de informa-
       ción en las humanidades y las ciencias sociales.
       San José: Universidad de Costa Rica, 1971. vii,
       121 ℓ. (Serie Bibliotecología, 26).

1669   Grupo de Trabajo para la Integración de la Información.
       Catálogo colectivo de publicaciones periódicas en
       desarrollo económico y social. Lima, 1972. xiii,
       185 p.

1670   "Indice bibliográfico; algunos trabajos publicados desde
       1960 hasta la fecha, donde se trata el problema
       de la marginalidad en algunas de sus dimensiones."
       Revista Latinoamericana de Sociología, 5:2 (jul.,
       1969), 447-456.

1671   Inter-American Center for Documentation and Agricul-
       ture Information. Bibliografia sobre juventudes
       rurales en América Latina. Turrialba, Costa
       Rica, 1972. 175 p. (Bibliografías, 11).

1672   Interamerican Children's Institute. Library. Biblio-
       grafía sobre "El aumento de la población y su in-
       cidencia sobre la infancia, la adolescencia, la ju-
       ventud y la família americana." Montevideo, 1968.
       92 p.

1673   _____. Bibliografía sobre servicio social. Monte-
       video.

1674   "Inventario de los estudios en ciencias sociales sobre
       America Latina: Sociología." Aportes. [Regular
       feature.]

1675   Leeds, Anthony and Elizabeth Leeds. A bibliography
       of urban settlement types in Latin America. Aus-
       tin, Texas, 1967? 1 v. unpaged.

1676 "Mestizaje y aculturación; bibliografía." Aportes, 14 (oct., 1969), 61-65.

1677 Monteforte Toledo, Mario. Bibliografía sociopolítica latinoamericana. México: Instituto de Investigaciones Sociales, UNAM, 1968. 157 p.

1678 Morales-Vergara, Julio. Bibliografía sobre temas de población en revistas especializadas. Santiago de Chile: Centro Latinoamericano de Demografía, 1974. 250 p.

1679 Nickel, Herbert J. Unterentwicklung als Marginalität in Lateinamerika; Einführung und Bibliographie zu einem lateinamerikanischen Thema. München: Weltforum Verlag, 1973. lxxix, 231 p. (Materialien zu Entwicklung und Politik, 5).

1680 Palais, Elliot. "A look at publications on Latin American history and social sciences." Latin American Digest, 7:4 (June, 1973), 22-24.

1681 Paris. Université. Institut des Hautes Etudes de l'Amérique Latine. Centre de Documentation. Bibliographie des recenseaments démographiques et économiques des pays d'Amérique Latine existant à Paris. 2. ed. revue et augmentée. Paris, 1969. 84 p.

1682 Peru. Oficina Nacional de Desarrollo Cooperativo. Biblioteca. Catálogo de publicaciones periódicas, 1965-1970, por Alicia Ibáñez. Lima, 1971. 41 p. (Serie bibliográfica, 4).

1683 Pescatello, Ann. "The female in Ibero-America; an essay on research bibliography and research directions." Latin American research review, 7:2 (Summer, 1972), 125-141.

1684 Porzecanski, Leopoldo. A selected bibliography on urban housing in Latin America. Monticello, Ill.: Council of Planning Librarians, 1973. 31 p. (Exchange bibliography, 412).

1685 "Problemas atuais da juventude na América Latina; levantamento bibliográfico." América Latina, 13:1 (jan./mar., 1970), 129-142.

1686   Puerto Rico.   University.   Centro de Investigaciones
       Pedagógicas.   Bibliografía anotada de artículos
       acerca de la juventud.   Preparada por Francisca
       Chardon de Ferrer et al.   Río Piedras, 1971.
       143 ℓ.   (Monografías del Centro de Investigaciones
       Pedagógicas.   Serie A: Bibliografía, 1).

1687   Redclift, Michael.   "A short survey and bibliography
       of British sociological work on Latin America."
       Bulletin of the Society for Latin American Studies,
       18 (Oct., 1973), 12-15.

1688   Resúmenes analíticos sobre defensa y seguridad na-
       cional; publicado con la colaboración y los auspicios
       del Consejo Nacional de Seguridad.   Abstracts of
       military bibliography; journal published with the col-
       laboration and under the auspices of the National
       Security Council.   v. 1, no. 1, 1968- .   Buenos
       Aires: Instituto de Publicaciones Navales, Centro
       Naval.

1689   Sable, Martin Howard.   Latin American urbanization:
       a guide to the literature, organizations, and per-
       sonnel.   Metuchen, N.J.:   Scarecrow Press, 1971.
       1077 p.

1690   Sanguinetti Vargas, Yolanda.   Bibliografía general
       sobre desarrollo de la comunidad.   Juseín, Vene-
       zuela: Centro Nacional de Capacitación e Investi-
       gación Aplicada para el Desarrollo de la Comuni-
       dad, 1969.   149 p.   (Serie divulgativa, 1).

1691   _____.   _____.   Caracas: Fondo Editorial
       Común, 1970.   118 p.

1692   Sepúlveda, Orlando and Francisco Fernández.   "Biblio-
       grafía sociológica iberoamericana."   Anuario de
       sociología de los pueblos ibéricos, 1 (1967).

1693   Solano, Francisco de.   "El proceso urbano iberoameri-
       cano desde sus orígenes hasta los principios del
       siglo XIX: estudio bibliográfico," por ... con la
       colaboración de Richard M. Morse, Jorge Enrique
       Hardoy y Richard P. Schaedel.   Revista de Indias,
       33/34:131/138 (ene. 1973/dic. 1974), 727-880.

1694   Solow, Anatole A.   National urbanization politics in

Latin America: a preliminary annotated bibliography with evaluative comments. Pittsburgh: University Center for International Studies, University
of Pittsburgh, 1974. iv, 41 p.

1695 Thomé, Joseph R. Derecho y cambio social en América Latina; materiales de curso. Santiago de Chile:
Instituto de Docencia e Investigación Jurídica, 1972.
2 v.

1696 Vaughan, Denton R. Urbanization in twentieth century
Latin America: a working bibliography. Austin:
Institute of Latin American Studies, Population Research Center, University of Texas, 1970. iv,
122 p.

1697 Vivó, Paquita. A guide to writings on the Alliance for
Progress. Washington: Department of Information
and Public Affairs, O. A. S. , 1970. 18 ℓ.

ARGENTINA

1698 Culebra de Soberanes, Cecilia. La bibliografía latinoamericana de ciencias sociales: Argentina, Chile
y Uruguay; proyecto de investigación. México:
Colegio de México, Biblioteca, 1972. 41 ℓ.

1699 Marsal, Juan Francisco. Contribución a una bibliografía del ensayo socio-político argentino y mexicano
contemporáneo. Buenos Aires: Instituto Torcuato
Di Tella, Centro de Investigaciones Sociales, 1969.
25 ℓ. (Documento de trabajo, 66).

1700 Villascuerna, Inés. Bibliografía para el estudio histórico de la marginalidad en el noroeste de Argentina. Buenos Aires: Instituto Torcuato Di Tella,
Centro de Investigaciones Sociales, 1970. 88 p.
(Documento de trabajo, 71).

BOLIVIA

1701 Arze, José Roberto. "Acotaciones para una bibliografía selecta sobre sociología boliviana." Inter-
American review of bibliography, 20:3 (Jul./Sept.,
1970), 294-308.

1702 Siles Guevara, Juan. "Bibliografía selecta de ciencias sociales bolivianas." Aportes, 17 (jul., 1970), 121-132.

1703 Torrico Arze, Armando and Irma Aliaga de Vizcarra. Bibliografía boliviana de colonización. La Paz: Sociedad de Ingenieros Agrónomos de Bolivia, 1967. 7 ℓ.

BRAZIL

1704 Camargo, Ana Maria de Almeida. "Estudos sôbre cidades: uma coleção de exemplos." Revista de história, São Paulo, 41:38 (jul./set., 1970), 213-235.

1705 Centro Latinoamericano de Pesquisas em Ciências Sociais. Serviço de Documentação. Levantamento das pesquisas sociais em curso na América Latina (Brasil: lista provisória). Rio de Janeiro, 1969. 29 ℓ.

1706 Colóquio de Estudos Teuto-Brasileiros, 2d., Recife, 1968. Catálogo da exposição bibliográfica do II Colóquio de Estúdos Teuto-Brasileiros realizada no Recife, de 4 a 10 de abril de 1968. Recife: Universidade Federal de Pernambuco, 1968. 4 ℓ.

1707 "Eve in a democracy: women and politics in Brazil; a selected bibliography." Occasional papers, New York University, Ibero American Language and Area Center, 5 (1975), 16-23.

1708 Margulies, Marcos. Iudaica brasiliensis; repertório bibliográfico comentado dos livros relacionados com o judaismo e questões afins, publicados no Brasil desde os primóridios das atividades editoriais no país até o presente momento. Rio de Janeiro: Editora Documentário, 1974. 159 p.

1709 Moura, Valdiki. Bibliografia brasileira do cooperativismo. Rio de Janeiro: Casa do Estudante.

1710 Parisse, Lucien. "Bibliografia cronológica sôbre a favela do Rio de Janeiro a partir de 1940." América latina, 12:3 (jul./set., 1969), 221-232.

1711   Rio de Janeiro.   Instituto Brasileiro de Bibliografia
e Documentação.   Pesquisas em proceso no Brasil.
1967- . Rio de Janeiro.

CENTRAL AMERICA

1712   Snarr, D. N. and E. L. Brown.   "Social and economic
change in Central America and Panama; an annotated bibliography."   International review of modern
sociology, 2 (Mar. , 1972), 102-115.

COLOMBIA

1713   Riascos Sánchez, Blanca.   Indice militar colombiano.
Medellín: Editorial Universidad de Antioquia,
1968. vii, 163 ℓ.

CUBA

1714   Fermoselle López, Rafael.   "The blacks in Cuba; a
bibliography."   Caribbean studies, 12:3 (Oct. ,
1972), 103-112.

1715   Trelles y Govin, Carlos Manuel.   Bibliografía social
cubana.   La Habana: Biblioteca Nacional José
Martí, 1969.   x, 50-106, xi-xxxiii p.   Reprint of
the 1925 ed.

1716   Valdés, Nelson P.   "A bibliography on Cuban women
in the 20th century."   Cuban studies newsletter/
Boletín de estudios sobre Cuba, 4:2 (Jun. 1974),
1-31.

ECUADOR

1717   Ecuador.   Junta Nacional de Planificación y Coordinación Económica.   Sección Estudios Sociales.   Lis-
tado parcial de la bibliografía social, socio-eco-
nómica y política del Ecuador: sección obras generales y sección histórica.   Versión preliminar.
Quito, 1972.   147 p.

1718   Navas C. , B. and Armando Cardozo.   Bibliografía

ecuatoriana de ciencias sociales aplicadas a la vida
rural. Quito: Universidad Central, Facultad de
Ingeniería y Medicina Veterinaría, 1971. 17 p.

GUYANA

1719   Mckenzie, H. I. "Race and class in Guyana; bibliography." Study encounter, 8:4 (1972), 1-13.

HAITI

1720   Mintz, Sidney W. and Vern Canol. "A selective social
science bibliography of the Republic of Haiti." Revista Interamericana de Ciencias Sociales, 2:3
(1963), 405-419.

MEXICO

1721   Mexico (City) Universidad Nacional. Instituto de Investigaciones Sociales. Investigaciones en proceso.
México, 1970. 95 p.

1722   Sáenz Cirlos, Vicente Javier. Guía de obras de con-
sulta sobre México, en el campo de las ciencias
sociales. Monterrey: Instituto Tecnológico y de
Estudios Superiores de Monterrey, 1974. vi,
180 p. (Publicaciones. Serie Catálogos de biblioteca, 5).

1723   Unikel, Luis. Bibliografía sobre desarrollo urbano y
regional de México. México: Universidad Nacional
Autónoma de México, Instituto Nacional de Antropología e Historia, 1972. 265 p. (Fuentes para
la historia de la ciudad de México, 2).

1724   Villa Aguilera, Manuel. "Los rasgos de la sociología
crítica en México." Revista paraguaya de sociología, 11:30 (mayo/ago., 1974), 7-56. Appended is
a bibliography of works on Mexican sociology published between 1950 and 1974.

PANAMA

1725   Arosemena Moreno, Julio. "Documentación relativa

213   SOCIAL SCIENCES

al negro en Panamá." Lotería, 14:164 (jul., 1969), 49-60.

PARAGUAY

1726 "Bibliografía: la población en el Paraguay." Revista paraguaya de sociología, 5:12 (ago., 1968), 136-140.

1727 "Bibliografía sobre la sociedad rural en el Paraguay." Revista paraguaya de sociología, 5:11 (abr., 1968), 129-134.

1728 Centro Paraguayo de Documentación Social. Bibliografía de las publicaciones del CPDS y del CPES. Asunción, 1973. 15 p. (Estudios bibliográficos, EB-73).

1729 _____. Documentos y estudios bibliográficos. Asunción, 1972- .

1730 Rivarola, Domingo M. Estudios y datos sobre la población en el Paraguay: bibliografía. Asunción: Centro Paraguayo de Estudios Sociológicos, 1970. 27 p.

PERU

1731 Herbold, Carl and Steve Stein. Guía bibliográfica para la historia social y política del Perú en el siglo XX (1895-1960). Lima: Instituto de Estudios Peruanos, 1971. 165 p.

1732 Matos Mar, José and Roger Ravines. Bibliografía peruana de ciencias sociales, 1957-1969; antropología, sociología, ciencia política, economía, educación, lingüística, psicología social, psiquiatría social. Lima: Instituto de Estudios Peruanos, 1971. 453 p.

1733 Welsh, Eileen. Bibliografía sobre el crecimiento dinámico de Lima referente al proceso de urbanización en el Perú. Lima: Centro de Estudios y Promoción del Desarrollo, 1970. 88 p. (Cuadernos Desco, A 5).

PUERTO RICO

1734   Bibliografía puertorriqueña de ciencias sociales,
       1930-1968. Río Piedras, Puerto Rico: Universi-
       dad de Puerto Rico, Centro de Investigaciones
       Sociales, n. d.

1735   Miranda, Altagracia. Fuentes puertorriqueñas de
       referencia en el area de las ciencias sociales.
       San Juan: Sociedad de Bibliotecarios de Puerto
       Rico, 1975. 14 p. (Cuadernos bibliotecarios, 11).

1736   Puerto Rico. University. Social Science Research
       Center. Investigaciones en proceso en el Centro
       de Investigaciones Sociales. Río Piedras, 1969.
       24 p.

VENEZUELA

1737   Centro Nacional de Capacitación e Investigación Apli-
       cada para el Desarrollo de la Comunidad. Biblio-
       grafía general sobre desarrollo de la comunidad.
       Caracas, 197? 118 p.

1738   Fundación para el Desarrollo de la Comunidad y Fo-
       mento Municipal, Caracas. Boletín bibliográfico
       de divulgación municipal. Caracas.

1739   Venezuela. Ministerio de Justicia. Bibliografía vene-
       zolana sobre criminología. Recopilación: Arnoldo
       García Iturbe. Caracas, 1970. 33 p. (Papeles
       de trabajo, 1).

STATISTICS

1740   Inter-American Statistical Institute. Bibliography of
       selected statistical sources of the American nations:
       a guide to the principal statistical materials of the
       22 American nations, including data, analyses,
       methodology, and laws and organization of statisti-
       cal agencies. Bibliografía de fuentes estadísticas
       escogidas de las naciones americanas: una guía
       de las principales materiales estadísticos de las
       22 naciones americanas incluyendo datos, análisis,

metodología y leyes y organización de los organismos de estadística. Detroit: Blaine-Ethridge
Books, 1974. xvi, 689 p. Reprint of 1947 ed.

1741　Koberstein, Gerhard. "Bibliografía de estadísticas
referente al estado de Puebla y al municipio de
Calpan, Pue. (1930-1967)." Revista mexicana de
sociología, 30:2 (abr./jun., 1968), 477-500.

1742　"Publicações editadas pelo Instituto Brasileiro de Estatística...." Revista brasileira de estatística.
[Regular feature.]

1743　Rosso, Hespéria Zuma de and Célia Maria Pereira
Pizzóquero. "Indicações bibliográficas sôbre re-
censeamento." Revista brasileira de estatística,
30:119 (jul./set., 1969), 314-347.

THEATER

1744　"Bibliografia de/sobre teatro." Revista do Livro, 11:
34 (1968), 139-170.

1745　Christensen, George K. "A bibliography of Latin
American plays in English translation." Latin
American Theatre Review, 6:2 (Spring, 1973),
29-39.

1746　Foster, Virginia Ramos. "Contemporary Argentine
dramatists: a bibliography." Theatre Documentation, 4:1 (1971/1972), 13-20.

1747　Huerta, Jorge A. A bibliography of Chicano and Mexican dance, drama, and music. Oxnard, Calif.:
Colegio Quetzalcoatl, 1972. iii, 59 p.

1748　Monteverde García Icazbalceta, Francisco. Bibliografía del teatro en México. New York: Burt Franklin, 1970. lxxx, 649 p. (Theater and drama
series, 11). Reprint of 1933 ed.

1749　Olavarría y Ferrari, Enrique de. Reseña histórica
del teatro en México, 1538, 1911.... Indices.
México: Ed. Porrúa, 1968- .

1750   Pepe, Luz E. and María Luisa Punte.   La crítica
         teatral argentina, 1880-1962.   Buenos Aires:
         Fondo Nacional de las Artes, 1966.   78 p.

SUBJECT INDEX

Libraries and archives (cont.)
  Archivo Histórico Nacional, Madrid   1315-16
  Ministerio de Asuntos Exteriores.   Archivo   881,
    1232
  Stanford University.   Hoover Institution on War, Revolu-
    tion, and Peace   1322
  Sweden   1320
  Syracuse University.   Library   1369
  Texas.   University.   Library   1331, 1368, 1370-88
  Tucumán, Argentina (Province).   Arquivo Histórico   1164
  Tulane University of Luisiana.   Library   1389-90
  United States   897-98, 1023, 1142, 1332-34, 1342, 1349-59
    Air University.   Library   1329
    Library of Congress   242, 1391
    National Archives   1392-98
    National Student Association.   Archives   750
  University of Guyana.   Library   1251, 1253-54
  Uruguay   1416
    Archivo General de la Nación   1417
  Valencia (City)
    Archivo Municipal   1308
    Universidad.   Biblioteca   1308
  Valparaiso, Chile.   Archivo de Escribanos   1217
  Vatican
    Archivio Vaticano   1419
    Biblioteca Vaticana   1418
  Venezuela   1435
    Archivo General de la Nación   1432
    Biblioteca Nacional   1422-23
  Washington University, St. Louis.   Library   650, 1399-
    1400
  West Indies   1436
  Wisconsin.   University.   Land Tenure Center.   Library
    1401-15
  Zulia, Venezuela (State).   Archivo General   1430
Library Science (see also Information science)   628, 961,
    967, 1421, 1440-41, 1446-48, 1451-53
  Argentina   1441, 1453, 1455
  Colombia   1449-50
  Periodicals   1158, 1445
  Uruguay   1454
  Venezuela   1024
Lima   1733
  Museo Nacional.   Revista   998
Limeira, Brazil--History   1215
Linguistics--Latin America   1059, 1063
Lins, Alvaro   453

Urbaneja Achelpohl, Luis Manuel   575
Urbanization
  Latin America   1657, 1667, 1675, 1684, 1689, 1693-94,
    1696
  Mexico   901, 1723
  Peru   1733
  Venezuela   1738
  Uruguay   112, 1376
  Government publications   1359
  History   1417
  Imprints   258
  Politics and government   1571
Usigli, Rodolfo   576
Uslar Pietri, Arturo   577-78

Valle Arizpe, Artemio de   579
Vallejo, César   580-81
Valparaiso, Chile--History   1217
Vedia y Mitre, Mariano   582
Vega, Carlos   583
Venezuela   116, 223, 1387, 1583
  Economy   737, 1583
  History   881, 939-42, 944-46, 1232, 1424-26, 1431-35,
    1529, 1646-47
  Imprints   113, 115, 259-63, 1423, 1628
  Ministerio de Justicia.   Revista   1025a
  Rural conditions   1414
  Social conditions   737
  Universidad Central
    Centro de Investigaciones Pedagógicas.   Boletín
      1026
    Instituto de Antropología e Historia.   Anuario   1027
    Instituto de Investigaciones de Prensa.   Boletín   1481
Vespucci, Amerigo   584
Viana, Helio   585
Villavicencio, Pablo de   586
Villegas Basavilbaso, Benjamín   587

Water resources--Rio de la Plata Region   684
Weitlaner, Roberto J.   588-89
West Indies   18, 866, 1256
  Government publications   1574
  History   1237
  Imprints   1437-38
  Politics and government   1573

AUTHOR INDEX